Learning Node

Shelley Powers

O'REILLY®

Beijing · Cambridge · Farnham · Köln · Sebastopol · Tokyo

Learning Node
by Shelley Powers

Copyright © 2012 Shelley Powers. All rights reserved.
Printed in the United States of America.

Published by O'Reilly Media, Inc., 1005 Gravenstein Highway North, Sebastopol, CA 95472.

O'Reilly books may be purchased for educational, business, or sales promotional use. Online editions are also available for most titles (*http://my.safaribooksonline.com*). For more information, contact our corporate/institutional sales department: 800-998-9938 or *corporate@oreilly.com*.

Editor: Simon St. Laurent	**Indexer:** Aaron Hazelton, BIM Publishing Services
Production Editor: Rachel Steely	**Cover Designer:** Karen Montgomery
Copyeditor: Rachel Monaghan	**Interior Designer:** David Futato
Proofreader: Kiel Van Horn	**Illustrators:** Robert Romano and Rebecca Demarest

September 2012:   First Edition.

Revision History for the First Edition:
2012-08-24   First release
See *http://oreilly.com/catalog/errata.csp?isbn=9781449323073* for release details.

ISBN: 978-1-449-32307-3

[LSI]

1345838343

Table of Contents

Preface

Not Your Ordinary JavaScript

You picked the perfect time to learn Node.

The technology evolving around Node is still young and vibrant, with interesting new variations and twists popping up on a regular basis. At the same time, the technology has reached a level of maturity that assures you your time learning Node will be well spent: installation has never been easier, even on Windows; the "best of breed" modules are beginning to surface from the seeming hundreds available for use; the infrastructure is becoming robust enough for production use.

There are two important things to keep in mind when you work with Node. The first is that it is based in JavaScript, more or less the same JavaScript you're used to working with in client-side development. True, you can use another language variation, such as CoffeeScript, but JavaScript is the *lingua franca* of the technology.

The second important thing to remember is that Node isn't your ordinary JavaScript. This is server-side technology, which means some of the functionality—and safeguards —you've come to expect in your browser environment just won't be there, and all sorts of new and potentially very unfamiliar capabilities will.

Of course, if Node were like JavaScript in the browser, what fun would that be?

Why Node?

If you explore the source code for Node, you'll find the source code for Google's V8, the JavaScript (technically, ECMAScript) engine that's also at the core of Google's Chrome browser. One advantage to Node.js, then, is that you can develop Node applications for just one implementation of JavaScript—not half a dozen different browsers and browser versions.

Node is designed to be used for applications that are heavy on input/output (I/O), but light on computation. More importantly, it provides this functionality directly out of the box. You don't have to worry about the application blocking any further processing while waiting for a file to finish loading or a database to finish updating, because most of the functionality is *asynchronous I/O* by default. And you don't have to worry about working with threads, because Node is implemented on a single thread.

 Asynchronous I/O means that applications don't wait for an input/output process to finish before going on to the next step in the application code. Chapter 1 goes into more detail on the asynchronous nature of Node.

Most importantly, Node is written in a language that many traditional web developers are familiar with: JavaScript. You may be learning how to use new technologies, such as working with WebSockets or developing to a framework like Express, but at least you won't have to learn a new language along with the concepts. This language familiarity makes it a lot easier to just focus on the new material.

This Book's Intended Audience

One of the challenges associated with working with Node is that there is an assumption that most people coming into Node development have come from a Ruby or Python environment, or have worked with Rails. I don't have this assumption, so I won't explain a Node component by saying it's "just like Sinatra."

This book's only assumption is that you, the reader, have worked with JavaScript and are comfortable with it. You don't have to be an expert, but you should know what I'm talking about when I mention *closures*, and have worked with Ajax and are familiar with event handling in the client environment. In addition, you'll get more from this book if you have done some traditional web development and are familiar with concepts such as HTTP methods (GET and POST), web sessions, cookies, and so on. You'll also need to be familiar with working either with the Console in Windows, or the Unix command line in Mac OS X or Linux.

You'll also enjoy the book more if you're interested in some of the new technologies such as WebSockets, or working with frameworks to create applications. I cover these as a way of introducing you to how Node can be used in real-world applications.

Most importantly, as you progress through the book, keep an open mind. Be prepared to hit an occasional alpha/beta wall and run into the gotchas that plague a dynamic technology. Above all, meet the prospect of learning Node with anticipation, because it really can be a lot of fun.

 If you're not sure you're familiar enough with JavaScript, you might want to check out my introductory text on JavaScript, *Learning JavaScript*, Second Edition (O'Reilly).

How to Best Use This Book

You don't have to read this book's chapters in order, but there are paths through the book that are dependent on what you're after and how much experience you have with Node.

If you've never worked with Node, then you're going to want to start with Chapter 1 and read through at least Chapter 5. These chapters cover getting both Node and the package manager (npm) installed, how to use them, creating your first applications, and utilizing modules. Chapter 5 also covers some of the style issues associated with Node, including how to deal with Node's unique approach to asynchronous development.

If you have had some exposure to Node, have worked with both the built-in Node modules and a few external ones, and have also used REPL (read-eval-print loop—the interactive console), you could comfortably skip Chapter 1–Chapter 4, but I still recommend starting no later than Chapter 5.

I incorporate the use of the Express framework, which also utilizes the Connect middleware, throughout the book. If you've not worked with Express, you're going to want to go through Chapter 6–Chapter 8, which cover the concepts of routing, proxies, web servers, and middleware, and introduce Express. In particular, if you're curious about using Express in a Model-View-Controller (MVC) framework, definitely read Chapter 7 and Chapter 8.

After these foundation chapters, you can skip around a bit. For instance, if you're primarily working with key/value pairs, you'll want to read the Redis discussion in Chapter 9; if you're interested in document-centric data, check out Chapter 10, which introduces how to use MongoDB with Node. Of course, if you're going to work only with a relational database, you can go directly to Chapter 11 and skip the Redis and MongoDB chapters, though do check them out sometime—they might provide a new viewpoint to working with data.

After those three data chapters, we get into specialized application use. Chapter 12 focuses purely on graphics and media access, including how to provide media for the new HTML5 video element, as well as working with PDF documents and Canvas. Chapter 13 covers the very popular Sockets.io module, especially for working with the new web socket functionality.

After the split into two different specialized uses of Node in Chapter 12 and Chapter 13, we come back together again at the end of the book. After you've had some time to work with the examples in the other chapters, you're going to want to spend some in Chapter 14, learning in-depth practices for Node debugging and testing.

Chapter 15 is probably one of the tougher chapters, and also one of the more important. It covers issues of security and authority. I don't recommend that it be one of the first chapters you read, but it is essential that you spend time in this chapter before you roll a Node application out for general use.

Chapter 16 is the final chapter, and you can safely leave it for last, regardless of your interest and experience. It focuses on how to prepare your application for production use, including how to deploy your Node application not only on your own system, but also in one of the cloud servers that are popping up to host Node applications. I'll also cover how to deploy a Node application to your server, including how to ensure it plays well with another web server such as Apache, and how to ensure your application survives a crash and restarts when the system is rebooted.

Node is heavily connected with the Git source control technique, and most (if not all) Node modules are hosted on GitHub. The Appendix provides a Git/GitHub survival guide for those who haven't worked with either.

I mentioned earlier that you don't *have to* follow the chapters in order, but I recommend that you do. Many of the chapters work off effort in previous chapters, and you may miss out on important points if you skip around. In addition, though there are numerous standalone examples all throughout the book, I do use one relatively simple Express application called Widget Factory that begins life in Chapter 7 and is touched on, here and there, in most of the rest of the chapters. I believe you'll have a better time with the book if you start at the beginning and then lightly skim the sections that you know, rather than skip a chapter altogether.

As the king says in *Alice in Wonderland*, "Begin at the beginning and go on till you come to the end: then stop."

The Technology

The examples in this book were created in various releases of Node 0.6.x. Most were tested in a Linux environment, but should work, as is, in any Node environment.

Node 0.8.x released just as this book went to production. The examples in the chapters do work with Node 0.8.x for the most part; I have indicated the instances where you'll need to make a code change to ensure that the application works with the newest Node release.

The Examples

You can find the examples as a compressed file at the O'Reilly web page for this book (*http://oreil.ly/Learning_node*). Once you've downloaded and uncompressed it, and you have Node installed, you can install all the dependency libraries for the examples by changing to the *examples* directory and typing:

```
npm install -d
```

I'll cover more on using the Node package manager (npm) in Chapter 4.

Conventions Used in This Book

The following typographical conventions are used in this book:

Plain text
> Indicates menu titles, menu options, menu buttons, and keyboard accelerators (such as Alt and Ctrl).

Italic
> Indicates new terms, URLs, email addresses, filenames, file extensions, pathnames, directories, and Unix utilities.

`Constant width`
> Indicates commands, options, switches, variables, attributes, keys, functions, types, classes, namespaces, methods, modules, properties, parameters, values, objects, events, event handlers, XML tags, HTML tags, macros, the contents of files, or the output from commands.

`Constant width bold`
> Shows commands or other text that should be typed literally by the user.

`Constant width italic`
> Shows text that should be replaced with user-supplied values.

 This icon signifies a tip, suggestion, or general note.

 This icon indicates a warning or caution.

Using Code Examples

This book is here to help you get your job done. In general, you may use the code in this book in your programs and documentation. You do not need to contact us for permission unless you're reproducing a significant portion of the code. For example, writing a program that uses several chunks of code from this book does not require permission. Selling or distributing a CD-ROM of examples from O'Reilly books does require permission. Answering a question by citing this book and quoting example code does not require permission. Incorporating a significant amount of example code from this book into your product's documentation does require permission.

We appreciate, but do not require, attribution. An attribution usually includes the title, author, publisher, and ISBN. For example: "*Learning Node* by Shelley Powers (O'Reilly). Copyright 2012 Shelley Powers, 978-1-449-32307-3."

If you feel your use of code examples falls outside fair use or the permission given above, feel free to contact us at *permissions@oreilly.com*.

Safari® Books Online

Safari Books Online (*www.safaribooksonline.com*) is an on-demand digital library that delivers expert content in both book and video form from the world's leading authors in technology and business.

Technology professionals, software developers, web designers, and business and creative professionals use Safari Books Online as their primary resource for research, problem solving, learning, and certification training.

Safari Books Online offers a range of product mixes and pricing programs for organizations, government agencies, and individuals. Subscribers have access to thousands of books, training videos, and prepublication manuscripts in one fully searchable database from publishers like O'Reilly Media, Prentice Hall Professional, Addison-Wesley Professional, Microsoft Press, Sams, Que, Peachpit Press, Focal Press, Cisco Press, John Wiley & Sons, Syngress, Morgan Kaufmann, IBM Redbooks, Packt, Adobe Press, FT Press, Apress, Manning, New Riders, McGraw-Hill, Jones & Bartlett, Course Technology, and dozens more. For more information about Safari Books Online, please visit us online.

How to Contact Us

Please address comments and questions concerning this book to the publisher:

O'Reilly Media, Inc.
1005 Gravenstein Highway North
Sebastopol, CA 95472
800-998-9938 (in the United States or Canada)
707-829-0515 (international or local)
707-829-0104 (fax)

We have a web page for this book, where we list errata, examples, and any additional information. You can access this page at *http://oreil.ly/Learning_node*.

To comment or ask technical questions about this book, please send email to *bookquestions@oreilly.com*.

For more information about our books, courses, conferences, and news, see our website at *http://www.oreilly.com*.

Find us on Facebook: *http://facebook.com/oreilly*

Follow us on Twitter: *http://twitter.com/oreillymedia*

Watch us on YouTube: *http://www.youtube.com/oreillymedia*

Acknowledgments

Thanks, as always, to friends and family who help keep me sane when I work on a book. Special thanks to my editor, Simon St. Laurent, who listened to me vent more than once.

My thanks also to the production crew who helped take this book from an idea to the work you're now holding: Rachel Steely, Rachel Monaghan, Kiel Van Horn, Aaron Hazelton, and Rebecca Demarest.

When you work with Node, you're the recipient of a great deal of generosity, starting with the creator of Node.js, Ryan Dahl, and including the creator of npm, Isaac Schlueter, who is also now the Node.js gatekeeper.

Others who provided extremely useful code and modules in this book are Bert Belder, TJ Holowaychuk, Jeremy Ashkenas, Mikeal Rogers, Guillermo Rauch, Jared Hanson, Felix Geisendörfer, Steve Sanderson, Matt Ranney, Caolan McMahon, Remy Sharp, Chris O'Hara, Mariano Iglesias, Marco Aurélio, Damián Suárez, Jeremy Ashkenas, Nathan Rajlich, Christian Amor Kvalheim, and Gianni Chiappetta. My apologies for any module developers I have inadvertently omitted.

And what would Node be without the good people who provide tutorials, how-tos, and helpful guides? Thanks to Tim Caswell, Felix Geisendörfer, Mikato Takada, Geo Paul, Manuel Kiessling, Scott Hanselman, Peter Krumins, Tom Hughes-Croucher, Ben Nadel, and the entire crew of Nodejitsu and Joyent.

CHAPTER 1

Node.js: Up and Running

Node.js is a server-side technology that's based on Google's V8 JavaScript engine. It's a highly scalable system that uses asynchronous, event-driven I/O (input/output), rather than threads or separate processes. It's ideal for web applications that are frequently accessed but computationally simple.

If you're using a traditional web server, such as Apache, each time a web resource is requested, Apache creates a separate thread or invokes a new process in order to handle the request. Even though Apache responds quickly to requests, and cleans up after the request has been satisfied, this approach can still tie up a lot of resources. A popular web application is going to have serious performance issues.

Node, on the other hand, doesn't create a new thread or process for every request. Instead, it listens for specific events, and when the event happens, responds accordingly. Node doesn't block any other request while waiting for the event functionality to complete, and events are handled—first come, first served—in a relatively uncomplicated *event loop*.

Node applications are created with JavaScript (or an alternative language that compiles to JavaScript). The JavaScript is the same as you'd use in your client-side applications. However, unlike JavaScript in a browser, with Node you have to set up a development environment.

Node can be installed in a Unix/Linux, Mac OS, or Windows environment. This chapter will walk you through setting up a development environment for Node in Windows 7 and Linux (Ubuntu). Installation on a Mac should be similar to installation on Linux. I'll also cover any requirements or preparation you need to take before installing the application.

Once your development environment is operational, I'll demonstrate a basic Node application and walk you through the important bit—the event loop I mentioned earlier.

Setting Up a Node Development Environment

There is more than one way to install Node in most environments. Which approach you use is dependent on your existing development environment, your comfort level working with source code, or how you plan to use Node in your existing applications.

Package installers are provided for both Windows and Mac OS, but you can install Node by grabbing a copy of the source and compiling the application. You can also use Git to *clone* (check out) the Node *repo* (repository) in all three environments.

In this section I'm going to demonstrate how to get Node working in a Linux system (an Ubuntu 10.04 VPS, or virtual private server), by retrieving and compiling the source directly. I'll also demonstrate how to install Node so that you can use it with Microsoft's WebMatrix on a Windows 7 PC.

Download source and basic package installers for Node from *http://no dejs.org/#download*. There's a wiki page providing some basic instruction for installing Node in various environments at *https://github.com/ joyent/node/wiki/Installing-Node-via-package-manager*. I also encourage you to search for the newest tutorials for installing Node in your environment, as Node is very dynamic.

Installing Node on Linux (Ubuntu)

Before installing Node in Linux, you need to prepare your environment. As noted in the documentation provided in the Node wiki, first make sure Python is installed, and then install libssl-dev if you plan to use SSL/TLS (Secure Sockets Layer/Transport Layer Security). Depending on your Linux installation, Python may already be installed. If not, you can use your systems package installer to install the most stable version of Python available for your system, as long as it's version 2.6 or 2.7 (required for the most recent version of Node).

This book assumes only that you have previous experience with Java-Script and traditional web development. Given that, I'm erring on the side of caution and being verbose in descriptions of what you need to do to install Node.

For both Ubuntu and Debian, you'll also need to install other libraries. Using the Advanced Packaging Tool (APT) available in most Debian GNU/Linux systems, you can ensure the libraries you need are installed with the following commands:

```
sudo apt-get update
sudo apt-get upgrade
sudo apt-get install build-essential openssl libssl-dev pkg-config
```

The update command just ensures the package index on your system is up to date, and the upgrade command upgrades any existing outdated packages. The third command line is the one that installs all of the necessary packages. Any existing package dependencies are pulled in by the package manager.

Once your system is prepared, download the Node *tarball* (the compressed, archived file of the source) to your system. I use wget to access tarballs, though you can also use curl. At the time I'm writing this, the most recent source for Node is version 0.8.2:

```
wget http://nodejs.org/dist/v0.8.2/node-v0.8.2.tar.gz
```

Once you've downloaded it, unzip and untar the file:

```
tar -zxf node-v0.8.2.tar.gz
```

You now have a directory labeled *node-v0.6.18*. Change into the directory and issue the following commands to compile and install Node:

```
./configure
make
sudo make install
```

If you've not used the make utility in Unix before, these three commands set up the *makefile* based on your system environment and installation, run a preliminary make to check for dependencies, and then perform a final make with installation. After processing these commands, Node should now be installed and accessible globally via the command line.

 The fun challenge of programming is that no two systems are alike. This sequence of actions should be successful in most Linux environments, but the operative word here is *should*.

Notice in the last command that you had to use sudo to install Node. You need root privileges to install Node this way (see the upcoming note). However, you can install Node locally by using the following, which installs Node in a given local subdirectory:

```
mkdir ~/working
./configure --prefix=~/working
make
make install
echo 'export PATH=~/working/bin:${PATH}' >> ~/.bashrc
. ~/.bashrc
```

So, as you can see here, setting the prefix configuration option to a specified path in your home directory installs Node locally. You'll need to remember to update your PATH environmental variable accordingly.

To use sudo, you have to be granted root, or *superuser*, privileges, and your username must be listed in a special file located at */etc/sudoers*.

Although you can install Node locally, if you're thinking of using this approach to use Node in your shared hosting environment, think again. Installing Node is just one part of using Node in an environment. You also need privileges to compile an application, as well as run applications off of certain ports (such as port 80). Most shared hosting environments will not allow you to install your own version of Node.

Unless there's a compelling reason, I recommend installing Node using sudo.

At one time there was a security concern about running the Node package manager (npm), covered in Chapter 4, with root privilege. However, those security issues have since been addressed.

Partnering Node with WebMatrix on Windows 7

You can install Node in Windows using a very basic installation sequence as outlined in the wiki installation page provided earlier. However, chances are that if you're going to use Node in a Windows environment, you're going to use it as part of a Windows web development infrastructure.

There are two different Windows infrastructures you can use Node with at this time. One is the new Windows Azure cloud platform, which allows developers to host applications in a remote service (called a *cloud*). Microsoft provides instructions for installing the Windows Azure SDK for Node, so I won't be covering that process in this chapter (though I will examine and demonstrate the SDK later in the book).

You can find the Windows Azure SDK for Node and installation instructions at *https://www.windowsazure.com/en-us/develop/nodejs/*.

The other approach to using Node on Windows—in this case, Windows 7—is by integrating Node into Microsoft's WebMatrix, a tool for web developers integrating open source technologies. Here are the steps we'll need to take to get Node up and running with WebMatrix in Windows 7:

1. Install WebMatrix.
2. Install Node using the latest Windows installation package.
3. Install iisnode for IIS Express 7.x, which enables Node applications with IIS on Windows.
4. Install Node templates for WebMatrix; these simplify Node development.

You install WebMatrix using the Microsoft Web Platform Installer, as shown in Figure 1-1. The tool also installs IIS Express, which is a developer version of Microsoft's web server. Download WebMatrix from *http://www.microsoft.com/web/webmatrix/*.

Figure 1-1. Installing WebMatrix in Windows 7

Once the WebMatrix installation is finished, install the latest version of Node using the installer provided at the primary Node site (*http://nodejs.org/#download*). Installation is one-click, and once you're finished you can open a Command window and type **node** to check for yourself that the application is operational, as shown in Figure 1-2.

For Node to work with IIS in Windows, install iisnode, a native IIS 7.x module created and maintained by Tomasz Janczuk. As with Node, installation is a snap using the prebuilt installation package, available at *https://github.com/tjanczuk/iisnode*. There are x86 and x64 installations, but for x64, you'll need to install both.

```
Command Prompt                                                    _ □ X
C:\Users\Shelley>node -h
Usage: node [options] [ -e script ! script.js ] [arguments]
       node debug script.js [arguments]

Options:
  -v, --version          print node's version
  -e, --eval script      evaluate script
  -p, --print            print result of --eval
  --v8-options           print v8 command line options
  --vars                 print various compiled-in variables
  --max-stack-size=val   set max v8 stack size (bytes)

Environment variables:
NODE_PATH                ';'-separated list of directories
                         prefixed to the module search path.
NODE_MODULE_CONTEXTS     Set to 1 to load modules in their own
                         global contexts.
NODE_DISABLE_COLORS      Set to 1 to disable colors in the REPL

Documentation can be found at http://nodejs.org/

C:\Users\Shelley>node -v
v0.6.8

C:\Users\Shelley>
```

Figure 1-2. Testing in the Command window to ensure Node is properly installed

During the iisnode installation, a window may pop up telling you that you're missing the Microsoft Visual C++ 2010 Redistributable Package, as shown in Figure 1-3. If so, you'll need to install this package, making sure you get the one that matches the version of iisnode you're installing—either the x86 package (available at *http://www.microsoft .com/download/en/details.aspx?id=5555*) or the x64 package (available at *http://www .microsoft.com/download/en/details.aspx?id=14632*), or both. Once you've installed the requisite package, run the iisnode installation again.

iisnode for iis express 7.x Setup   ⚠

⚠ Microsoft Visual C++ 2010 Redistributable Package
    (x86) is required but not installed. Please install it then
    rerun this installer.

                    [OK]

Figure 1-3. Message warning us that we need to install the C++ redistributable package

If you want to install the iisnode samples, open a Command window with administrator privileges, go to the directory where iisnode is installed—either *Program Files* for 64-bit, or *Program Files (x86)*—and run the *setupsamples.bat* file.

To complete the WebMatrix/Node setup, download and install the Node templates for WebMatrix, created by Steve Sanderson and found at *https://github.com/SteveSan derson/Node-Site-Templates-for-WebMatrix*.

You can test that everything works by running WebMatrix, and in the opening pages, select the "Site from Template" option. In the page that opens, shown in Figure 1-4, you'll see two Node template options: one for Express (introduced in Chapter 7) and one for creating a basic, empty site configured for Node. Choose the latter option, giving the site a name of First Node Site, or whatever you want to use.

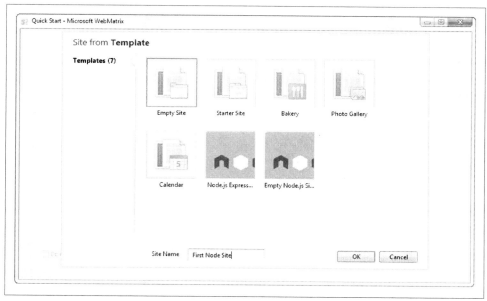

Figure 1-4. Creating a new Node site using a template in WebMatrix

Figure 1-5 shows WebMatrix once the site has been generated. Click the Run button, located in the top left of the page, and a browser page should open with the ubiquitous "Hello, world!" message displayed.

If you're running the Windows Firewall, the first time you run a Node application, you may get a warning like that shown in Figure 1-6. You need to let the Firewall know this application is acceptable by checking the "Private networks" option and then the "Allow access" button. You want to restrict communication to just your private network on your development machine.

Figure 1-5. Newly generated Node site in WebMatrix

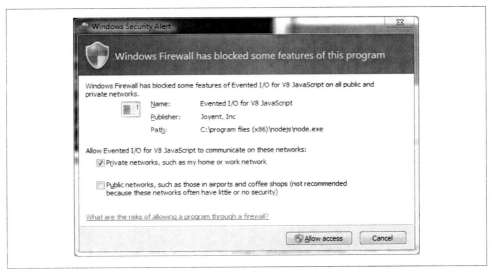

Figure 1-6. Warning that the Windows Firewall blocked Node application, and the option to bypass

If you look at the generated files for your new WebMatrix Node project, you'll see one named *app.js*. This is the Node file, and it contains the following code:

```
var http = require('http');

http.createServer(function (req, res) {

    res.writeHead(200, { 'Content-Type': 'text/html' });
    res.end('Hello, world!');

}).listen(process.env.PORT || 8080);
```

What this all means, I'll get into in the second part of this chapter. The important item to take away from this code right now is that we can run this same application in any operating system where Node is installed and get the exact same functionality: a service that returns a simple message to the user.

 To access the iisnode examples from WebMatrix, select the WebMatrix option "Site from Folder," and then input the following into the dialog that opens: **%localappdata%\iisnode\www**.

Updating Node

Node stable releases are even numbered, such as the current 0.8.x, while the development releases are odd numbered (currently 0.9.x). I recommend sticking with stable releases only—at least until you have some experience with Node.

Updating your Node installation isn't complicated. If you used the package installer, using it for the new version should just override the old installation. If you're working directly with the source, you can always uninstall the old source and install the new if you're concerned about potential clutter or file corruption. In the Node source directory, just issue the uninstall make option:

```
make uninstall
```

Download the new source, compile it, and install it, and you're ready to go again.

The challenge with updating Node is determining whether a specific environment, module, or other application works with the new version. In most cases, you shouldn't have version troubles. However, if you do, there is an application you can use to "switch" Node versions. The application is the Node Version Manager (Nvm).

You can download Nvm from GitHub, at *https://github.com/creationix/nvm*. Like Node, Nvm must be compiled and installed on your system.

To install a specific version of Node, install it with Nvm:

```
nvm install v0.4.1
```

To switch to a specific version, use the following:

```
nvm run v0.4.1
```

To see which versions are available, use:

```
nvm ls
```

Node: Jumping In

Now that you have Node installed, it's time to jump into your first application.

Hello, World in Node

As is typical for testing out any new development environment, language, or tool, the first application we'll create is "Hello, World"—a simple application that prints out a greeting to whomever accesses it.

Example 1-1 shows all the text needed to create Hello, World in Node.

Example 1-1. Hello, World in Node

```
// load http module
var http = require('http');

// create http server
http.createServer(function (req, res) {

  // content header
  res.writeHead(200, {'content-type': 'text/plain'});

  // write message and signal communication is complete
  res.end("Hello, World!\n");
}).listen(8124);

console.log('Server running on 8124');
```

The code is saved in a file named *helloworld.js*. As server-side functionality goes, this Node application is neither too verbose, nor too cryptic; one can intuit what's happening, even without knowing Node. Best of all, it's familiar since it's written in a language we know well: JavaScript.

To run the application, from the command line in Linux, the Terminal window in Mac OS, or the Command window in Windows, type:

```
node helloworld.js
```

The following is printed to the command line once the program has successfully started:

```
Server running at 8124
```

Now, access the site using any browser. If the application is running on your local machine, you'll use localhost:8124. If it's running remotely, use the URL of the remote site, with the 8124 port. A web page with the words "Hello, World!" is displayed. You've now created your first complete and working Node application.

If you're installing Node in a Fedora system, be aware that Node is renamed due to name conflicts with existing functionality. There's more on this at *http://nodejs.tchol.org/*.

Since we didn't use an ampersand (&) following the node command—telling the application to run in the background—the application starts and doesn't return you to the command line. You can continue accessing the application, and the same words get displayed. The application continues until you type Ctrl-C to cancel it, or otherwise kill the process.

If you want to run the application in the background within a Linux system, use the following:

```
node helloworld.js &
```

However, you'll then have to find the process identifier using ps -ef, and manually kill the right process—in this case, the one with the process identifier 3747—using kill:

```
ps -ef | grep node
kill 3747
```

Exiting the terminal window will also kill the process.

In Chapter 16, I cover how to create a persistent Node application installation.

You won't be able to start another Node application listening at the same port: you can run only one Node application against one port at a time. If you're running Apache at port 80, you won't be able to run the Node application at this port, either. You must use a different port for each application.

You can also add *helloworld.js* as a new file to the existing WebMatrix website you created earlier, if you're using WebMatrix. Just open the site, choose the "New File..." option from the menu bar, and add the text shown in Example 1-1 to the file. Then click the Run button.

WebMatrix overrides the port in the application. When you run the application, you'll access the application from the port defined for the project, not specified in the http.Server.listen method.

Hello, World from the Top

I'll get more in depth on the anatomy of Node applications in the next couple of chapters, but for now, let's take a closer look at the Hello, World application.

Returning to the text in Example 1-1, the first line of code is:

```
var http = require('http');
```

Most Node functionality is provided through external applications and libraries called *modules*. This line of JavaScript loads the HTTP module, assigning it to a local variable. The HTTP module provides basic HTTP functionality, enabling network access of the application.

The next line of code is:

```
http.createServer(function (req, res) { ...
```

In this line of code, a new server is created with `createServer`, and an anonymous function is passed as the parameter to the function call. This anonymous function is the `requestListener` function, and has two parameters: a server request (`http.Server Request`) and a server response (`http.ServerResponse`).

Within the anonymous function, we have the following line:

```
res.writeHead(200, {'content-Type': 'text/plain'});
```

The `http.ServerResponse` object has a method, `writeHead`, that sends a response header with the response status code (200), as well as provides the `content-type` of the response. You can also include other response header information within the `headers` object, such as `content-length` or `connection`:

```
{ 'content-length': '123',
  'content-type': 'text/plain',
  'connection': 'keep-alive',
  'accept': '*/*' }
```

A second, optional parameter to `writeHead` is a `reasonPhrase`, which is a textual description of the status code.

Following the code to create the header is the command to write the "Hello, World!" message:

```
res.end("Hello, World!\n");
```

The `http.ServerResponse.end` method signals that the communication is finished; all headers and the response body have been sent. This method *must* be used with every `http.ServerResponse` object.

The end method has two parameters:

- A chunk of data, which can be either a string or a buffer.
- If the chunk of data is a string, the second parameter specifies the encoding.

Both parameters are optional, and the second parameter is required only if the encoding of the string is anything other than `utf8`, which is the default.

Instead of passing the text in the end function, I could have used another method, `write`:

```
res.write("Hello, World!\n");
```

and then:

```
    res.end();
```

The anonymous function and the `createServer` function are both finished on the next line in the code:

```
    }).listen(8124);
```

The `http.Server.listen` method chained at the end of the `createServer` method listens for incoming connections on a given port—in this case, port 8124. Optional parameters are a hostname and a *callback* function. If a hostname isn't provided, the server accepts connections to web addresses, such as *http://oreilly.com* or *http://examples.burningbird .net*.

 More on the callback function later in this chapter.

The `listen` method is *asynchronous*, which means the application doesn't block program execution, waiting for the connection to be established. Whatever code following the `listen` call is processed, and the `listen` callback function is invoked when the `listening` event is fired—when the port connection is established.

The last line of code is:

```
    console.log('Server running on 8124/');
```

The `console` object is one of the objects from the browser world that is incorporated into Node. It's a familiar construct for most JavaScript developers, and provides a way to output text to the command line (or development environment), rather than to the client.

Asynchronous Functions and the Node Event Loop

The fundamental design behind Node is that an application is executed on a single thread (or process), and all events are handled asynchronously.

Consider how the typical web server, such as Apache, works. Apache has two different approaches to how it handles incoming requests. The first is to assign each request to a separate process until the request is satisfied; the second is to spawn a separate thread for each request.

The first approach (known as the *prefork multiprocessing model*, or prefork MPM) can create as many child processes as specified in an Apache configuration file. The advantage to creating a separate process is that applications accessed via the request, such as a PHP application, don't have to be thread-safe. The disadvantage is that each process is memory intensive and doesn't scale very well.

The second approach (known as the *worker* MPM), implements a hybrid process-thread approach. Each incoming request is handled via a new thread. It's more efficient from a memory perspective, but also requires that all applications be thread-safe. Though the popular web language PHP is now thread-safe, there's no guarantee that the many different libraries used with it are also thread-safe.

Regardless of the approach used, both types respond to requests in parallel. If five people access a web application at the exact same time, and the server is set up accordingly, the web server handles all five requests simultaneously.

Node does things differently. When you start a Node application, it's created on a single thread of execution. It sits there, waiting for an application to come along and make a request. When Node gets a request, no other request can be processed until it's finished processing the code for the current one.

You might be thinking that this doesn't sound very efficient, and it wouldn't be except for one thing: Node operates asynchronously, via an event loop and callback functions. An event loop is nothing more than functionality that basically polls for specific events and invokes event handlers at the proper time. In Node, a callback function is this event handler.

Unlike with other single-threaded applications, when you make a request to a Node application and it must, in turn, make some request of resources (such as a database request or file access), Node initiates the request, but doesn't wait around until the request receives a response. Instead, it attaches a callback function to the request. When whatever has been requested is ready (or finished), an event is emitted to that effect, triggering the associated callback function to do something with either the results of the requested action or the resources requested.

If five people access a Node application at the exact same time, and the application needs to access a resource from a file, Node attaches a callback function to a response event for each request. As the resource becomes available for each, the callback function is called, and each person's request is satisfied in turn. In the meantime, the Node application can be handling other requests, either for the same applications or a different application.

Though the application doesn't process the requests in parallel, depending on how busy it is and how it's designed, most people usually won't perceive any delay in the response. Best of all, the application is very frugal with memory and other limited resources.

Reading a File Asynchronously

To demonstrate Node's asynchronous nature, Example 1-2 modifies the Hello, World application from earlier in the chapter. Instead of just typing out "Hello, World!" it actually opens up the previously created *helloworld.js* and outputs the contents to the client.

Example 1-2. Asynchronously opening and writing out contents of a file

```
// load http module
var http = require('http');
var fs = require('fs');

// create http server
http.createServer(function (req, res) {

    // open and read in helloworld.js
    fs.readFile('helloworld.js', 'utf8', function(err, data) {

        res.writeHead(200, {'Content-Type': 'text/plain'});
        if (err)
            res.write('Could not find or open file for reading\n');
        else

            // if no error, write JS file to client
            res.write(data);
        res.end();
    });
}).listen(8124, function() { console.log('bound to port 8124');});});

console.log('Server running on 8124/');
```

A new module, File System (`fs`), is used in this example. The File System module wraps standard POSIX file functionality, including opening up and accessing the contents from a file. The method used is `readFile`. In Example 1-2, it's passed the name of the file to open, the encoding, and an anonymous function.

The two instances of asynchronous behavior I want to point out in Example 1-2 are the callback function that's attached to the `readFile` method, and the callback function attached to the `listen` method.

As discussed earlier, the `listen` method tells the HTTP server object to begin listening for connections on the given port. Node doesn't block, waiting for the connection to be established, so if we need to do something once the connection is established, we provide a callback function, as shown in Example 1-2.

When the connection is established, a `listening` event is emitted, which then invokes the callback function, outputting a message to the console.

The second, more important callback instance is the one attached to `readFile`. Accessing a file is a time-consuming operation, relatively speaking, and a single-threaded application accessed by multiple clients that blocked on file access would soon bog down and be unusable.

Instead, the file is opened and the contents are read asynchronously. Only when the contents have been read into the data buffer—or an error occurs during the process— is the callback function passed to the `readFile` method called. It's passed the error (if any), and the data if no error occurs.

In the callback function, the error is checked, and if there is no error, the data is then written out to the response back to the client.

Taking a Closer Look at Asynchronous Program Flow

Most people who have developed with JavaScript have done so in client applications, meant to be run by one person at a time in a browser. Using JavaScript in the server may seem odd. Creating a JavaScript application accessed by multiple people at the same time may seem even odder.

Our job is made easier because of the Node event loop and being able to put our trust in asynchronous function calls. However, we're no longer in Kansas, Dorothy—we are developing for a different environment.

To demonstrate the differences in this new environment, I created two new applications: one as a service, and one to test the new service. Example 1-3 shows the code for the service application.

In the code, a function is called, synchronously, to write out numbers from 1 to 100. Then a file is opened, similar to what happened in Example 1-2, but this time the name of the file is passed in as a query string parameter. In addition, the file is opened only after a timer event.

Example 1-3. New service that prints out a sequence of numbers and then the contents of a file

```
var http = require('http');
var fs = require('fs');

// write out numbers
function writeNumbers(res) {

  var counter = 0;

  // increment global, write to client
  for (var i = 0; i<100; i++) {
    counter++;
    res.write(counter.toString() + '\n');
  }
}

// create http server
http.createServer(function (req, res) {

    var query = require('url').parse(req.url).query;
    var app = require('querystring').parse(query).file + ".txt";

    // content header
    res.writeHead(200, {'Content-Type': 'text/plain'});

    // write out numbers
    writeNumbers(res);
```

```
    // timer to open file and read contents
    setTimeout(function() {

        console.log('opening ' + app);
        // open and read in file contents
        fs.readFile(app, 'utf8', function(err, data) {
            if (err)
                res.write('Could not find or open file for reading\n');
            else {
                res.write(data);
            }
            // response is done
            res.end();
        });
    },2000);
}).listen(8124);

console.log('Server running at 8124');
```

The loop to print out the numbers is used to delay the application, similar to what could happen if you performed a computationally intensive process and then blocked until the process was finished. The setTimeout function is another asynchronous function, which in turn invokes a second asynchronous function: readFile. The application combines both asynchronous and synchronous processes.

Create a text file named *main.txt*, containing any text you want. Running the application and accessing the page from Chrome with a query string of file=main generates the following console output:

```
Server running at 8124/
opening main.txt
opening undefined.txt
```

The first two lines are expected. The first is the result of running console.log at the end of the application, and the second is a printout of the file being opened. But what's *undefined.txt* in the third line?

When processing a web request from a browser, be aware that browsers may send more than one request. For instance, a browser may also send a second request, looking for a *favicon.ico*. Because of this, when you're processing the query string, you must check to see if the data you need is being provided, and ignore requests without the data.

 The browser sending multiple requests can impact your application if you're expecting values via a query string. You must adjust your application accordingly. And yes, you'll still need to test your application with several different browsers.

So far, all we've done is test our Node applications from a browser. This isn't really putting much stress on the asynchronous nature of the Node application.

Example 1-4 contains the code for a very simple test application. All it does is use the HTTP module to request the example server several times in a loop. The requests aren't asynchronous. However, we'll also be accessing the service using the browser as we run the test program. Both, combined, asynchronously test the application.

 I'll cover creating asynchronous testing applications in Chapter 14.

Example 1-4. Simple application to call the new Node application 2,000 times

```
var http = require('http');

//The url we want, plus the path and options we need
var options = {
    host: 'localhost',
    port: 8124,
    path: '/?file=secondary',
    method: 'GET'
};

var processPublicTimeline = function(response) {
    // finished? ok, write the data to a file
    console.log('finished request');
};

for (var i = 0; i < 2000; i++) {
    // make the request, and then end it, to close the connection
    http.request(options, processPublicTimeline).end();
}
```

Create the second text file, named *secondary.txt*. Put whatever you wish in it, but make the contents obviously different from *main.txt*.

After making sure the Node application is running, start the test application:

```
node test.js
```

As the test application is running, access the application using your browser. If you look at the console messages being output by the application, you'll see it process both your manual and the test application's automated requests. Yet the results are consistent with what we would expect, a web page with:

- The numbers 1 through 100 printed out
- The contents of the text file—in this case, *main.txt*

Now, let's mix things up a bit. In Example 1-3, make the counter global rather than local to the loop function, and start the application again. Then run the test program and access the page in the browser.

The results have definitely changed. Rather than the numbers starting at 1 and going to 100, they start at numbers like 2,601 and 26,301. They still print out the next sequential 99 numbers, but the starting value is different.

The reason is, of course, the use of the global counter. Since you're accessing the same application in the browser manually as the test program is doing automatically, you're both updating counter. Both the manual and automated application requests are processed, in turn, so there's no contention for the shared data (a major problem with thread safety in a multithreaded environment), but if you're expecting a consistent beginning value, you might be surprised.

Now change the application again, but this time remove the var keyword in front of the app variable—"accidentally" making it a global variable. We all have, from time to time, forgotten the var keyword with our client-side JavaScript applications. The only time we get bit by this mistake is if any libraries we're using are using the same variable name.

Run the test application and access the Node service in your browser a couple of times. Chances are, you'll end up with the text from the *secondary.txt* file in your browser window, rather than the requested *main.txt* file. The reason is that in the time between when you processed the query for the filename and when you actually opened the file, the automatic application modified the app variable. The test application is able to do so because you made an asynchronous function request, basically ceding program control to another request while your request was still mid-process.

 This example demonstrates how absolutely critical the use of var is with Node.

Benefits of Node

By now you have a working Node installation—possibly even more than one.

You've also had a chance to create a couple of Node applications and test out the differences between synchronous and asynchronous code (and what happens if you accidentally forget the var keyword).

Node isn't all asynchronous function calls. Some objects may provide both synchronous and asynchronous versions of the same function. However, Node works best when you use asynchronous coding as much as possible.

The Node event loop and callback functions have two major benefits.

First, the application can easily scale, since a single thread of execution doesn't have an enormous amount of overhead. If we were to create a PHP application similar to the Node application in Example 1-3, the user would see the same page—but your system would definitely notice the difference. If you ran the PHP application in Apache with the default prefork MPM, each time the application was requested, it would have to be handled in a separate child process. Chances are, unless you have a significantly loaded system, you'll only be able to run—at most—a couple of hundred child processes in parallel. More than that number of requests means that a client needs to wait for a response.

A second benefit to Node is that you minimize resource usage, but without having to resort to multithreaded development. In other words, you don't have to create a thread-safe application. If you've ever developed a thread-safe application previously, you're probably feeling profoundly glad at this statement.

However, as was demonstrated in the last example application, you aren't developing JavaScript applications for single users to run in the browser, either. When you work with asynchronous applications, you need to make sure that you don't build in dependencies on one asynchronous function call finishing ahead of another, because there are no guarantees—not unless you call the second function call within the code of the first. In addition, global variables are extremely hazardous in Node, as is forgetting the var keyword.

Still, these are issues we can work with—especially considering the benefits of Node's low resource requirements and not having to worry about threads.

 A final reason for liking Node? You can code in JavaScript without having to worry about IE6.

CHAPTER 2

Interactive Node with REPL

While you're exploring the use of Node and figuring out the code for your custom module or Node application, you don't have to type JavaScript into a file and run it with Node to test your code. Node also comes with an interactive component known as *REPL*, or *read-eval-print loop*, which is the subject of this chapter.

REPL (pronounced "repple") supports a simplified Emacs style of line editing and a small set of basic commands. Whatever you type into REPL is processed no differently than if you had typed the JavaScript into a file and run the file using Node. You can actually use REPL to code your entire application—literally testing the application on the fly.

In this chapter, I'll also cover some interesting quirks of REPL, along with some ways you can work around them. These workarounds include replacing the underlying mechanism that persists commands, as well as using some command-line editing.

Lastly, if the built-in REPL doesn't provide exactly what you need for an interactive environment, there's also an API to create your own custom REPL, which I'll demonstrate in the latter part of the chapter.

 You'll find a handy guide for using REPL at *http://docs.nodejitsu.com/ articles/REPL/how-to-use-nodejs-repl*. The Nodejitsu site also provides a nice tutorial on how to create a custom REPL at *http://docs.nodejitsu .com/articles/REPL/how-to-create-a-custom-repl*.

REPL: First Looks and Undefined Expressions

To begin REPL, simply type **node** without providing any Node application file, like so:

```
$ node
```

REPL then provides a command-line prompt—an angle bracket (>)—by default. Anything you type from this point on is processed by the underlying V8 JavaScript engine.

REPL is very simple to use. Just start typing in your JavaScript, like you'd add it to a file:

```
> a = 2;
2
```

The tool prints out the result of whatever expression you just typed. In this session excerpt, the value of the expression is 2. In the following, the expression result is an array with three elements:

```
> b = ['a','b','c'];
[ 'a', 'b', 'c' ]
```

To access the last expression, use the underscore/underline character (_). In the following, a is set to 2, and the resulting expression is incremented by 1, and then 1 again:

```
> a = 2;
2
> _ ++;
3
> _ ++;
4
```

You can even access properties or call methods on the underscored expression:

```
> ['apple','orange','lime']
[ 'apple', 'orange', 'lime' ]
> _.length
3
> 3 + 4
7
> _.toString();
'7'
```

You can use the var keyword with REPL in order to access an expression or value at a later time, but you might get an unexpected result. For instance, the following line in REPL:

```
var a = 2;
```

doesn't return the value 2, it returns a value of undefined. The reason is that the result of the expression is undefined, since variable assignment doesn't return a result when evaluated.

Consider the following instead, which is what's happening, more or less, under the hood in REPL:

```
console.log(eval('a = 2'));
console.log(eval('var a = 2'));
```

Typing the preceding lines into a file and running that file using Node returns:

```
2
undefined
```

There is no result from the second call to eval, and hence the value returned is undefined. Remember, REPL is a read-eval-print loop, with emphasis on the *eval*.

Still, you can use the variable in REPL, just as you would in a Node application:

```
> var a = 2;
undefined
> a++;
2
> a++;
3
```

The latter two command lines do have results, which are printed out by REPL.

 I'll demonstrate how to create your own custom REPL—one that doesn't output undefined—in the section "Custom REPL" on page 29.

To end the REPL session, either press Ctrl-C twice, or Ctrl-D once. We'll cover other ways to end the session later, in "REPL Commands" on page 27.

Benefits of REPL: Getting a Closer Understanding of JavaScript Under the Hood

Here's a typical demonstration of REPL:

```
> 3 > 2 > 1;
false
```

This code snippet is a good example of how REPL can be useful. At first glance, we might expect the expression we typed to evaluate to true, since 3 is greater than 2, which is greater than 1. However, in JavaScript, expressions are evaluated left to right, and each expression's result is returned for the next evaluation.

A better way of looking at what's happening with the preceding code snippet is this REPL session:

```
> 3 > 2 > 1;
false
> 3 > 2;
true
> true > 1;
false
```

Now the result makes more sense. What's happening is that the expression 3 > 2 is evaluated, returning true. But then the value of true is compared to the numeric 1. JavaScript provides automatic data type conversion, after which true and 1 are equivalent values. Hence, true is not greater than 1, and the result is false.

REPL's helpfulness is in enabling us to discover these little interesting quirks in JavaScript. Hopefully, after testing our code in REPL, we don't have unexpected side effects in our applications (such as expecting a result of true but getting a result of false).

Multiline and More Complex JavaScript

You can type the same JavaScript into REPL just like you'd type it into a file, including require statements to import modules. A session to try out the Query String (qs) module is repeated in the following text:

```
$ node
> qs = require('querystring');
{ unescapeBuffer: [Function],
  unescape: [Function],
  escape: [Function],
  encode: [Function],
  stringify: [Function],
  decode: [Function],
  parse: [Function] }
> val = qs.parse('file=main&file=secondary&test=one').file;
[ 'main', 'secondary' ]
```

Since you didn't use the var keyword, the expression result is printed out—in this instance, the interface for the querystring object. How's that for a bonus? Not only are you getting access to the object, but you're also learning more about the object's interface while you're at it. However, if you want to forgo the potentially lengthy output of text, use the var keyword:

```
> var qs = require('querystring');
```

You'll be able to access the querystring object with the qs variable with either approach.

In addition to being able to incorporate external modules, REPL gracefully handles multiline expressions, providing a textual indicator of code that's nested following an opening curly brace ({):

```
> var test = function (x, y) {
... var val = x * y;
... return val;
... };
undefined
> test(3,4);
12
```

REPL provides repeating dots to indicate that everything that's being typed follows an open curly brace and hence the command isn't finished yet. It does the same for an open parenthesis, too:

```
> test(4,
... 5);
20
```

Increasing levels of nesting generates more dots; this is necessary in an interactive environment, where you might lose track of where you are, as you type:

```
> var test = function (x, y) {
... var test2 = function (x, y) {
..... return x * y;
```

```
..... }
... return test2(x,y);
... }
undefined
> test(3,4);
12
>
```

You can type in, or copy and paste in, an entire Node application and run it from REPL:

```
> var http = require('http');
undefined
> http.createServer(function (req, res) {
...
...    // content header
...    res.writeHead(200, {'Content-Type': 'text/plain'});
...
...    res.end("Hello person\n");
... }).listen(8124);
{ connections: 0,
  allowHalfOpen: true,
  _handle:
   { writeQueueSize: 0,
     onconnection: [Function: onconnection],
     socket: [Circular] },
  _events:
   { request: [Function],
     connection: [Function: connectionListener] },
  httpAllowHalfOpen: false }
>
undefined
> console.log('Server running at http://127.0.0.1:8124/');
Server running at http://127.0.0.1:8124/
Undefined
```

You can access this application from a browser no differently than if you had typed the text into a file and run it using Node. And again, the responses back from REPL can provide an interesting look at the code, as shown in the boldfaced text.

In fact, my favorite use of REPL is to get a quick look at objects. For instance, the Node core object global is sparsely documented at the Node.js website. To get a better look, I opened up a REPL session and passed the object to the console.log method like so:

```
> console.log(global)
```

I could have done the following, which has the same result:

```
> gl = global;
```

I'm not replicating what was displayed in REPL; I'll leave that for you to try on your own installation, since the interface for global is so large. The important point to take away from this exercise is that we can, at any time, quickly and easily get a quick look at an object's interface. It's a handy way of remembering what a method is called, or what properties are available.

There's more on `global` in Chapter 3.

You can use the up and down arrow keys to traverse through the commands you've typed into REPL. This can be a handy way of reviewing what you've done, as well as a way of editing what you've done, though in a somewhat limited capacity.

Consider the following session in REPL:

```
> var myFruit = function(fruitArray,pickOne) {
... return fruitArray[pickOne - 1];
... }
undefined
> fruit = ['apples','oranges','limes','cherries'];
[ 'apples',
  'oranges',
  'limes',
  'cherries' ]
> myFruit(fruit,2);
'oranges'
> myFruit(fruit,0);
undefined
> var myFruit = function(fruitArray,pickOne) {
... if (pickOne <= 0) return 'invalid number';
... return fruitArray[pickOne - 1];
... };
undefined
> myFruit(fruit,0);
'invalid number'
> myFruit(fruit,1);
'apples'
```

Though it's not demonstrated in this printout, when I modified the function to check the input value, I actually arrowed up through the content to the beginning function declaration, and then hit Enter to restart the function. I added the new line, and then again used the arrow keys to repeat previously typed entries until the function was finished. I also used the up arrow key to repeat the function call that resulted in an `undefined` result.

It seems like a lot of work just to avoid retyping something so simple, but consider working with regular expressions, such as the following:

```
> var ssRe = /^\d{3}-\d{2}-\d{4}$/;
undefined
> ssRe.test('555-55-5555');
true
> var decRe = /^\s*(\+|-)?((\d+(\.\d+)?)|(\.\d+))\s*$/;
undefined
> decRe.test(56.5);
true
```

I'm absolutely useless when it comes to regular expressions, and have to tweak them several times before they're just right. Using REPL to test regular expressions is very attractive. However, retyping long regular expressions would be a monstrous amount of work.

Luckily, all we have to do with REPL is arrow up to find the line where the regular expression was created, tweak it, hit Enter, and continue with the next test.

In addition to the arrow keys, you can also use the Tab key to *autocomplete* text. As an example, type **va** at the command line and then press Tab; REPL will autocomplete *var*. You can also use the Tab key to autocomplete any global or local variable. Table 2-1 offers a quick summary of keyboard commands that work with REPL.

Table 2-1. Keyboard control in REPL

Keyboard entry	What it does
Ctrl-C	Terminates current command. Pressing Ctrl-C twice forces an exit.
Ctrl-D	Exits REPL.
Tab	Autocompletes global or local variable.
Up arrow	Traverses up through command history.
Down arrow	Traverses down through command history.
Underscore (_)	References result of last expression.

If you're concerned about spending a lot of time coding in REPL with nothing to show for it when you're done, no worries: you can save the results of the current context with the .save command. It and the other REPL commands are covered in the next section.

REPL Commands

REPL has a simple interface with a small set of useful commands. In the preceding section, I mentioned .save. The .save command saves your inputs in the current object context into a file. Unless you specifically created a new object context or used the .clear command, the context should comprise all of the input in the current REPL session:

```
> .save ./dir/session/save.js
```

Only your inputs are saved, as if you had typed them directly into a file using a text editor.

Here is the complete list of REPL commands and their purposes:

.break

> If you get lost during a multiline entry, typing .break will start you over again. You'll lose the multiline content, though.

`.clear`

>   Resets the context object and clears any multiline expression. This command basically starts you over again.

`.exit`

>   Exits REPL.

`.help`

>   Displays all available REPL commands.

`.save`

>   Saves the current REPL session to a file.

`.load`

>   Loads a file into the current session (`.load /path/to/file.js`).

If you're working on an application using REPL as an editor, here's a hint: save your work often using `.save`. Though current commands are persisted to history, trying to recreate your code from history would be a painful exercise.

Speaking of persistence and history, now let's go over how to customize both with REPL.

REPL and rlwrap

The Node.js website documentation for REPL mentions setting up an environmental variable so you can use REPL with `rlwrap`. What is `rlwrap`, and why would you use it with REPL?

The `rlwrap` utility is a wrapper that adds GNU `readline` library functionality to command lines that allow increased flexibility with keyboard input. It intercepts keyboard input and provides additional functionality, such as enhanced line editing, as well as a persistent history of commands.

You'll need to install `rlwrap` and `readline` to use this facility with REPL, though most flavors of Unix provide an easy package installation. For instance, in my own Ubuntu system, installing `rlwrap` was this simple:

```
apt-get install rlwrap
```

Mac users should use the appropriate installer for these applications. Windows users have to use a Unix environmental emulator, such as Cygwin.

Here's a quick and visual demonstration of using REPL with `rlwrap` to change the REPL prompt to purple:

```
env NODE_NO_READLINE=1 rlwrap -ppurple node
```

If I always want my REPL prompt to be purple, I can add an alias to my *bashrc* file:

```
alias node="env NODE_NO_READLINE=1 rlwrap -ppurple node"
```

To change both the prompt and the color, I'd use the following:

```
env NODE_NO_READLINE=1 rlwrap -ppurple -S "::>" node
```

Now my prompt would be:

```
::>
```

in purple.

The especially useful component of `rlwrap` is its ability to persist history across REPL sessions. By default, we have access to command-line history only within a REPL session. By using `rlwrap`, the next time we access REPL, not only will we have access to a history of commands within the current session, but also a history of commands in past sessions (and other command-line entries). In the following session output, the commands shown were not typed in, but were instead pulled from history with the up arrow key:

```
# env NODE_NO_READLINE=1 rlwrap -ppurple -S "::>" node
::>e = ['a','b'];
[ 'a', 'b' ]
::>3 > 2 > 1;
false
```

As helpful as `rlwrap` is, we still end up with `undefined` every time we type in an expression that doesn't return a value. However, we can adjust this, and other functionality, just by creating our own custom REPL, discussed next.

Custom REPL

Node provides us access to creating our own custom REPL. To do so, first we need to include the REPL module (`repl`):

```
var repl = require("repl");
```

To create a new REPL, we call the `start` method on the `repl` object. The syntax for this method is:

```
repl.start([prompt], [stream], [eval], [useGlobal], [ignoreUndefined]);
```

All of the parameters are optional. If not provided, default values will be used for each as follows:

prompt
> Default is >.

stream
> Default is `process.stdin`.

eval
> Default is the `async` wrapper for `eval`.

useGlobal
> Default is `false` to start a new context rather than use the global object.

ignoreUndefined
Default is `false`; don't ignore the `undefined` responses.

I find the `undefined` expression result in REPL to be unedifying, so I created my own REPL. It took exactly two lines of code (not including the comment):

```
repl = require("repl");

// start REPL with ignoreUndefined set to true
repl.start("node via stdin> ", null, null, null, true);
```

I ran the file, *repl.js*, using Node:

```
node repl.js
```

Then I used the custom REPL just like I use the built-in version, except now I have a different prompt and no longer get the annoying `undefined` after the first variable assignment. I do still get the other responses that aren't `undefined`:

```
node via stdin> var ct = 0;
node via stdin> ct++;
0
node via stdin> console.log(ct);
1
node via stdin> ++ct;
2
node via stdin> console.log(ct);
2
```

In my code, I wanted the defaults for all but `prompt` and `ignoreUndefined`. Setting the other parameters to `null` triggers Node to use the default values for each.

You can replace the `eval` function with your custom REPL. The only requirement is that it has a specific format:

```
function eval(cmd, callback) {
    callback(null, result);
}
```

The `stream` option is interesting. You can run multiple versions of REPL, taking input from both the standard input (the default), as well as sockets. The documentation for REPL at the Node.js site provides an example of a REPL listening in on a TCP socket, using code similar to the following:

```
var repl = require("repl"),
    net = require("net");

// start REPL with ignoreUndefined set to true
repl.start("node via stdin> ", null, null, null, true);

net.createServer(function (socket) {
  repl.start("node via TCP socket> ", socket);

}).listen(8124);
```

When you run the application, you get the standard input prompt where the Node application is running. However, you can also access REPL via TCP. I used PuTTY as a Telnet client to access this TCP-enabled version of REPL. It does work...to a point. I had to issue a `.clear` first, the formatting is off, and when I tried to use the underscore to reference the last expression, Node didn't know what I was talking about, as shown in Figure 2-1.

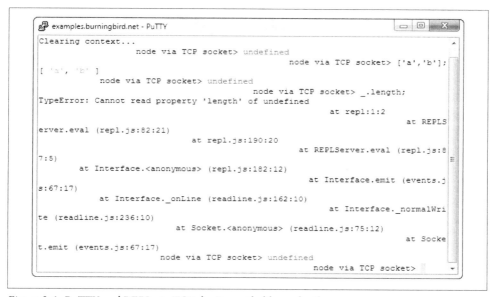

Figure 2-1. PuTTY and REPL via TCP don't exactly like each other

I also tried with the Windows 7 Telnet client, and the response was even worse. However, using my Linux Telnet client worked without a hitch.

The problem here, as you might expect, is Telnet client settings. However, I didn't pursue it further, because running REPL from an exposed Telnet socket is not something I plan to implement, and not something I would recommend, either—at least, not without heavy security. It's like using `eval()` in your client-side code, and not scrubbing the text your users send you to run—but worse.

You could keep a running REPL and communicate via a Unix socket with something like the GNU Netcat utility:

```
nc -U /tmp/node-repl-sock
```

You can type in commands no differently than typing them in using `stdin`. Be aware, though, if you're using either a TCP or Unix socket, that any `console.log` commands are printed out to the server console, not to the client:

```
console.log(someVariable); // actually printed out to server
```

An application option that I consider to be more useful is to create a REPL application that preloads modules. In the application in Example 2-1, after the REPL is started, the http, os, and util modules are loaded and assigned to context properties.

Example 2-1. Creating a custom REPL that preloads modules

```
var repl = require('repl');
var context = repl.start(">>", null, null, null, true).context;

// preload in modules
context.http = require('http');
context.util = require('util');
context.os = require('os');
```

Running the application with Node brings up the REPL prompt, where we can then access the modules:

```
>>os.hostname();
'einstein'
>>util.log('message');
5 Feb 11:33:15 - message
>>
```

If you want to run the REPL application like an executable in Linux, add the following line as the first line in the application:

```
#!/usr/local/bin/node
```

Modify the file to be an executable and run it:

```
# chmod u+x replcontext.js
# ./replcontext.js
>>
```

Stuff Happens—Save Often

Node's REPL is a handy interactive tool that can make our development tasks a little easier. REPL allows us not only to try out JavaScript before including it in our files, but also to actually create our applications interactively and then save the results when we're finished.

Another useful REPL feature is that it enables us to create a custom REPL so that we can eliminate the unhelpful undefined responses, preload modules, change the prompt or the eval routine we use, and more.

I also strongly recommend that you look into using REPL with rlwrap in order to persist commands across sessions. This could end up being a major time saver. Plus, who among us doesn't like additional editing capability?

As you explore REPL further, there's one very important thing to keep in mind from this chapter:

Stuff happens. Save often.

If you'll be spending a lot of time developing in REPL, even with the use of `rlwrap` to persist history, you're going to want to frequently save your work. Working in REPL is no different than working in other editing environments, so I'll repeat: *stuff happens —save often.*

 REPL has had a major facelift in Node 0.8. For instance, just typing the built-in module name, such as `fs`, loads the module now. Other improvements are noted in the new REPL documentation at the primary Node.js website.

CHAPTER 3

The Node Core

Chapter 1 provided a first look at a Node application with the traditional (and always entertaining) Hello, World application. The examples in the chapter made use of a couple of modules from what is known as the *Node core*: the API providing much of the functionality necessary for building Node applications.

In this chapter, I'm going to provide more detail on the Node core system. It's not an exhaustive overview, since the API is quite large and dynamic in nature. Instead, we'll focus on key elements of the API, and take a closer look at those that we'll use in later chapters and/or are complex enough to need a more in-depth review.

Topics covered in this chapter include:

- Node global objects, such as `global`, `process`, and `Buffer`
- The timer methods, such as `setTimeout`
- A quick overview of socket and stream modules and functionality
- The `Utilities` object, especially the part it plays in Node inheritance
- The `EventEmitter` object and events

 Node.js documentation for the current stable release is available at *http: //nodejs.org/api/*.

Globals: global, process, and Buffer

There are several objects available to all Node applications without the user having to incorporate any module. The Node.js website groups these items under the descriptive label of *globals*.

We've been using one global, `require`, to include modules into our applications. We've also made extensive use of another global, `console`, to log messages to the console. Other globals are essential to the underlying implementation of Node, but aren't necessarily anything we'd access or need to know about directly. Some, though, are important enough for us to take a closer look at, because they help define key aspects of how Node works.

In particular, we're going to explore:

- The `global` object—that is, the global namespace
- The `process` object, which provides essential functionality, such as wrappers for the three STDIO (Standard IO) streams, and functionality to transform a synchronous function into an asynchronous callback
- The `Buffer` class, a global object that provides raw data storage and manipulation
- Child processes
- Modules useful for domain resolution and URL processing

global

`global` is the global *namespace* object. In some ways, it's similar to `windows` in a browser environment, in that it provides access to global properties and methods and doesn't have to be explicitly referenced by name.

From REPL, you can print out the `global` object to the console like so:

```
> console.log(global)
```

What prints out is the interface for all of the other global objects, as well as a good deal of information about the system in which you're running.

I mentioned that `global` is like the `windows` object in a browser, but there are key differences—and not just the methods and properties available. The `windows` object in a browser is truly global in nature. If you define a global variable in client-side JavaScript, it's accessible by the web page and by every single library. However, if you create a variable at the top-level scope in a Node module (a variable outside a function), it only becomes global to the module, not to all of the modules.

You can actually see what happens to the `global` object when you define a module/ global variable in REPL. First, define the top-level variable:

```
> var test = "This really isn't global, as we know global";
```

Then print out `global`:

```
> console.log(global);
```

You should see your variable, as a new property of `global`, at the bottom. For another interesting perspective, assign `global` to a variable, but don't use the `var` keyword:

```
gl = global;
```

The `global` object interface is printed out to the console, and at the bottom you'll see the local variable assigned as a *circular reference*:

```
> g1 = global;
...
    g1: [Circular],
    _: [Circular] }
```

Any other global object or method, including `require`, is part of the `global` object's interface.

When Node developers discuss *context*, they're really referring to the `global` object. In Example 2-1 in Chapter 2, the code accessed the `context` object when creating a custom REPL object. The context object is a `global` object. When an application creates a custom REPL, it exists within a new context, which in this case means it has its own `global` object. The way to override this and use the existing `global` object is to create a custom REPL and set the `useGlobal` flag to `true`, rather than the default of `false`.

Modules exist in their own global namespace, which means that if you define a top-level variable in one module, it is not available in other modules. More importantly, it means that only what is explicitly exported from the module becomes part of whatever application includes the module. In fact, you can't access a top-level module variable in an application or other module, even if you deliberately try.

To demonstrate, the following code contains a very simple module that has a top-level variable named `globalValue`, and functions to set and return the value. In the function that returns the value, the `global` object is printed out using a `console.log` method call.

```
var globalValue;

exports.setGlobal = function(val) {
    globalValue = val;
};

exports.returnGlobal = function() {
    console.log(global);
    return globalValue;
};
```

We might expect that in the printout of the `global` object we'll see `globalValue`, as we do when we set a variable in our applications. This doesn't happen, though.

Start a REPL session and issue a `require` call to include the new module:

```
> var mod1 = require('./mod1.js');
```

Set the value and then ask for the value back:

```
> mod1.setGlobal(34);
> var val = mod1.returnGlobal();
```

The `console.log` method prints out the `global` object before returning its globally defined value. We can see at the bottom the new variable holding a reference to the imported module, but `val` is `undefined` because the variable hasn't yet been set. In addition, the output includes no reference to that module's own top-level `globalValue`:

```
mod1: { setGlobal: [Function], returnGlobal: [Function] },
_: undefined,
val: undefined }
```

If we ran the command again, then the outer application variable would be set, but we still wouldn't see globalValue:

```
mod1: { setGlobal: [Function], returnGlobal: [Function] },
_: undefined,
val: 34 }
```

The only access we have to the module data is by whatever means the module provides. For JavaScript developers, this means no more unexpected and harmful data collisions because of accidental or intentional global variables in libraries.

process

Each Node application is an instance of a Node process object, and as such, comes with certain built-in functionality.

Many of the process object's methods and properties provide identification or information about the application and its environment. The process.execPath method returns the execution path for the Node application; process.version provides the Node version; and process.platform identifies the server platform:

```
console.log(process.execPath);
console.log(process.version);
console.log(process.platform);
```

This code returns the following in my system (at the time of this writing):

```
/usr/local/bin/node
v0.6.9
linux
```

The process object also wraps the STDIO streams stdin, stdout, and stderr. Both stdin and stdout are asynchronous, and are readable and writable, respectively. stderr, however, is a synchronous, blocking stream.

To demonstrate how to read and write data from stdin and stdout, in Example 3-1 the Node application listens for data in stdin, and repeats the data to stdout. The stdin stream is paused by default, so we have to issue a resume call before sending data.

Example 3-1. Reading and writing data to stdin and stdout, respectively

```
process.stdin.resume();

process.stdin.on('data', function (chunk) {
  process.stdout.write('data: ' + chunk);
});
```

Run the application using Node, and then start typing into the terminal. Every time you type something and press Enter, what you typed is reflected back to you.

Another useful `process` method is `memoryUsage`, which tells us how much memory the Node application is using. This could be helpful for performance tuning, or just to satisfy your general curiosity about the application. The response has the following structure:

```
{ rss: 7450624, heapTotal: 2783520, heapUsed: 1375720 }
```

The `heapTotal` and `heapUsed` properties refer to the V8 engine's memory usage.

The last `process` method I'm going to cover is `process.nextTick`. This method attaches a callback function that's fired during the next tick (loop) in the Node event loop.

You would use `process.nextTick` if you wanted to delay a function for some reason, but you wanted to delay it asynchronously. A good example would be if you're creating a new function that has a callback function as a parameter and you want to ensure that the callback is truly asynchronous. The following code is a demonstration:

```
function asynchFunction = function (data, callback) {
    process.nextTick(function() {
        callback(val);
    });
);
```

If we just called the callback function, then the action would be synchronous. Now, the callback function won't be called until the next tick in the event loop, rather than right away.

You could use `setTimeout` with a zero (0) millisecond delay instead of `process.nextTick`:

```
setTimeout(function() {
    callback(val);
}, 0);
```

However, `setTimeout` isn't as efficient as `process.nextTick`. When they were tested against each other, `process.nextTick` was called far more quickly than `setTimeout` with a zero-millisecond delay. You might also use `process.nextTick` if you're running an application that has a function performing some computationally complex, and time-consuming, operation. You could break the process into sections, each called via `process.nextTick`, to allow other requests to the Node application to be processed without waiting for the time-consuming process to finish.

Of course, the converse of this is that you don't want to break up a process that you need to ensure executes sequentially, because you may end up with unexpected results.

Buffer

The `Buffer` class, also a global object, is a way of handling binary data in Node. In the section "Servers, Streams, and Sockets" on page 41 later in the chapter, I'll cover the fact that streams are often binary data rather than strings. To convert the binary data to a string, the data encoding for the stream socket is changed using `setEncoding`.

As a demonstration, you can create a new buffer with the following:

```
var buf = new Buffer(string);
```

If the buffer holds a string, you can pass in an optional second parameter with the encoding. Possible encodings are:

ascii
:   Seven-bit ASCII

utf8
:   Multibyte encoded Unicode characters

usc2
:   Two bytes, little-endian-encoded Unicode characters

base64
:   Base64 encoding

hex
:   Encodes each byte as two hexadecimal characters

You can also write a string to an existing buffer, providing an optional offset, length, and encoding:

```
buf.write(string); // offset defaults to 0, length defaults to
                   buffer.length - offset, encoding is utf8
```

Data sent between sockets is transmitted as a buffer (in binary format) by default. To send a string instead, you either need to call setEncoding directly on the socket, or specify the encoding in the function that writes to the socket. By default, the TCP (Transmission Control Protocol) socket.write method sets the second parameter to utf8, but the socket returned in the connectionListener callback to the TCP create Server function sends the data as a buffer, not a string.

The Timers: setTimeout, clearTimeout, setInterval, and clearInterval

The timer functions in client-side JavaScript are part of the global windows object. They're not part of JavaScript, but have become such a ubiquitous part of JavaScript development that the Node developers incorporated them into the Node core API.

The timer functions operate in Node just like they operate in the browser. In fact, they operate in Node exactly the same as they would in Chrome, since Node is based on Chrome's V8 JavaScript engine.

The Node setTimeout function takes a callback function as first parameter, the delay time (in milliseconds) as second parameter, and an optional list of arguments:

```
// timer to open file and read contents to HTTP response object
function on_OpenAndReadFile(filename, res) {

    console.log('opening ' + filename);
```

```
   // open and read in file contents
   fs.readFile(filename, 'utf8', function(err, data) {
      if (err)
         res.write('Could not find or open file for reading\n');
      else {
         res.write(data);
      }
   // reponse is done
   res.end();
}

   setTimeout(openAndReadFile, 2000, filename, res);
```

In the code, the callback function on_OpenAndReadFile opens and reads a file to the HTTP response when the function is called after approximately 2,000 milliseconds have passed.

> As the Node documentation carefully notes, there's no guarantee that the callback function will be invoked in exactly *n* milliseconds (whatever *n* is). This is no different than the use of setTimeout in a browser—we don't have absolute control over the environment, and factors could slightly delay the timer.

The function clearTimeout clears a preset setTimeout. If you need to have a repeating timer, you can use setInterval to call a function every *n* milliseconds—*n* being the second parameter passed to the function. Clear the interval with clearInterval.

Servers, Streams, and Sockets

Much of the Node core API has to do with creating services that listen to specific types of communications. In the examples in Chapter 1, we used the HTTP module to create an HTTP web server. Other methods can create a TCP server, a TLS (Transport Layer Security) server, and a UDP (User Datagram Protocol)/datagram socket. I'll cover TLS in Chapter 15, but in this section I want to introduce the TCP and UDP Node core functionality. First, though, I'll offer a brief introduction to the terms used in this section.

A *socket* is an endpoint in a communication, and a *network socket* is an endpoint in a communication between applications running on two different computers on the network. The data flows between the sockets in what's known as a *stream*. The data in the stream can be transmitted as binary data in a buffer, or in Unicode as a string. Both types of data are transmitted as *packets*: parts of the data split off into specifically sized pieces. There is a special kind of packet, a finish packet (FIN), that is sent by a socket to signal that the transmission is done. How the communication is managed, and how reliable the stream is, depends on the type of socket created.

TCP Sockets and Servers

We can create a basic TCP server and client with the Node Net module. TCP forms the basis for most Internet applications, such as web service and email. It provides a way of reliably transmitting data between client and server sockets.

Creating the TCP server is a little different than creating the HTTP server in Example 1-1 in Chapter 1. We create the server, passing in a callback function. The TCP server differs from the HTTP server in that, rather than passing a requestListener, the TCP callback function's sole argument is an instance of a socket listening for incoming connections.

Example 3-2 contains the code to create a TCP server. Once the server socket is created, it listens for two events: when data is received, and when the client closes the connection.

Example 3-2. A simple TCP server, with a socket listening for client communication on port 8124

```
var net = require('net');

var server = net.createServer(function(conn) {
   console.log('connected');

   conn.on('data', function (data) {
      console.log(data + ' from ' + conn.remoteAddress + ' ' +
        conn.remotePort);
      conn.write('Repeating: ' + data);
   });

   conn.on('close', function() {
       console.log('client closed connection');
   });

}).listen(8124);

console.log('listening on port 8124');
```

There is an optional parameter for createServer: allowHalfOpen. Setting this parameter to true instructs the socket not to send a FIN when it receives a FIN packet from the client. Doing this keeps the socket open for writing (not reading). To close the socket, you'd then need to explicitly use the end method. By default, allowHalfOpen is false.

Notice how a callback function is attached to the two events via the on method. Many objects in Node that emit events provide a way to attach a function as an event listener by using the on method. This method takes the name of the event as first parameter, and the function listener as the second.

 Node objects that inherit from a special object, the EventEmitter, expose the on method event handling, as discussed later in this chapter.

The TCP client is just as simple to create as the server, as shown in Example 3-3. The call to the setEncoding method on the client changes the encoding for the received data. As discussed earlier in the section "Buffer" on page 39, data is transmitted as a buffer, but we can use setEncoding to read it as a utf8 string. The socket's write method is used to transmit the data. It also attaches listener functions to two events: data, for received data, and close, in case the server closes the connection.

Example 3-3. The client socket sending data to the TCP server

```
var net = require('net');

var client = new net.Socket();
client.setEncoding('utf8');

// connect to server
client.connect ('8124','localhost', function () {
    console.log('connected to server');
    client.write('Who needs a browser to communicate?');
});

// prepare for input from terminal
process.stdin.resume();

// when receive data, send to server
process.stdin.on('data', function (data) {
    client.write(data);
});

// when receive data back, print to console
client.on('data',function(data) {
    console.log(data);
});

// when server closed
client.on('close',function() {
    console.log('connection is closed');
});
```

The data being transmitted between the two sockets is typed in at the terminal, and transmitted when you press Enter. The client application first sends the string you just typed, which the TCP server writes out to the console. The server repeats the message back to the client, which in turn writes the message out to the console. The server also prints out the IP address and port for the client using the socket's remoteAddress and remotePort properties. Following is the console output for the server after several strings were sent from the client (with the IP address edited out for security):

```
Hey, hey, hey, hey-now.
  from #ipaddress 57251
Don't be mean, we don't have to be mean.
  from #ipaddress 57251
Cuz remember, no matter where you go,
  from #ipaddress 57251
```

```
there you are.
 from #ipaddress 57251
```

The connection between the client and server is maintained until you kill one or the other using Ctrl-C. Whichever socket is still open receives a `close` event that's printed out to the console. The server can also serve more than one connection from more than one client, since all the relevant functions are asynchronous.

As I mentioned earlier, TCP is the underlying transport mechanism for much of the functionality we use on the Internet today, including HTTP, which we'll cover next.

HTTP

You had a chance to work with the HTTP module in Chapter 1. We created servers using the `createServer` method, passing in the function that will act as the `requestLis` `tener`. Requests are processed as they come, asynchronously.

In a network, TCP is the transportation layer and HTTP is the application layer. If you scratch around in the modules included with Node, you'll see that when you create an HTTP server, you're inheriting functionality from the TCP-based `net.Server`.

For the HTTP server, the `requestListener` is a socket, while the `http.ServerRequest` object is a readable stream and the `http.ServerResponse` is a writable stream. HTTP adds another level of complexity because of the *chunked transfer encoding* it supports. The chunked transfer encoding allows transfer of data when the exact size of the response isn't known until it's fully processed. Instead, a zero-sized chunk is sent to indicate the end of a query. This type of encoding is useful when you're processing a request such as a large database query output to an HTML table: writing the data can begin before the rest of the query data has been received.

 More on streams in the upcoming section titled, appropriately enough, "Streams, Pipes, and Readline" on page 48.

The TCP examples earlier in this chapter, and the HTTP examples in Chapter 1, were both coded to work with network sockets. However, all of the server/socket modules can also connect to a Unix socket, rather than a specific network port. Unlike a network socket, a Unix or IPC (interprocess communication) socket enables communication between processes within the same system.

To demonstrate Unix socket communication, I duplicated Example 1-3's code, but instead of binding to a port, the new server binds to a Unix socket, as shown in Example 3-4. The application also makes use of `readFileSync`, the synchronous version of the function to open a file and read its contents.

Example 3-4. HTTP server bound to a Unix socket

```
// create server
// and callback function
var http = require('http');
var fs = require('fs');

http.createServer(function (req, res) {

  var query = require('url').parse(req.url).query;
  console.log(query);
  file = require('querystring').parse(query).file;

  // content header
  res.writeHead(200, {'Content-Type': 'text/plain'});

  // increment global, write to client
  for (var i = 0; i<100; i++) {
    res.write(i + '\n');
  }

  // open and read in file contents
  var data = fs.readFileSync(file, 'utf8');
  res.write(data);
  res.end();
}).listen('/tmp/node-server-sock');
```

The client is based on a code sample provided in the Node core documentation for the `http.request` object at the Node.js site. The `http.request` object, by default, makes use of `http.globalAgent`, which supports pooled sockets. The size of this pool is five sockets by default, but you can adjust it by changing the `agent.maxSockets` value.

The client accepts the chunked data returned from the server, printing out to the console. It also triggers a response on the server with a couple of minor writes, as shown in Example 3-5.

Example 3-5. Connecting to the Unix socket and printing out received data

```
var http = require('http');

var options = {
    method: 'GET',
    socketPath: '/tmp/node-server-sock',
    path: "/?file=main.txt"
};

var req = http.request(options, function(res) {
  console.log('STATUS: ' + res.statusCode);
  console.log('HEADERS: ' + JSON.stringify(res.headers));
  res.setEncoding('utf8');
  res.on('data', function (chunk) {
    console.log('chunk o\' data: ' + chunk);
  });
});
```

```
req.on('error', function(e) {
  console.log('problem with request: ' + e.message);
});

// write data to request body
req.write('data\n');
req.write('data\n');
req.end();
```

I didn't use the asynchronous file read function with the `http.request` object because the connection is already closed when the asynchronous function is called and no file contents are returned.

Before leaving this section on the HTTP module, be aware that much of the behavior you've come to expect with Apache or other web servers isn't built into a Node HTTP server. For instance, if you password-protect your website, Apache will pop up a window asking for your username and password; a Node HTTP server will not. If you want this functionality, you're going to have to code for it.

 Chapter 15 covers the SSL version of HTTP, *HTTPS*, along with Crypto and TLS/SSL.

UDP/Datagram Socket

TCP requires a dedicated connection between the two endpoints of the communication. UDP is a connectionless protocol, which means there's no guarantee of a connection between the two endpoints. For this reason, UDP is less reliable and robust than TCP. On the other hand, UDP is generally faster than TCP, which makes it more popular for real-time uses, as well as technologies such as VoIP (Voice over Internet Protocol), where the TCP connection requirements could adversely impact the quality of the signal.

Node core supports both types of sockets. In the last couple of sections, I demonstrated the TCP functionality. Now, it's UDP's turn.

The UDP module identifier is `dgram`:

```
require ('dgram');
```

To create a UDP socket, use the `createSocket` method, passing in the type of socket—either `udp4` or `udp6`. You can also pass in a callback function to listen for events. Unlike messages sent with TCP, messages sent using UDP must be sent as buffers, not strings.

Example 3-6 contains the code for a demonstration UDP client. In it, data is accessed via `process.stdin`, and then sent, as is, via the UDP socket. Note that we don't have to set the encoding for the string, since the UDP socket accepts only a buffer, and the `process.stdin` data *is* a buffer. We do, however, have to convert the buffer to a string, using the buffer's `toString` method, in order to get a meaningful string for the `console.log` method call that echoes the input.

Example 3-6. A datagram client that sends messages typed into the terminal

```
var dgram = require('dgram');

var client = dgram.createSocket("udp4");

// prepare for input from terminal
process.stdin.resume();

process.stdin.on('data', function (data) {
   console.log(data.toString('utf8'));
   client.send(data, 0, data.length, 8124, "examples.burningbird.net",
      function (err, bytes) {
        if (err)
          console.log('error: ' + err);
        else
          console.log('successful');
   });
});
```

The UDP server, shown in Example 3-7, is even simpler than the client. All the server application does is create the socket, bind it to a specific port (8124), and listen for the `message` event. When a message arrives, the application prints it out using `console.log`, along with the IP address and port of the sender. Note especially that no encoding is necessary to print out the message—it's automatically converted from a buffer to a string.

We didn't have to bind the socket to a port. However, without the binding, the socket would attempt to listen in on every port.

Example 3-7. A UDP socket server, bound to port 8124, listening for messages

```
var dgram = require('dgram');

var server = dgram.createSocket("udp4");

server.on ("message", function(msg, rinfo) {
   console.log("Message: " + msg + " from " + rinfo.address + ":"
                + rinfo.port);
});

server.bind(8124);
```

I didn't call the `close` method on either the client or the server after sending/receiving the message. However, no connection is being maintained between the client and server —just the sockets capable of sending a message and receiving communication.

Streams, Pipes, and Readline

The communication stream between the sockets discussed in the previous sections is an implementation of the underlying abstract stream interface. Streams can be readable, writable, or both, and all streams are instances of EventEmitter, discussed in the upcoming section "Events and EventEmitter" on page 59.

It's important to take away from this section that all of these communication streams, including process.stdin and process.stdout, are implementations of the abstract stream interface. Because of this underlying interface, there is basic functionality available in all streams in Node:

- You can change the encoding for the stream data with setEncoding.
- You can check whether the stream is readable, writable, or both.
- You can capture stream events, such as data received or connection closed, and attach callback functions for each.
- You can pause and resume the stream.
- You can pipe data from a readable stream to a writable stream.

The last capability is one we haven't covered yet. A simple way to demonstrate a *pipe* is to open a REPL session and type in the following:

```
> process.stdin.resume();
> process.stdin.pipe(process.stdout);
```

...and then enjoy the fact that everything you type from that point on is echoed back to you.

If you want to keep the output stream open for continued data, pass an option, { end: false }, to the output stream:

```
process.stdin.pipe(process.stdout, { end : false });
```

There is one additional object that provides a specific functionality to readable streams: readline. You include the Readline module with code like the following:

```
var readline = require('readline');
```

The Readline module allows line-by-line reading of a stream. Be aware, though, that once you include this module, the Node program doesn't terminate until you close the interface and the stdin stream. The Node site documentation contains an example of how to begin and terminate a Readline interface, which I adapted in Example 3-8. The application asks a question as soon as you run it, and then outputs the answer. It also listens for any "command," which is really any line that terminates with \n. If the command is .leave, it leaves the application; otherwise, it just repeats the command and prompts the user for more. A Ctrl-C or Ctrl-D key combination also causes the application to terminate.

Example 3-8. Using Readline to create a simple, command-driven user interface

```
var readline = require('readline');

// create a new interface
var interface = readline.createInterface(process.stdin, process.stdout, null);

// ask question
interface.question(">>What is the meaning of life?  ", function(answer) {
   console.log("About the meaning of life, you said " + answer);
   interface.setPrompt(">>");
   interface.prompt();
});

// function to close interface
function closeInterface() {
   console.log('Leaving interface...');
   process.exit();
}
// listen for .leave
interface.on('line', function(cmd) {
   if (cmd.trim() == '.leave') {
      closeInterface();
      return;
   } else {
      console.log("repeating command: " + cmd);
   }
   interface.setPrompt(">>");
   interface.prompt();
});

interface.on('close', function() {
   closeInterface();
});
```

Here's an example session:

```
>>What is the meaning of life?  ===
About the meaning of life, you said ===
>>This could be a command
repeating command: This could be a command
>>We could add eval in here and actually run this thing
repeating command: We could add eval in here and actually run this thing
>>And now you know where REPL comes from
repeating command: And now you know where REPL comes from
>>And that using rlwrap replaces this Readline functionality
repeating command: And that using rlwrap replaces this Readline functionality
>>Time to go
repeating command: Time to go
>>.leave
Leaving interface...
```

This should look familiar. Remember from Chapter 2 that we can use rlwrap to override the command-line functionality for REPL. We use the following to trigger its use:

```
env NODE_NO_READLINE=1 rlwrap node
```

And now we know what the flag is triggering—it's instructing REPL not to use Node's Readline module for command-line processing, but to use `rlwrap` instead.

This is a quick introduction to the Node stream modules. Now it's time to change course, and check out Node's child processes.

Child Processes

Operating systems provide access to a great deal of functionality, but much of it is only accessible via the command line. It would be nice to be able to access this functionality from a Node application. That's where *child processes* come in.

Node enables us to run a system command within a new child process, and listen in on its input/output. This includes being able to pass arguments to the command, and even pipe the results of one command to another. The next several sections explore this functionality in more detail.

 All but the last example demonstrated in this section use Unix commands. They work on a Linux system, and should work in a Mac. They won't, however, work in a Windows Command window.

child_process.spawn

There are four different techniques you can use to create a child process. The most common one is using the `spawn` method. This launches a command in a new process, passing in any arguments. In the following, we create a child process to call the Unix `pwd` command to print the current directory. The command takes no arguments:

```
var spawn = require('child_process').spawn,
    pwd = spawn('pwd');

pwd.stdout.on('data', function (data) {
  console.log('stdout: ' + data);
});

pwd.stderr.on('data', function (data) {
  console.log('stderr: ' + data);
});

pwd.on('exit', function (code) {
  console.log('child process exited with code ' + code);
});
```

Notice the events that are captured on the child process's `stdout` and `stderr`. If no error occurs, any output from the command is transmitted to the child process's `stdout`, triggering a `data` event on the process. If an error occurs, such as in the following where we're passing an invalid option to the command:

```
var spawn = require('child_process').spawn,
    pwd = spawn('pwd', ['-g']);
```

Then the error gets sent to `stderr`, which prints out the error to the console:

```
stderr: pwd: invalid option -- 'g'
Try `pwd --help' for more information.

child process exited with code 1
```

The process exited with a code of 1, which signifies that an error occurred. The exit code varies depending on the operating system and error. When no error occurs, the child process exits with a code of 0.

The earlier code demonstrated sending output to the child process's `stdout` and `stderr`, but what about `stdin`? The Node documentation for child processes includes an example of directing data to `stdin`. It's used to emulate a Unix pipe (|) whereby the result of one command is immediately directed as input to another command. I adapted the example in order to demonstrate one of my favorite uses of the Unix pipe—being able to look through all subdirectories, starting in the local directory, for a file with a specific word (in this case, *test*) in its name:

```
find . -ls | grep test
```

Example 3-9 implements this functionality as child processes. Note that the first command, which performs the `find`, takes two arguments, while the second one takes just one: a term passed in via user input from `stdin`. Also note that, unlike the example in the Node documentation, the `grep` child process's `stdout` encoding is changed via `setEncoding`. Otherwise, when the data is printed out, it would be printed out as a buffer.

Example 3-9. Using child processes to find files in subdirectories with a given search term, "test"

```
var spawn = require('child_process').spawn,
    find = spawn('find',['.','-ls']),
    grep = spawn('grep',['test']);

grep.stdout.setEncoding('utf8');

// direct results of find to grep
find.stdout.on('data', function(data) {
   grep.stdin.write(data);
});

// now run grep and output results
grep.stdout.on('data', function (data) {
  console.log(data);
});

// error handling for both
find.stderr.on('data', function (data) {
  console.log('grep stderr: ' + data);
});
grep.stderr.on('data', function (data) {
  console.log('grep stderr: ' + data);
});
```

```
// and exit handling for both
find.on('exit', function (code) {
  if (code !== 0) {
    console.log('find process exited with code ' + code);
  }

  // go ahead and end grep process
  grep.stdin.end();
});

grep.on('exit', function (code) {
  if (code !== 0) {
    console.log('grep process exited with code ' + code);
  }
});
```

When you run the application, you'll get a listing of all files in the current directory and any subdirectories that contain *test* in their filename.

All of the example applications up to this point work the same in Node 0.8 as in Node 0.6. Example 3-9 is an exception because of a change in the underlying API.

In Node 0.6, the exit event would not be emitted until the child process exits and all STDIO pipes are closed. In Node 0.8, the event is emitted as soon as the child process finishes. This causes the application to crash, because the grep child process's STDIO pipe is closed when it tries to process its data. For the application to work in Node 0.8, the application needs to listen for the close event on the find child process, rather than the exit event:

```
// and exit handling for both
find.on('close', function (code) {
  if (code !== 0) {
    console.log('find process exited with code ' + code);
  }

  // go ahead and end grep process
  grep.stdin.end();
});
```

In Node 0.8, the close event is emitted when the child process exits and all STDIO pipes are closed.

child_process.exec and child_process.execFile

In addition to spawning a child process, you can also use child_process.exec and child_process.execFile to run a command in a shell and buffer the results. The only difference between child_process.exec and child_process.execFile is that execFile runs an application in a file, rather than running a command.

The first parameter in the two methods is either the command or the file and its location; the second parameter is options for the command; and the third is a callback function.

The callback function takes three arguments: `error`, `stdout`, and `stderr`. The data is buffered to `stdout` if no error occurs.

If the executable file contains:

```
#!/usr/local/bin/node

console.log(global);
```

the following application prints out the buffered results:

```
var execfile = require('child_process').execFile,
    child;

child = execfile('./app.js', function(error, stdout, stderr) {
  if (error == null) {
    console.log('stdout: ' + stdout);
  }
});
```

child_process.fork

The last child process method is `child_process.fork`. This variation of `spawn` is for spawning Node processes.

What sets the `child_process.fork` process apart from the others is that there's an actual communication channel established to the child process. Note, though, that each process requires a whole new instance of V8, which takes both time and memory.

 The Node documentation for `fork` provides several good examples of its use.

Running a Child Process Application in Windows

Earlier I warned you that child processes that invoke Unix system commands won't work with Windows, and vice versa. I know this sounds obvious, but not everyone knows that, unlike with JavaScript in browsers, Node applications can behave differently in different environments.

It wasn't until recently that the Windows binary installation of Node even provided access to child processes. You also need to invoke whatever command you want to run via the Windows command interpreter, `cmd.exe`.

Example 3-10 demonstrates running a Windows command. In the application, Windows `cmd.exe` is used to create a directory listing, which is then printed out to the console via the data event handler.

Example 3-10. Running a child process application in Windows

```
var cmd = require('child_process').spawn('cmd', ['/c', 'dir\n']);

cmd.stdout.on('data', function (data) {
    console.log('stdout: ' + data);
});

cmd.stderr.on('data', function (data) {
    console.log('stderr: ' + data);
});

cmd.on('exit', function (code) {
    console.log('child process exited with code ' + code);
});
```

The /c flag passed as the first argument to cmd.exe instructs it to carry out the command and then terminate. The application doesn't work without this flag. You especially don't want to pass in the /K flag, which tells cmd.exe to execute the application and then remain because your application won't terminate.

 I provide more demonstrations of child processes in Chapter 9 and Chapter 12.

Domain Resolution and URL Processing

The DNS module provides DNS resolution using *c-ares*, a C library that provides asynchronous DNS requests. It's used by Node with some of its other modules, and can be useful for applications that need to discover domains or IP addresses.

To discover the IP address given a domain, use the dns.lookup method and print out the returned IP address:

```
var dns = require('dns');
dns.lookup('burningbird.net',function(err,ip) {
   if (err) throw err;
   console.log(ip);
});
```

The dns.reverse method returns an array of domain names for a given IP address:

```
dns.reverse('173.255.206.103', function(err,domains) {
domains.forEach(function(domain) {
  console.log(domain);
  });
});
```

The dns.resolve method returns an array of record types by a given type, such as A, MX, NS, and so on. In the following code, I'm looking for the name server domains for my domain name, *burningbird.net*:

```
var dns = require('dns');
dns.resolve('burningbird.net', 'NS', function(err,domains) {
domains.forEach(function(domain) {
  console.log(domain);
  });
});
```

This returns:

```
ns1.linode.com
ns3.linode.com
ns5.linode.com
ns4.linode.com
```

We used the URL module in Example 1-3 in Chapter 1. This simple module provides a way of parsing a URL and returning an object with all of the URL components. Passing in the following URL:

```
var url = require('url');
var urlObj = url.parse('http://examples.burningbird.net:8124/?file=main');
```

returns the following JavaScript object:

```
{ protocol: 'http:',
  slashes: true,
  host: 'examples.burningbird.net:8124',
  port: '8124',
  hostname: 'examples.burningbird.net',
  href: 'http://examples.burningbird.net:8124/?file=main',
  search: '?file=main',
  query: 'file=main',
  pathname: '/',
  path: '/?file=main' }
```

Each of the components can then be discretely accessed like so:

```
var qs = urlObj.query; // get the query string
```

Calling the URL.format method performs the reverse operation:

```
console.log(url.format(urlObj)); // returns original URL
```

The URL module is often used with the Query String module. The latter module is a simple utility module that provides functionality to parse a received query string, or prepare a string for use as a query string.

To chunk out the key/value pairs in the query string, use the querystring.parse method. The following:

```
var vals = querystring.parse('file=main&file=secondary&type=html");
```

results in a JavaScript object that allows for easy access of the individual query string values:

```
{ file: [ 'main', 'secondary' ], type: 'html' }
```

Since file is given twice in the query string, both values are grouped into an array, each of which can be accessed individually:

```
console.log(vals.file[0]); // returns main
```

You can also convert an object into a query string, using `querystring.stringify`:

```
var qryString = querystring.stringify(vals)
```

The Utilities Module and Object Inheritance

The Utilities module provides several useful functions. You include this module with:

```
var util = require('util');
```

You can use Utilities to test if an object is an array (`util.isArray`) or regular expression (`util.isRegExp`), and to format a string (`util.format`). A new experimental addition to the module provides functionality to pump data from a readable stream to a writable stream (`util.pump`):

```
util.pump(process.stdin, process.stdout);
```

However, I wouldn't type this into REPL, as anything you type from that point on is echoed as soon as you type it—making the session a little awkward.

I make extensive use of `util.inspect` to get a string representation of an object. I find it's a great way to discover more about an object. The first required argument is the object; the second optional argument is whether to display the nonenumerable properties; the third optional argument is the number of times the object is recursed (depth); and the fourth, also optional, is whether to style the output in ANSI colors. If you assign a value of `null` to the depth, it recurses indefinitely (the default is two times)—as much as necessary to exhaustively inspect the object. From experience, I'd caution you to be careful using `null` for the depth because you're going to get a large output.

You can use `util.inspect` in REPL, but I recommend a simple application, such as the following:

```
var util = require('util');
var jsdom = require('jsdom');

console.log(util.inspect(jsdom, true, null, true));
```

When you run it, pipe the result to a file:

```
node inspectjsdom.js > jsdom.txt
```

Now you can inspect and reinspect the object interface at your leisure. Again, if you use `null` for depth, expect a large output file.

The Utilities module provides several other methods, but the one you're most likely to use is `util.inherits`. The `util.inherits` function takes two parameters, `constructor` and `superConstructor`. The result is that the constructor will inherit the functionality from the superconstructor.

Example 3-11 demonstrates all the nuances associated with using `util.inherits`. The explanation of the code follows.

Example 3-11 and its explanation cover some core JavaScript functionality you might already be familiar with. However, it's important that
all readers come away from this section with the same understanding of
what's happening.

Example 3-11. Enabling object inheritance via the util.inherits method

```
var util = require('util');

// define original object
function first() {
  var self = this;
  this.name = 'first';
  this.test = function() {
    console.log(self.name);
  };
}

first.prototype.output = function() {
    console.log(this.name);
}

// inherit from first
function second() {
  second.super_.call(this);
  this.name = 'second';
}
util.inherits(second,first);

var two = new second();


function third(func) {
    this.name = 'third';
    this.callMethod = func;
}

var three = new third(two.test);

// all three should output "second"
two.output();
two.test();
three.callMethod();
```

The application creates three objects named `first`, `second`, and `third`, respectively.

The `first` object has two methods: `test` and `output`. The `test` method is defined directly in the object, while the `output` method is added later via the `prototype` object. The reason I used both techniques for defining a method on the object is to demonstrate an important aspect of inheritance with `util.inherits` (well, of JavaScript, but enabled by `util.inherits`).

The `second` object contains the following line:

```
    second.super_.call(this);
```

If we eliminate this line from the second object constructor, any call to output on the second object would succeed, but a call to test would generate an error and force the Node application to terminate with a message about test being undefined.

The call method chains the constructors between the two objects, ensuring that the superconstructor is invoked as well as the constructor. The superconstructor is the constructor for the inherited object.

We need to invoke the superconstructor since the test method doesn't exist until first is created. However, we didn't need the call method for the output method, because it's defined directly on the first object's prototype object. When the second object inherits properties from the first, it also inherits the newly added method.

If we look under the hood of util.inherits, we see where super_ is defined:

```
exports.inherits = function(ctor, superCtor) {
  ctor.super_ = superCtor;
  ctor.prototype = Object.create(superCtor.prototype, {
    constructor: {
      value: ctor,
      enumerable: false,
      writable: true,
      configurable: true
    }
  });
};
```

super_ is assigned as a property to the second object when util.inherits is called:

```
    util.inherits (second, first);
```

The third object in the application, third, also has a name property. It doesn't inherit from either first or second, but does expect a function passed to it when it's instantiated. This function is assigned to its own callMethod property. When the code creates an instance of this object, the two object instance's test method is passed to the constructor:

```
    var three = new third(two.test);
```

When three.callMethod is called, "second" is output, not "third" as you might expect at first glance. And that's where the self reference in the first object comes in.

In JavaScript, this is the object context, which can change as a method is passed around, or passed to an event handler. The only way you can preserve data for an object's method is to assign this to an object variable—in this case, self—and then use the variable within any functions in the object.

Running this application results in the following output:

```
    second
    second
    second
```

Much of this is most likely familiar to you from client-side JavaScript development, though it's important to understand the Utilities part in the inheritance. The next section, which provides an overview of Node's EventEmitter, features functionality that is heavily dependent on the inheritance behavior just described.

Events and EventEmitter

Scratch underneath the surface of many of the Node core objects, and you'll find EventEmitter. Anytime you see an object emit an event, and an event handled with on, you're seeing EventEmitter in action. Understanding how EventEmitter works and how to use it are two of the more important components of Node development.

The EventEmitter object is what provides the asynchronous event handling to objects in Node. To demonstrate its core functionality, we'll try a quick test application.

First, include the Events module:

```
var events = require('events');
```

Next, create an instance of EventEmitter:

```
var em = new events.EventEmitter();
```

Use the newly created EventEmitter instance to do two essential tasks: attach an event handler to an event, and emit the actual event. The on event handler is triggered when a specific event is emitted. The first parameter to the method is the name of the event, the second a function to process the event:

```
em.on('someevent', function(data) { ... });
```

The event is emitted on the object, based on some criteria, via the emit method:

```
if (somecriteria) {
    en.emit('data');
}
```

In Example 3-12, we create an EventEmitter instance that emits an event, timed, every three seconds. In the event handler function for this event, a message with a counter is output to the console.

Example 3-12. Very basic test of the EventEmitter functionality

```
var eventEmitter = require('events').EventEmitter;
var counter = 0;

var em = new eventEmitter();

setInterval(function() { em.emit('timed', counter++); }, 3000);

em.on('timed', function(data) {
  console.log('timed ' + data);
});
```

Running the application outputs timed event messages to the console until the application is terminated.

This is an interesting example, but not particularly helpful. What we need is the ability to add `EventEmitter` functionality to our existing objects—not use instances of `EventEmitter` throughout our applications.

To add this necessary `EventEmitter` functionality to an object, use the `util.inherits` method, described in the preceding section:

```
util.inherits(someobj, EventEmitter);
```

By using `util.inherits` with the object, you can call the `emit` method within the object's methods, and code event handlers on the object instances:

```
someobj.prototype.somemethod = function() { this.emit('event'); };
...
someobjinstance.on('event', function() { });
```

Rather than attempt to decipher how `EventEmitter` works in the abstract sense, let's move on to Example 3-13, which shows a working example of an object inheriting `EventEmitter`'s functionality. In the application, a new object, `inputChecker`, is created. The constructor takes two values, a person's name and a filename. It assigns the person's name to an object variable, and also creates a reference to a writable stream using the File System module's `createWriteStream` method (for more on the File System module, see the sidebar "Readable and Writable Stream" on page 60).

Readable and Writable Stream

The Node File System module (`fs`) enables us to open a file for reading and writing, to watch specific files for new activity, and to manipulate directories. It also provides us with readable and writable stream capability.

You create a readable stream using `fs.createReadStream`, passing in the name and path for the file and other options. You create a writable stream with `fs.createWriteStream`, also passing in a filename and path.

You'd use a writable and readable stream over the more traditional read and write methods in situations when you're reading and writing from a file based on events where the reads and writes can occur frequently. The streams are opened in the background, and reads (and writes) are queued.

The object also has a method, `check`, that checks incoming data for specific commands. One command (`wr:`) triggers a write event, another (`en:`) an end event. If no command is present, then an echo event is triggered. The object instance provides event handlers for all three events. It writes to the output file for the write event, it echoes the input for the commandless input, and it terminates the application with an end event, using the `process.exit` method.

All input comes from standard input (`process.stdin`).

Example 3-13. Creating an event-based object that inherits from EventEmitter

```
var util = require('util');
var eventEmitter = require('events').EventEmitter;
var fs = require('fs');

function inputChecker (name, file) {
   this.name = name;
   this.writeStream = fs.createWriteStream('./' + file + '.txt',
      {'flags' : 'a',
       'encoding' : 'utf8',
       'mode' : 0666});
};

util.inherits(inputChecker,eventEmitter);

inputChecker.prototype.check = function check(input) {
  var command = input.toString().trim().substr(0,3);
  if (command == 'wr:') {
    this.emit('write',input.substr(3,input.length));
  } else if (command == 'en:') {
    this.emit('end');
  } else {
    this.emit('echo',input);
  }
};
// testing new object and event handling
var ic = new inputChecker('Shelley','output');

ic.on('write', function(data) {
   this.writeStream.write(data, 'utf8');
});

ic.on('echo', function( data) {
   console.log(this.name + ' wrote ' + data);
});

ic.on('end', function() {
   process.exit();
});

process.stdin.resume();
process.stdin.setEncoding('utf8');
process.stdin.on('data', function(input) {
    ic.check(input);
});
```

The EventEmitter functionality is bolded in the example. Note that the functionality also includes the process.stdin.on event handler method, since process.stdin is one of the many Node objects that inherit from EventEmitter.

We don't have to chain the constructors from the new object to EventEmitter, as demonstrated in the earlier example covering util.inherits, because the functionality we need—on and emit—consists of prototype methods, not object instance properties.

The on method is really a shortcut for the `EventEmitter.addListener` method, which takes the same parameters. So this:

```
ic.addListener('echo', function( data) {
    console.log(this.name + ' wrote ' + data);
});
```

is exactly equivalent to:

```
ic.on('echo', function( data) {
    console.log(this.name + ' wrote ' + data);
});
```

You can listen only to the first event with:

```
ic.once(event, function);
```

When you exceed 10 listeners for an event, you'll get a warning by default. Use `setMax` `Listeners`, passing in a number, to change the number of listeners. Use a value of zero (0) for an unlimited amount of listeners.

Many of the core Node objects, as well as third-party modules, make use of `EventEmit` `ter`. In Chapter 4, I'll demonstrate how to convert the code in Example 3-13 into a module.

The Node Module System

Node's basic implementation is kept as streamlined as possible. Rather than incorporate every possible component of use directly into Node, developers offer additional functionality via Node's modules.

Node's module system is patterned after the *CommonJS module system*, a way of creating modules so that they're interoperable. The core of the system is a contract that developers adhere to in order to ensure that their modules play well with others.

Among the CommonJS module system requirements implemented with Node are:

- Support is included for a `require` function that takes the module identifier and returns the exported API.
- The module name is a string of characters, and may include forward slashes (for identification of path).
- The module must specifically export that which is to be exposed outside the module.
- Variables are private to the module.

In the next several sections, we'll see how Node adheres to these requirements.

Loading a Module with require and Default Paths

Node supports a simple module loading system: there is a one-to-one correspondence between the file and module.

To include a module within a Node application, use the `require` statement, passing in a string with the identifier for the module:

```
var http = require ('http');
```

You can also just include a specific object, rather than all objects, from a module:

```
var spawn = require('child_process').spawn;
```

You can load core modules—i.e., those native to Node—or modules from the *node_modules* folder just by providing the module identifier, such as `http` for the HTTP module. Modules not part of core, or not included in the *node_modules* folder, should include forward slashes to indicate the path. As an example, Node expects to find the module named *mymodule.js* in the same directory as the Node application in the following `require` statement:

```
require ('./mymodule');
```

Or you can use the full path:

```
require ('/home/myname/myapp/mymodule.js');
```

Module files can have either a *.js*, *.node*, or *.json* file extension. The *.node* extension assumes that the file is a compiled binary, not a text file containing JavaScript.

Node core modules have higher priority than external modules. If you're trying to load a custom module named `http`, Node loads the core version of the HTTP module. You'll have to provide either a different module identifier, or you'll need to provide the full path.

Earlier I mentioned the *node_modules* folder. If you specify the node identifier without providing a path, and the module isn't a core module, Node first looks for a *node_modules* folder local to the application, and searches for the module in this folder. If it doesn't find the module, Node then looks in the parent subdirectory for a *node_modules* folder and the node, and so on.

If the module is named `mymodule`, and the application is located in a subdirectory with the following path:

```
/home/myname/myprojects/myapp
```

then Node looks for the module using the following searches, in turn:

- */home/myname/myprojects/myapp/node_modules/mymodule.js*
- */home/myname/myprojects/node_modules/mymodule.js*
- */home/myname/node_modules/mymodule.js*
- */node_modules/mymodule.js*

Node can optimize the search depending on where the file issuing the `require` statement resides. For instance, if the file making the `require` statement is itself a module in a subdirectory of the *node_modules* folder, Node begins the search for the required module in the topmost *node_modules* folder.

There are two additional variations of `require`: `require.resolve` and `require.cache`. The `require.resolve` method performs the lookup for the given module but, rather than load the module, just returns the resolved filename. The `resolve.cache` object contains a cached version of all loaded modules. When you try to load the module again in the same context, it's loaded from the cache. If you want to force a new load, delete the item from the cache.

If the item's path is:

```
var circle = require('./circle.js');
```

delete it with:

```
delete require.cache('./circle.js');
```

This code forces a reload of the module the next time a `require` is called on it.

External Modules and the Node Package Manager

As mentioned earlier, much of the rich functionality associated with Node comes in via third-party modules. There are router modules, modules for working with relational or document database systems, template modules, testing modules, and even modules for payment gateways.

Though there is no formal Node module developer system, developers are encouraged to upload their modules to GitHub. Following are good resources for finding Node modules:

- npm registry (*http://search.npmjs.org/*)
- Node module wiki (*https://github.com/joyent/node/wiki/modules*)
- The node-toolbox (*http://toolbox.no.de/*)
- Nipster! (*http://eirikb.github.com/nipster/*)

The modules are roughly categorized into different types such as the aforementioned routers, database, templating, payment gateway, and so on.

To use a module, you can download the source from GitHub (or wherever the source is located), and then install it manually into your application environment. Most modules provide basic installation instructions, or, at a minimum, you can deduce the installation requirements by examining the files and directories included in the module. However, there is a far easier way to install a Node module: using the Node Package Manager (npm).

 The npm site is at *http://npmjs.org/*. You can find basic instructions on npm at *http://npmjs.org/doc/README.html*. Essential reading for Node module developers is the Developers section of the npm manual, found at *http://npmjs.org/doc/developers.html*. For a useful post explaining the differences between local and global installation, see *http://blog.nodejs .org/2011/03/23/npm-1-0-global-vs-local-installation/*.

Modern installations include npm, but you can double-check for its existence by typing **npm** at the command line in the same environment that you use to access Node.

To get an overview of npm commands, use the following:

```
$ npm help npm
```

Modules can be installed globally or locally. The local installation is the best approach if you're working on a project and not everyone sharing the system needs access to this module. A local installation, which is the default, installs the module in the current location in the *node_modules* directory.

```
$ npm install modulename
```

As an example, to install Connect, a very popular middleware framework, use the following:

```
$ npm install connect
```

npm not only installs Connect, it also discovers its module dependencies and installs them, too, as shown in Figure 4-1.

Once it's installed, you can find the module in your local directory's *node_modules* directory. Any dependencies are installed in that module's *node_modules* directory.

If you want to install the package globally, use the -g or --global option:

```
$ npm -g install connect
```

These examples install packages that are registered at the npm site. You can also install a module that's in a folder on the filesystem, or a tarball that's either local or fetched via a URL:

```
npm install http://somecompany.com/somemodule.tgz
```

If the package has versions, you can install a specific version:

```
npm install modulename@0.1
```

 npm can also work with Git, as demonstrated in the Appendix.

You can even install an old friend, jQuery:

```
npm install jquery
```

Now you can make use of a familiar syntax in your Node application development.

If you're no longer using a module, you can uninstall it:

```
npm uninstall modulename
```

The following command tells npm to check for new modules, and perform an update if any are found:

```
npm update
```

Or you can update a single module:

```
npm update modulename
```

If you just want to check to see if any packages are outdated, use the following:

```
npm outdated
```

Again, you can run this command against a single module.

List installed packages and dependencies with list, ls, la, or ll:

```
npm ls
```

The la and ll options provide extended descriptions. The following is the text I get running npm ll in my Windows 7 machine:

```
C:\Users\Shelley>npm ls ll
npm WARN jsdom >= 0.2.0 Unmet dependency in C:\Users\Shelley\node_modules\html5
C:\Users\Shelley
├── async@0.1.15
├── colors@0.6.0-1
├── commander@0.5.2
├─┬ connect@1.8.5
│ ├── formidable@1.0.8
│ ├── mime@1.2.4
│ └── qs@0.4.1
├─┬ html5@v0.3.5
│ ├── UNMET DEPENDENCY jsdom >= 0.2.0
│ ├── opts@1.2.2
│ └─┬ tap@0.0.13
│   ├── inherits@1.0.0
│   ├── tap-assert@0.0.10
│   ├── tap-consumer@0.0.1
│   ├── tap-global-harness@0.0.1
│   ├── tap-harness@0.0.3
│   ├── tap-producer@0.0.1
│   ├── tap-results@0.0.2
│   ├─┬ tap-runner@0.0.7
│   │ ├── inherits@1.0.0
│   │ ├── slide@1.1.3
│   │ ├── tap-assert@0.0.10
│   │ ├── tap-consumer@0.0.1
│   │ ├── tap-producer@0.0.1
│   │ ├── tap-results@0.0.2
│   │ └── yamlish@0.0.3
│   ├── tap-test@0.0.2
│   └── yamlish@0.0.2
└─┬ optimist@0.3.1
  └── wordwrap@0.0.2
```

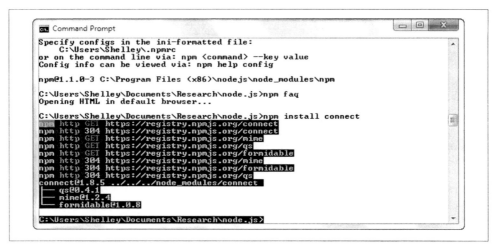

Figure 4-1. Installing Connect in Windows 7 using npm

Note the warning about an unmet dependency for the HTML5 module. The HTML5 module requires an older version of the JSDOM library. To correct this, I installed the necessary version of the module:

```
npm install jsdom@0.2.0
```

You can also directly install all dependencies with the -d flag. For instance, in the directory for the module, type the following:

```
npm install -d
```

If you want to install a version of the module that hasn't yet been uploaded to the npm registry, you can install directly from the Git repository:

```
npm install https://github.com/visionmedia/express/tarball/master
```

Use caution, though, as I've found that when you install a not-yet-released version of a module, and you do an npm update, the npm registry version can overwrite the version you're using.

To see which modules are installed globally, use:

```
npm ls -g
```

You can learn more about your npm installation using the config command. The following lists the npm configuration settings:

```
npm config list
```

You can get a more in-depth look at all configuration settings with:

```
npm config ls -l
```

You can modify or remove configuration settings either by using a command line:

```
npm config delete keyname
npm config set keyname value
```

or by directly editing the configuration file:

```
$ npm config edit
```

 I would strongly recommend you leave your npm configuration settings alone, unless you're very sure of a change's effect.

You can also search for a module using whatever terms you think might return the best selection:

```
npm search html5 parser
```

The first time you do a search, npm builds an index, which can take a few minutes. When it's finished, though, you'll get a list of possible modules that match the term or terms you provided. The search terms *html5* and *parser* returned just two modules: HTML5, an HTML parser that includes support for SVG and MathML; and Fabric, an object model with support for HTML5 Canvas and an SVG-to-Canvas parser.

The npm website provides a registry of modules you can browse through, and an up-to-date listing of modules most depended on—that is, modules most used by other modules or by Node applications. In the next section, I'll cover a sampling of these modules.

 I'll cover other npm commands later in this chapter, in the section "Creating Your Own Custom Module" on page 74.

Finding Modules

Though Node.js has been active only for a few years, it's already attracted a large body of work. When you look at the Node.js modules wiki page, you'll find a significant number of modules. The good thing is, you can find a lot of useful modules that implement the functionality you need. The bad news is, it's difficult to determine which module to use—in other words, which modules are "best of breed."

Using a search tool like Google can give you a fair idea of which modules are popular. For example, it quickly became apparent when I was exploring middleware and framework modules that Connect and Express were very popular.

In addition, when you look at the GitHub registry for the item, you can see if it's actively supported and up to date with the current Node installation. As another example, I was checking out a tool named Apricot, which does HTML parsing and is recommended in the Node documentation, but then I noticed it hadn't been updated for some time, and when I tried to use the module, I found it didn't work with my installation of Node (at least, not when this book was written).

 Many of the modules provide example applications, and a quick test of these will let you know if you can use the module in your current environment.

As mentioned, the Node documentation site does provide a listing of recommended third-party modules, starting with the npm, which is now incorporated into the Node installation. However, the npm website and its module registry provide us with a better view of what modules are used in most applications.

At the npm registry page, you can search for modules, but you can also review a list of the "most depended on" modules, which are modules used either in other modules or in Node applications. At the time of this writing, the top modules were:

Underscore
Provides general JavaScript utility functions

Coffee-script
Enables use of CoffeeScript, a language that compiles to JavaScript

Request
A simplified HTTP request client

Express
A framework

Optimist
Offers lightweight option parsing

Async
Provides functions and patterns for asynchronous code

Connect
Middleware

Colors
Adds colors to the console

Uglify-js
A parser and compressor/beautifier

Socket.IO
Enables real-time client/server communication

Redis
A Redis client

Jade
A templating engine

Commander
> For command-line programs

Mime
> Offers support for file extensions and MIME mapping

JSDOM
> Implements the W3C DOM

I'll cover several of these modules in future chapters, but I want to cover three now—both because they give us a chance to better understand how Node works, and because they are especially useful. They are:

- Colors
- Optimist
- Underscore

Colors: Simple Is Best

Colors is one of the simpler modules. You can use it to provide different color and style effects to the `console.log` output, and that's it. However, it's also a good demonstration of an effective module because it is simple to use, focuses on providing one service, and does a good job with that one service.

Testing how a module works is a great reason for using REPL. To try Colors, install it using npm like so:

```
$ npm install colors
```

Open a new REPL session and include the `colors` library:

```
> var colors = require('colors');
```

Because the Colors module is included in the current location's *node_modules* subdirectory, Node is able to find it rather quickly.

Now try something out, such as the following:

```
console.log('This Node kicks it!'.rainbow.underline);
```

The result is a colorful, underlined rendering of your message. The style applies only for the one message—you'll need to apply another style for another message.

If you've worked with jQuery, you recognize the chaining used to combine effects. The example makes use of two: a font effect, `underlined`, and a font color, `rainbow`.

Try another, this time `zebra` and `bold`:

```
console.log('We be Nodin'.zebra.bold);
```

You can change the style for sections of the console message:

```
console.log('rainbow'.rainbow, 'zebra'.zebra);
```

Why would something like Colors be useful? One reason is that it enables us to specify formatting for various events, such as displaying one color for errors in one module, another color or effect for warnings in a second module, and so on. To do this, you can use the Colors presets or create a custom theme:

```
> colors.setTheme({
....... mod1_warn: 'cyan',
....... mod1_error: 'red',
....... mod2_note: 'yellow'
....... });
> console.log("This is a helpful message".mod2_note);
This is a helpful message
> console.log("This is a bad message".mod1_error);
This is a bad message
```

 Find more on Colors at *https://github.com/Marak/colors.js*.

Optimist: Another Short and Simple Module

Optimist is another module focused on solving a specific problem: parsing command options. That's it, that's all it does—but it does it very well.

As an example, this simple application uses the Optimist module to print command-line options to the console.

```
#!/usr/local/bin/node
var argv = require('optimist').argv;
console.log(argv.o + " " + argv.t);
```

You can run the application with short options. The following prints the values of 1 and 2 out to the console:

```
./app.js -o 1 -t 2
```

You can also process long options:

```
#!/usr/local/bin/node
var argv = require('optimist').argv;
console.log(argv.one + " " + argv.two);
```

and test with the following, resulting in a printout of My Name:

```
./app2.js --one="My" --two="Name"
```

You can also use the Optimist module to process Boolean and unhyphenated options.

 Read more about Optimist at *https://github.com/substack/node-optimist*.

Underscore

Install the Underscore module with:

```
npm install underscore
```

According to the developers, Underscore is a utility-belt library for Node. It provides a lot of extended JavaScript functionality we're used to with third-party libraries, such as jQuery or Prototype.js.

Underscore is so named because, traditionally, its functionality is accessed with an underscore (_), similar to jQuery's $. Here's an example:

```
var _ = require('underscore');
_.each(['apple','cherry'], function (fruit) { console.log(fruit); });
```

Of course, the problem with the underscore is that this character has a specific meaning in REPL. No worries, though—we can just use another variable, us:

```
var us = require('underscore');
us.each(['apple','cherry'], function(fruit) { console.log(fruit); });
```

Underscore provides expanded functionality for arrays, collections, functions, objects, chaining, and general utility. Fortunately, there's also excellent documentation for all of its functionality, so I'll forgo detailing any of it here.

However, I do want to mention one nice capability: a controlled way to extend Underscore with your own utility functions, via the mixin function. We can quickly try this method, and the others, in a REPL session:

```
> var us = require('underscore');
undefined
> us.mixin({
```

```
... betterWithNode: function(str) {
..... return str + ' is better with Node';
..... }
... });
> console.log(us.betterWithNode('chocolate'));
chocolate is better with Node
```

 You'll see the term *mixin* used in several Node modules. It's based on a pattern where properties of one object are added ("mixed in") to another.

Of course, it makes more sense to extend Underscore from a module that we can reuse in our applications, which leads us to our next topic—creating our own custom modules.

Creating Your Own Custom Module

Just as you do for your client-side JavaScript, you'll want to split off reusable JavaScript into its own libraries. The only difference is that you need to take a couple of extra steps to convert your JavaScript library into a module for use with Node.

Let's say you have a JavaScript library function, concatArray, that takes a string and an array of strings, and concatenates the first string to each string in the array:

```
function concatArray(str, array) {
  return array.map(function(element) {
      return str + ' ' + element;
  });
}
```

You want to use this function, as well as others, in your Node applications.

To convert your JavaScript library for use in Node, you'll need to export all of your exposed functions using the exports object, as shown in the following code:

```
exports.concatArray = function(str, array) {
  return array.map(function(element) {
      return str + ' ' + element;
  });
};
```

To use concatArray in a Node application, import the library using require, assigning the library to a variable name. Once the library is assigned, you can call any of the exposed functions in your code:

```
var newArray = require ('./arrayfunctions.js');

console.log(newArray.concatArray('hello', ['test1','test2']));
```

It's not very complicated, as long as you remember two things:

- Use the `exports` object to export the function.
- Treat the library as a single imported object, assigned to a variable, in order to access the functions.

Packaging an Entire Directory

You can split your module into separate JavaScript files, all located within a directory. Node can load the directory contents, as long as you organize the contents in one of two ways.

The first way is to provide a JSON file named *package.json* with information about the directory. The structure can contain other information, but the only entries relevant to Node are:

```
{ "name" : "mylibrary",
  "main" : "./mymodule/mylibrary.js" }
```

The first property, `name`, is the name of the module. The second, `main`, indicates the entry point for the module.

The second way is to include either an *index.js* or *index.node* file in the directory to serve as the main module entry point.

Why would you provide a directory rather than just a single module? The most likely reason is that you're making use of existing JavaScript libraries, and just providing a "wrapper" file that wraps the exposed functions with `exports` statements. Another reason is that your library is so large that you want to break it down to make it easier to modify.

Regardless of the reason, be aware that all of the exported objects must be in the one main file that Node loads.

Preparing Your Module for Publication

If you want to make your package available to others, you can promote it on your website, but you'll be missing out on a significant audience. When you're ready to publish a module, you're going to want to add it to the list of modules at the Node.js website, and you'll also want to publish it to the npm registry.

Earlier I mentioned the *package.json* file. It's actually based on the CommonJS module system recommendations, which you can find at *http://wiki.commonjs.org/wiki/Pack ages/1.0#Package_Descriptor_File* (though check to see if there's a more up-to-date version).

Among the required fields for the *package.json* file are:

name
    The name of the package

description
> The package description

version
> The current version conforming to semantic version requirements

keywords
> An array of search terms

maintainers
> An array of package maintainers (includes name, email, and website)

contributors
> An array of package contributors (includes name, email, and website)

bugs
> The URL where bugs can be submitted

licenses
> An array of licenses

repositories
> An array of repositories where the package can be found

dependencies
> Prerequisite packages and their version numbers

The other fields are optional. Still, that's a lot of fields. Thankfully, npm makes it easier to create this file. If you type the following at the command line:

```
npm init
```

the tool will run through the required fields, prompting you for each. When it's done, it generates a *package.json* file.

In Chapter 3, Example 3-13, I started an object called inputChecker that checks incoming data for commands and then processes the command. The example demonstrated how to incorporate EventEmitter. Now we're going to modify this simple object to make it usable by other applications and modules.

First, we'll create a subdirectory in *node_modules* and name it *inputcheck*, and then move the existing inputChecker code file to it. We need to rename the file to *index.js*. Next, we need to modify the code to pull out the part that implements the new object. We'll save it for a future test file. The last modification we'll do is add the exports object, resulting in the code shown in Example 4-1.

Example 4-1. Application from Example 3-13 modified to be a module object

```
var util = require('util');
var eventEmitter = require('events').EventEmitter;
var fs = require('fs');

exports.inputChecker = inputChecker;

function inputChecker(name, file) {
```

```
    this.name = name;
    this.writeStream = fs.createWriteStream('./' + file + '.txt',
      {'flags' : 'a',
       'encoding' : 'utf8',
       'mode' : 0666});
};

util.inherits(inputChecker,eventEmitter);
inputChecker.prototype.check = function check(input) {
  var self = this;
  var command = input.toString().trim().substr(0,3);
  if (command == 'wr:') {
    self.emit('write',input.substr(3,input.length));
  } else if (command == 'en:') {
    self.emit('end');
  } else {
    self.emit('echo',input);
  }
};
```

We can't export the object function directly, because `util.inherits` expects an object
to exist in the file named `inputChecker`. We're also modifying the `inputChecker` object's
`prototype` later in the file. We could have changed these code references to use
`exports.inputChecker`, but that's *kludgy*. It's just as easy to assign the object in a separate statement.

To create the *package.json* file, I ran `npm init` and answered each of the prompts. The
resulting file is shown in Example 4-2.

Example 4-2. Generated package.json for inputChecker module

```
{
  "author": "Shelley Powers <shelleyp@burningbird.net> (http://burningbird.net)",
  "name": "inputcheck",
  "description": "Looks for commands within the string and implements the commands",
  "version": "0.0.1",
  "homepage": "http://inputcheck.burningbird.net",
  "repository": {
    "url": "
  },
  "main": "inputcheck.js",
  "engines": {
    "node": "~0.6.10"
  },
  "dependencies": {},
  "devDependencies": {},
  "optionalDependencies": {}
}
```

The `npm init` command doesn't prompt for dependencies, so we need to add them
directly to the file. However, the `inputChecker` module isn't dependent on any external
modules, so we can leave these fields blank in this case.

Chapter 16 has a more in-depth look at the *package.json* file.

At this point, we can test the new module to make sure it actually works as a module. Example 4-3 is the portion of the previously existing `inputChecker` application that tested the new object, now pulled out into a separate test application.

Example 4-3. InputChecker test application

```
var inputChecker = require('inputcheck').inputChecker;

// testing new object and event handling
var ic = new inputChecker('Shelley','output');

ic.on('write', function(data) {
   this.writeStream.write(data, 'utf8');
});

ic.addListener('echo', function( data) {
   console.log(this.name + ' wrote ' + data);
});

ic.on('end', function() {
   process.exit();
});

process.stdin.resume();
process.stdin.setEncoding('utf8');
process.stdin.on('data', function(input) {
    ic.check(input);
});
```

We can now move the test application into a new *examples* subdirectory within the module directory to be packaged with the module as an example. Good practice demands that we also provide a *test* directory with one or more testing applications, as well as a *doc* directory with documentation. For a module this small, a *README* file should be sufficient. Lastly, we create a gzipped tarball of the module.

Once we've provided all we need to provide, we can publish the module.

Publishing the Module

The folks who brought us npm also provide a really great source for Node developers: the Developer Guide. It outlines everything we need to know about how to publish our modules.

The Guide specifies some additional requirements for the *package.json* file. In addition to the fields already created, we also need to add in a `directories` field with a hash of folders, such as the previously mentioned *test* and *doc*:

```
"directories" : {
    "doc" : ".",
    "test" : "test",
    "example" : "examples"
}
```

Before publishing, the Guide recommends we test that the module can cleanly install. To test for this, type the following in the root directory for the module:

```
npm install . -g
```

At this point, we've tested the `inputChecker` module, modified the *package.json* package to add directories, and confirmed that the package successfully installs.

Next, we need to add ourselves as npm users if we haven't done so already. We do this by typing:

```
npm adduser
```

and following the prompts to add a username, a password, and an email address.

There's one last thing to do:

```
npm publish
```

We can provide the path to the tarball or the directory. As the Guide warns us, everything in the directory is exposed unless we use a `.npmignore` list in the *package.json* file to ignore material. It's better, though, just to remove anything that's not needed before publishing the module.

Once published—and once the source is also uploaded to GitHub (if that's the repository you're using)—the module is now officially ready for others to use. Promote the module on Twitter, Google+, Facebook, your website, and wherever else you think people would want to know about the module. This type of promotion isn't bragging—it's *sharing*.

CHAPTER 5

Control Flow, Asynchronous Patterns, and Exception Handling

Node might seem intimidating at times, with discussions about asynchronous events and callbacks and new objects such as `EventEmitter`—not to mention all that new server-side functionality we have to play with. If you've worked with any of the modern JavaScript libraries, though, you've experienced much of the functionality that goes into Node, at least when it comes to asynchronous development.

For instance, if you've used a timer in JavaScript, you've used an asynchronous function. If you've ever developed in Ajax, you've used an asynchronous function. Even the plain old `onclick` event handler is an asynchronous function, since we never know when the user is going to click that mouse or tap that keyboard.

Any method that doesn't block the control thread while waiting for some event or result is an asynchronous function. When it comes to the `onclick` handling, the application doesn't block all other application processing, waiting for that user's mouse click—just as it doesn't block all functionality while the timer is in effect, or while waiting for the server to return from an Ajax call.

In this chapter, we're going to look more closely at exactly what we mean by the term *asynchronous control*. In particular, we're going to look at some asynchronous design patterns, as well as explore some of the Node modules that provide finer control over program flow when we're working in this new environment. And since asynchronous control can add some new and interesting twists when it comes to error handling, we're also going to take a closer look at exception handling within an asynchronous Node environment.

Promises, No Promises, Callback Instead

In the earlier days of Node, asynchronous functionality was facilitated through the use of *promises*, a concept that arose in the 1970s. A promise is an object that represents the result of an asynchronous action. It's also known as a *future*, a *delay*, or simply *deferred*. The CommonJS design model embraced the concept of the promise.

In the earlier Node implementation, a promise was an object that emitted exactly two events: `success` and `error`. Its use was simple: if an asynchronous operation succeeded, the `success` event was emitted; otherwise, the `error` event was emitted. No other events were emitted, and the object would emit one or the other, but not both, and no more than once. Example 5-1 incorporates a previously implemented promise into a function that opens and reads in a file.

Example 5-1. Using a previously implemented Node promise

```
function test_and_load(filename) {
  var promise = new process.Promise();
  fs.stat(filename).addCallback(function (stat) {

    // Filter out non-files
    if (!stat.isFile()) { promise.emitSuccess(); return; }

    // Otherwise read the file in
    fs.readFile(filename).addCallback(function (data) {
      promise.emitSuccess(data);
    }).addErrback(function (error) {
      promise.emitError(error);
    });

  }).addErrback(function (error) {
    promise.emitError(error);
  });
  return promise;
}
```

Each object would return the promise object. The code to process a successful result would be passed as a function to the promise object's `addCallback` method, which had one parameter, the data. The code to process the error would be passed as a function to the promise object's `addErrback` method, which received the error as its one and only parameter:

```
var File = require('file');
var promise = File.read('mydata.txt');
promise.addCallback(function (data) {
  // process data
});
promise.addErrback(function (err) {
  // deal with error
})
```

The promise object ensured that the proper functionality was performed whenever the event finished—either the results could be manipulated, or the error processed.

The code for Example 5-1 is one of a number of examples of possible asynchronous function techniques documented at *http://groups.google .com/group/nodejs/browse_thread/thread/8dab9f0a5ad753d5* as part of the discussions about how Node would handle this concept in the future.

The promise object was pulled from Node in version 0.1.30. As Ryan Dahl noted at the time, the reasoning was:

> Because many people (myself included) only want a low-level interface to file system operations that does not necessitate creating an object, while many other people want something like promises but different in one way or another. So instead of promises we'll use last argument callbacks and consign the task of building better abstraction layers to user libraries.

Rather than the promise object, Node incorporated the *last argument callbacks* we've used in previous chapters. All asynchronous methods feature a callback function as the last argument. The first argument in this callback function is always an error object.

To demonstrate the fundamental structure of the callback functionality, Example 5-2 is a complete Node application that creates an object with one method, someMethod. This method takes three arguments, the second of which must be a string, and the third being the callback. In the method, if the second argument is missing or is not a string, the object creates a new Error object, which is passed to the callback function. Otherwise, whatever the result of the method is gets passed to the callback function.

Example 5-2. The fundamental structure of the last callback functionality

```
var obj =function() { };

obj.prototype.doSomething = function(arg1, arg2_) {
  var arg2 = typeof(arg2_) === 'string' ? arg2_ : null;

  var callback_ = arguments[arguments.length - 1];
  callback = (typeof(callback_) == 'function' ? callback_ : null);

  if (!arg2)
    return callback(new Error('second argument missing or not a string'));

  callback(arg1);
}
var test = new obj();

try {
  test.doSomething('test', 3.55, function(err,value) {
    if (err) throw err;

    console.log(value);
  });
} catch(err) {
```

```
    console.error(err);
}
```

The key elements of the callback functionality are in boldface in the code.

The first key functionality is to ensure the last argument is a callback function. Well, we can't determine the user's intent, but we can make sure the last argument is a function, and that will have to do. The second key functionality is to create the new Node `Error` object if an error occurs, and return it as the result to the callback function. The last critical functionality is to invoke the callback function, passing in the method's result if no error occurs. In short, everything else is changeable, as long as these three key functionalities are present:

- Ensure the last argument is a function.
- Create a Node `Error` and return it if an error occurs.
- If no error occurs, invoke the callback function, passing the method's result.

With the existing code in Example 5-1, the application output is the following error message printed out to the console:

```
[Error: second argument missing or not a string]
```

Changing the method call in the code to the following:

```
    test.doSomething('test','this',function(err,value) {
```

results in `test` being printed out to the console. Changing it then to the following:

```
    test.doSomething('test',function(err,value) {
```

again results in an error, this time because the second argument is missing.

If you look through the code in the *lib* directory of the Node installation, you'll see the last callback pattern repeated throughout. Though the functionality may change, this pattern remains the same.

This approach is quite simple and ensures consistent results from asynchronous methods. However, it also creates its own unique challenges, as we'll cover in the next section.

Sequential Functionality, Nested Callbacks, and Exception Handling

It's not unusual to find the following in a client-side JavaScript application:

```
val1 = callFunctionA();
val2 = callFunctionB(val1);
val3 = callFunctionC(val2);
```

The functions are called, in turn, passing the results from the earlier function to each subsequent function. Since all the functions are synchronous, we don't have to worry about the function calls getting out of sequence—no unexpected results.

Example 5-3 shows a relatively common case of this type of sequential programming. The application uses synchronous versions of Node's File System methods to open a file and get its data, modify the data by replacing all references to "apple" with "orange," and output the resulting string to a new file.

Example 5-3. A sequential synchronous application

```
var fs = require('fs');

try {
   var data = fs.readFileSync('./apples.txt','utf8');
   console.log(data);
   var adjData = data.replace(/[A|a]pple/g,'orange');

   fs.writeFileSync('./oranges.txt', adjData);
} catch(err) {
   console.error(err);
}
```

Since problems can occur and we can't be sure errors are handled internally in any module function, we wrap all of the function calls in a try block to allow for graceful —or at least, more informative—exception handling. The following is an example of what the error looks like when the application can't find the file to read:

```
{ [Error: ENOENT, no such file or directory './apples.txt']
  errno: 34,
  code: 'ENOENT',
  path: './apples.txt',
  syscall: 'open' }
```

While perhaps not very user-friendly, at least it's a lot better than the alternative:

```
node.js:201
        throw e; // process.nextTick error, or 'error' event on first tick
        ^
Error: ENOENT, no such file or directory './apples.txt'
    at Object.openSync (fs.js:230:18)
    at Object.readFileSync (fs.js:120:15)
    at Object.<anonymous> (/home/examples/public_html/node/read.js:3:18)
    at Module._compile (module.js:441:26)
    at Object..js (module.js:459:10)
    at Module.load (module.js:348:31)
    at Function._load (module.js:308:12)
    at Array.0 (module.js:479:10)
    at EventEmitter._tickCallback (node.js:192:40)
```

In the example, we're going to have expected results because each function call is performed in sequence.

Converting this synchronous sequential application pattern to an asynchronous implementation requires a couple of modifications. First, we have to replace all functions with their asynchronous counterparts. However, we also have to account for the fact that each function doesn't block when called, which means we can't guarantee the proper sequence if the functions are called independently of each other. The only way to ensure that each function is called in its proper sequence is to use *nested callbacks*.

Example 5-4 is an asynchronous version of the application from Example 5-3. All of the File System function calls have been replaced by their asynchronous versions, and the functions are called in the proper sequence via a nested callback.

Example 5-4. Application from Example 5-3 converted into asynchronous nested callbacks

```
var fs = require('fs');

try {
   fs.readFile('./apples2.txt','utf8', function(err,data) {

      if (err) throw err;

      var adjData = data.replace(/[A|a]pple/g,'orange');

      fs.writeFile('./oranges.txt', adjData, function(err) {

         if (err) throw err
      });
   });
} catch(err) {
   console.error(err);
}
```

In Example 5-4, the input file is opened and read, and only when both actions are finished does the callback function passed as the last parameter get called. In this function, the error is checked to make sure it's `null`. If not, the error is thrown for catching in the outer exception-handling block.

 Some style guides frown on throwing an error, and more complex frameworks provide error-handling objects and functions to ensure that all errors are resolved. My primary concern is that errors are handled.

If no error occurs, the data is processed and the asynchronous `writeFile` method is called. Its callback function has only one parameter, the error object. If it's not null, it's thrown for handling in the outer exception block.

If an error occurred, it would look similar to the following:

```
/home/examples/public_html/node/read2.js:11
         if (err) throw err;
                   ^
Error: ENOENT, no such file or directory './boogabooga/oranges.txt'
```

If you want the stack trace of the error, you can print out the `stack` property of the Node error object:

```
catch(err) {
    console.log(err.stack);
}
```

Including another sequential function call adds another level of callback nesting. In Example 5-5, we access a listing of files for a directory. In each of the files, we replace a generic domain name with a specific domain name using the string `replace` method, and the result is written *back* to the original file. A log is maintained of each changed file, using an open write stream.

Example 5-5. Retrieving directory listing for files to modify

```
var fs = require('fs');

var writeStream = fs.createWriteStream('./log.txt',
    {'flags' : 'a',
     'encoding' : 'utf8',
     'mode' : 0666});

try {
   // get list of files
   fs.readdir('./data/', function(err, files) {

      // for each file
      files.forEach(function(name) {

         // modify contents
         fs.readFile('./data/' + name,'utf8', function(err,data) {

            if (err) throw err;
            var adjData = data.replace(/somecompany\.com/g,'burningbird.net');

            // write to file
            fs.writeFile('./data/' + name, adjData, function(err) {

               if (err) throw err;

               // log write
               writeStream.write('changed ' + name + '\n', 'utf8', function(err) {

                  if(err) throw err;
               });
            });
         });
      });
   });
} catch(err) {
   console.error(util.inspect(err));
}
```

Though the application looks like it's processing each file individually before moving on to the next, remember that each of the methods used in this application is asynchronous. If you run the application several times and check the *log.txt* file, you'll see that the files are processed in a different, seemingly random order. In my *data* subdirectory I had five files. Running the application three times in a row resulted in the following output to *log.txt* (blank lines inserted for clarity):

```
changed data1.txt
changed data3.txt
changed data5.txt
changed data2.txt
changed data4.txt

changed data3.txt
changed data1.txt
changed data5.txt
changed data2.txt
changed data4.txt

changed data1.txt
changed data3.txt
changed data5.txt
changed data4.txt
changed data2.txt
```

Another issue arises if you want to check when all of the files have been modified in order to do something. The forEach method invokes the iterator callback functions asynchronously, so it doesn't block. Adding a statement following the use of forEach, like the following:

```
console.log('all done');
```

doesn't really mean the application is all finished, just that the forEach method didn't block. If you add a console.log statement at the same time you log the changed file:

```
writeStream.write('changed ' + name + '\n', 'utf8', function(err) {

    if(err) throw err;
    console.log('finished ' + name);
});
```

and add the following after the forEach method call:

```
console.log('all finished');
```

you'll actually get the following console output:

```
all done
finished data3.txt
finished data1.txt
finished data5.txt
finished data2.txt
finished data4.txt
```

To solve this challenge, add a counter that is incremented with each log message and then checked against the file array's length to print out the "all done" message:

```
// before accessing directory
var counter = 0;
...
                writeStream.write('changed ' + name + '\n', 'utf8', function(err) {

                    if(err) throw err;
                    console.log('finished ' + name);
                    counter++;
                    if (counter >= files.length)
                      console.log('all done');

                });
```

You'd then get the expected result: an "all done" message displays after all the files have been updated.

The application works quite well—except if the directory we're accessing has subdirectories as well as files. If the application encounters a subdirectory, it spits out the following error:

```
/home/examples/public_html/node/example5.js:20
          if (err) throw err;
                   ^
Error: EISDIR, illegal operation on a directory
```

Example 5-6 prevents this type of error by using the fs.stats method to return an object representing the data from a Unix stat command. This object contains information about the object, including whether it's a file or not. The fs.stats method is, of course, another asynchronous method, requiring yet more callback nesting.

Example 5-6. Adding in a stats check of each directory object to make sure it's a file

```
var fs = require('fs');

var writeStream = fs.createWriteStream('./log.txt',
      {'flags' : 'a',
       'encoding' : 'utf8',
       'mode' : 0666});

try {
   // get list of files
   fs.readdir('./data/', function(err, files) {

      // for each file
      files.forEach(function(name) {

         // check to see if object is file
         fs.stat('./data/' + name, function(err, stats) {

            if (err) throw err;

            if (stats.isFile())
```

```
        // modify contents
        fs.readFile('./data/' + name,'utf8', function(err,data) {

            if (err) throw err;
            var adjData = data.replace(/somecompany\.com/g,'burningbird.net');

            // write to file
            fs.writeFile('./data/' + name, adjData, function(err) {

                if (err) throw err;

                // log write
                writeStream.write('changed ' + name + '\n', 'utf8',
                                                    function(err) {
                    if(err) throw err;
                });
            });
        });
      });
    });
  });
} catch(err) {
  console.error(err);
}
```

Again, the application performs its purpose, and performs it well—but how difficult it is to read and maintain! I've heard this type of nested callback called *callback spaghetti* and the even more colorful *pyramid of doom*, both of which are apt terms.

The nested callbacks continue to push against the right side of the document, making it more difficult to ensure we have the right code in the right callback. However, we can't break the callback nesting apart because it's essential that the methods be called in turn:

1. Start the directory lookup.
2. Filter out subdirectories.
3. Read each file's contents.
4. Modify the contents.
5. Write back to the original file.

What we'd like to do is find a way of implementing this series of method calls but without having to depend on nested callbacks. For this, we need to look at third-party modules that provide asynchronous control flow.

 Another approach is to provide a named function as a callback function for each method. This way, you can flatten the pyramid, and it can simplify debugging. However, this approach doesn't solve some of the other problems, such as determining when all processes have finished. For this, you still need the third-party libraries.

Asynchronous Patterns and Control Flow Modules

The application in Example 5-6 is an example of an asynchronous pattern, where each function is called in turn and passes its results to the next function, and the entire chain stops only if an error occurs. There are several such patterns, though some are variations of others, and not everyone uses the exact same terminology.

One Node module, Async, provides names and support for the most extensive list of asynchronous control flow patterns:

waterfall
: Functions are called in turn, and results of all are passed as an array to the last callback (also called series and sequence by others).

series
: Functions are called in turn and, optionally, results are passed as an array to the last callback.

parallel
: Functions are run in parallel and when completed, results are passed to the last callback (though the result array isn't part of the pattern in some interpretations of the parallel pattern).

whilst
: Repeatedly calls one function, invoking the last callback only if a preliminary test returns false or an error occurs.

queue
: Calls functions in parallel up to a given limit of concurrency, and new functions are queued until one of the functions finishes.

until
: Repeatedly calls one function, invoking the last callback only if a post-process test returns false or an error occurs.

auto
: Functions are called based on requirements, each function receiving the results of previous callbacks.

iterator
: Each function calls the next, with the ability to individually access the next iterator.

apply
: A continuation function with arguments already applied combined with other control flow functions.

nextTick
: Calls the callback in the next loop of an event loop—based on process.nextTick in Node.

In the listing of modules provided at the Node.js website, there is a category titled "Control Flow/Async Goodies." In this list is the Async module, which provides the asynchronous control patterns I just listed. Though not every control flow module provides the capability to handle all possible patterns, most provide functionality for the most common patterns: `series` (also called `sequence` and sometimes referred to as `waterfall`—as in the preceding list—though Async lists `waterfall` separately from `series`) and `parallel`. In addition, some of the modules also reinstate the concept of promises from earlier editions of Node, while others implement a concept called *fibers*, which emulate threads.

In the next couple of sections, I'll demonstrate two of the more popular of the actively maintained control flow modules: Step and Async. Each offers its own unique perspective on asynchronous control flow management, though both provide a very useful—and likely essential—service.

Step

Step is a focused utility module that enables simplified control flow for serial and parallel execution. It can be installed using npm as follows:

```
npm install step
```

The Step module exports exactly one object. To use the object for serial execution, wrap your asynchronous function calls within functions that are then passed as parameters to the object. For instance, in Example 5-7, Step is used to read the contents of a file, modify the contents, and write them back to the file.

Example 5-7. Using Step to perform serial asynchronous tasks

```
var fs = require('fs'),
    Step = require('step');

try {

    Step (
        function readData() {
            fs.readFile('./data/data1.txt', 'utf8', this);
        },
        function modify(err, text) {
            if (err) throw err;
            return text.replace(/somecompany\.com/g,'burningbird.net');
        },
        function writeData(err, text) {
            if (err) throw err;
            fs.writeFile('./data/data1.txt', text, this);
        }
    );
} catch(err) {
    console.error(err);
}
```

The first function in the Step sequence, `readData`, reads a file's contents into a string, which is then passed to a second function. The second function modifies the string using replacement, and the result is passed to a third function. In the third function, the modified string is written back to the original file.

 For more information, see the Step GitHub site at *https://github.com/ creationix/step.*

In more detail, the first function wraps the asynchronous fs.readFile. However, rather than pass a callback function as the last parameter, the code passes the this context. When the function is finished, its data and any possible error are sent to the next function, modify. The modify function isn't an asynchronous function, as all it's doing is replacing one substring for another in the string. It doesn't require the this context, and just returns the result at the end of the function.

The last function gets the newly modified string and writes it back to the original file. Again, since it's an asynchronous function, it gets this in place of the callback function. If we didn't include this as the last parameter to the final function, any errors that occur wouldn't be thrown and caught in the outer loop. If the *boogabooga* subdirectory didn't exist with the following modified code:

```
function writeFile(err, text) {
    if (err) throw err;
    fs.writeFile('./boogabooga/data/data1.txt');
}
```

we'd never know that the write failed.

Even though the second function isn't asynchronous, every function but the first in Step requires the error object as the first parameter for consistency. It's just null by default in a synchronous function.

Example 5-7 performs part of the functionality of the application in Example 5-6. Could it do the rest of the functionality, especially handling modification to multiple files? The answer is yes, and no. Yes, it can do the work, but only if we throw in some kludgy code.

In Example 5-8, I added in the readir asynchronous function to get a list of files in a given subdirectory. The array of files is processed with a forEach command, like in Example 5-6, but the end of the call to readFile isn't a callback function or this. In Step, the call to create the group object signals to reserve a parameter for a group result; the call to the group object in the readFile asynchronous function results in each of the callbacks being called in turn, and the results being grouped into an array for the next function.

Example 5-8. Using Step's group() capability to handle grouped asynchronous processes

```
var fs = require('fs'),
    Step = require('step'),
```

```
    files,
    _dir = './data/';

try {

    Step (
        function readDir() {
            fs.readdir(_dir, this);
        },
        function readFile(err, results) {
            if (err) throw err;
            files = results;
            var group = this.group();
            results.forEach(function(name) {
                fs.readFile(_dir + name, 'utf8', group());
            });
        },
        function writeAll(err, data) {
            if (err) throw err;
            for (var i = 0; i < files.length; i++) {
                var adjdata = data[i].replace(/somecompany\.com/g,'burningbird.net');
                fs.writeFile(_dir + files[i], adjdata, 'utf8',this);
            }
        }
    );
} catch(err) {
    console.log(err);
}
```

To preserve the filenames, the readdir result is assigned to a global variable, files. In the last Step function, a regular for loop cycles through the data to modify it, and then cycles through the files variable to get the filename. Both the filename and modified data are used in the last asynchronous call to writeFile.

One other approach we could have used if we wanted to hardcode the change to each file is to use the Step parallel feature. Example 5-9 performs a readFile on a couple of different files, passing in this.parallel() as the last parameter. This results in a parameter being passed to the next function for each readFile in the first function. The parallel function call also has to be used in the writeFile function in the second function, to ensure that each callback is processed in turn.

Example 5-9. Reading and writing to a group of files using Step's group functionality

```
var fs = require('fs'),
    Step = require('step'),
    files;

try {

    Step (
        function readFiles() {
            fs.readFile('./data/data1.txt', 'utf8',this.parallel());
            fs.readFile('./data/data2.txt', 'utf8',this.parallel());
```

```
        fs.readFile('./data/data3.txt', 'utf8',this.parallel());
    },
    function writeFiles(err, data1, data2, data3) {
        if (err) throw err;
        data1 = data1.replace(/somecompany\.com/g,'burningbird.net');
        data2 = data2.replace(/somecompany\.com/g,'burningbird.net');
        data3 = data3.replace(/somecompany\.com/g,'burningbird.net');

        fs.writeFile('./data/data1.txt', data1, 'utf8', this.parallel());
        fs.writeFile('./data/data2.txt', data2, 'utf8', this.parallel());
        fs.writeFile('./data/data3.txt', data3, 'utf8', this.parallel());
    }
);
} catch(err) {
    console.log(err);
}
```

It works, but it's clumsy. It would be better to reserve the use of the parallel functionality for a sequence of different asynchronous functions that can be implemented in parallel, and the data processed post-callback.

As for our earlier application, rather than trying to force Step into contortions to fit our use case, we can use another library that provides the additional flexibility we need: Async.

Async

The Async module provides functionality for managing collections, such as its own variation of forEach, map, and filter. It also provides some utility functions, including ones for *memoization*. However, what we're interested in here are its facilities for handling control flow.

 There is both an Async and an Async.js module, so be careful not to confuse the two. The one covered in this section is Async, by Caolan McMahon. Its GitHub site is *https://github.com/caolan/async*.

Install Async using npm like so:

```
npm install async
```

As mentioned earlier, Async provides control flow capability for a variety of asynchronous patterns, including serial, parallel, and waterfall. Like Step, it gives us a tool to tame the wild nested callback pyramid, but its approach is quite different. For one, we don't insert ourselves between each function and its callback. Instead, we incorporate the callback as part of the process.

As an example, we've already identified that the pattern of the earlier application matches with Async's waterfall, so we'll be using the async.waterfall method. In Example 5-10, I used async.waterfall to open and read a data file using fs.readFile, perform the synchronous string substitution, and then write the string back to the file using `fs.writeFile`. Pay particular attention to the callback function used with each step in the application.

Example 5-10. Using async.waterfall to read, modify, and write a file's contents asynchronously

```
var fs = require('fs'),
    async = require('async');

try {
   async.waterfall([
      function readData(callback) {
         fs.readFile('./data/data1.txt', 'utf8', function(err, data){
            callback(err,data);
         });
      },
      function modify(text, callback) {
         var adjdata=text.replace(/somecompany\.com/g,'burningbird.net');
         callback(null, adjdata);
      },
      function writeData(text, callback) {
         fs.writeFile('./data/data1.txt', text, function(err) {
            callback(err,text);
         });
      }
   ], function (err, result) {
        if (err) throw err;
        console.log(result);
   });
} catch(err) {
   console.log(err);
}
```

The `async.waterfall` method takes two parameters: an array of tasks and an optional final callback function. Each asynchronous task function is an element of the `async.waterfall` method array, and each function requires a callback as the last of its parameters. It is this callback function that allows us to chain the asynchronous callback results without having to physically nest the functions. However, as you can see in the code, each function's callback is handled as we would normally handle it if we were using nested callbacks—other than the fact that we don't have to test the errors in each function. The callbacks look for an error object as first parameter. If we pass an error object in the callback function, the process is ended at this point, and the final callback routine is called. The final callback is when we can test for an error, and throw the error to the outer exception handling block (or otherwise handle).

The `readData` function wraps our `fs.readFile` call, which checks for an error, first. If an error is found, it throws the error, ending the process. If not, it issues a call to the callback as its last operation. This is the trigger to tell Async to invoke the next function, passing any relevant data. The next function isn't asynchronous, so it does its processing, passing `null` as the error object, and the modified data. The last function, `write Data`, calls the asynchronous `writeFile`, using the passed-in data from the previous callback and then testing for an error in its own callback routine.

Example 5-10 uses named functions, while the Async documentation shows anonymous functions. However, named functions can simplify debugging and error handling. Both work equally well.

The processing is very similar to what we had in Example 5-4, but without the nesting (and having to test for an error in each function). It may seem more complicated than what we had in Example 5-4, and I wouldn't necessarily recommend its use for such simple nesting, but look what it can do with a more complex nested callback. Example 5-11 duplicates the exact functionality from Example 5-6, but without the callback nesting and excessive indenting.

Example 5-11. Get objects from directory, test to look for files, read file test, modify, and write back out log results

```
var fs = require('fs'),
    async = require('async'),
    _dir = './data/';

var writeStream = fs.createWriteStream('./log.txt',
      {'flags' : 'a',
       'encoding' : 'utf8',
       'mode' : 0666});
try {
   async.waterfall([
       function readDir(callback) {
           fs.readdir(_dir, function(err, files) {
               callback(err,files);
           });
       },
       function loopFiles(files, callback) {
           files.forEach(function (name) {
               callback (null, name);
           });
       },
       function checkFile(file, callback) {
           fs.stat(_dir + file, function(err, stats) {
               callback(err, stats, file);
           });
       },
       function readData(stats, file, callback) {
           if (stats.isFile())
               fs.readFile(_dir + file, 'utf8', function(err, data){
                   callback(err,file,data);
               });
       },
       function modify(file, text, callback) {
           var adjdata=text.replace(/somecompany\.com/g,'burningbird.net');
           callback(null, file, adjdata);
       },
       function writeData(file, text, callback) {
           fs.writeFile(_dir + file, text, function(err) {
               callback(err,file);
```

```
            });
        },
        function logChange(file, callback) {
            writeStream.write('changed ' + file + '\n', 'utf8', function(err) {
                callback(err, file);
            });
        }
    ], function (err, result) {
        if (err) throw err;
        console.log('modified ' + result);
    });
} catch(err) {
   console.log(err);
}
```

Every last bit of functionality is present from Example 5-6. The `fs.readdir` method is used to get an array of directory objects. The Node `forEach` method (not the Async `forEach`) is used to access each specific object. The `fs.stats` method is used to get the `stats` for each object. `stats` is used to check for files, and when a file is found, it's opened and its data accessed. The data is then modified, and passed on to be written back to the file via `fs.writeFile`. The operation is logged in the logfile and also echoed to the console.

Note that there is more data passed in some of the callbacks. Most of the functions need the filename as well as the text, so this is passed in the last several methods. Any amount of data can be passed in the methods, as long as the first parameter is the error object (or `null`, if no error object) and the last parameter in each function is the callback function.

We don't have to check for an error in each asynchronous task function either, because Async tests the error object in each callback, and stops processing and calls the final callback function if an error is found. And we don't have to worry about using special processing when handling an array of items, as we did when we used Step earlier in the chapter.

The other Async control flow methods, such as `async.parallel` and `async.serial`, perform in a like manner, with an array of tasks as the first method parameter, and a final optional callback as the second. How they process the asynchronous tasks differs, though, as you would expect.

 We use the `async.serial` method with a Redis application in Chapter 9, in the section "Building a Game Leaderboard" on page 190.

The `async.parallel` method calls all of the asynchronous functions at once, and when they are each finished, calls the optional final callback. Example 5-12 uses `async.parallel` to read in the contents of three files in parallel. However, rather than an array of functions, this example uses an alternative approach that Async supports: passing in an object with each asynchronous task listed as a property of the object. The results are then printed out to the console when all three tasks have finished.

Example 5-12. Opening three files in parallel and reading in their contents

```
var fs = require('fs'),
    async = require('async');

try {
   async.parallel({
      data1 : function (callback) {
         fs.readFile('./data/data1.txt', 'utf8', function(err, data){
            callback(err,data);
         });
      },
      data2 : function (callback) {
         fs.readFile('./data/data2.txt', 'utf8', function(err, data){
            callback(err,data);
         });
      },
      data3 : function readData3(callback) {
         fs.readFile('./data/data3.txt', 'utf8', function(err, data){
            callback(err,data);
         });
      },

   }, function (err, result) {
       if (err) throw err;
       console.log(result);
   });
} catch(err) {
   console.log(err);
}
```

The results are returned as an array of objects, with each result tied to each of the properties. If the three data files in the example had the following content:

- *data1.txt*: apples
- *data2.txt*: oranges
- *data3.txt*: peaches

the result of running Example 5-12 is:

```
{ data1: 'apples\n', data2: 'oranges\n', data3: 'peaches\n' }
```

I'll leave the testing of the other Async control flow methods as a reader exercise. Just remember that when you're working with the Async control flow methods, all you need is to pass a callback to each asynchronous task and to call this callback when you're finished, passing in an error object (or null) and whatever data you need.

Node Style

A couple of times in the chapter I mentioned people recommending certain restraints, such as using named rather than anonymous functions in Node applications. Collectively, these restraints are known as *preferred Node style*, though there is no one style guide or definitive set of shared preferences. In fact, there are several different recommendations for proper Node style.

 One helpful Node.js style guide is Felix's Node.js Style Guide, at *http://nodeguide.com/style.html*.

Here are some of the recommendations, and my own take on each:

Use asynchronous functions over synchronous.
Yes, this is essential for Node applications.

Use a two-space indentation.
My take: Sorry, I'm used to three spaces, and I'll continue to use three spaces. I think it's more important to be consistent and *not* to use tabs; I'm not going to split hairs on the number of spaces.

Use semicolons/don't use semicolons.
Amazing how contentious this one is. I use semicolons, but follow your own instincts.

Use single quotes.
I'm rather used to double quotes, but have managed to kick the habit (more or less). Regardless, it's better to use double quotes than to escape a single quote in a string.

When defining several variables, use one var *keyword/don't use one* var *keyword.*
Some of the applications in this book use the var keyword for each variable; some don't. Again, old habits are hard to break, but I don't think this is as much an issue as some people make it.

Constants should be uppercase.
I agree with this one.

Variables should be camel case.
I more or less agree with this, but not religiously.

Use the strict equality operator (===).
Sound advice, but I repeat, old habits are hard to break. I mean to use strict equality, but frequently use just the regular equality (==). Don't be bad like me.

Name your closures.
My bad, again. This really is sound advice, and I'm trying to improve, but most of my code still uses anonymous functions.

Line length should be fewer than 80 characters.
    Again, sound advice.

Curly braces begin on the same line as what necessitates them.
    I do follow this religiously.

The most important rule to remember out of all of these is to use asynchronous functions whenever and wherever possible. After all, asynchronous functionality is the heart of Node.

CHAPTER 6

Routing Traffic, Serving Files, and Middleware

Click a link in a web page, and you expect something to happen. That something is typically a page being loaded. However, there's actually a lot that goes on before that web resource loads—some of which is mostly out of our control (such as packet routing), and some of which is dependent on us having software installed that understands how to respond based on the link's contents.

Of course, when we use web servers such as Apache, and software such as Drupal, much of the mechanics of serving a file or a resource are handled behind the scenes. However, when we're creating our own server-side applications in Node and bypassing our usual technology, we have to get more involved in ensuring that the right resource gets delivered at the right time.

This chapter focuses on the technology available to Node developers for providing the very basic routing and middleware functionality we need to ensure that resource A gets delivered to user B correctly and quickly.

Building a Simple Static File Server from Scratch

We have all the functionality we need to build a simple router or to serve static files built directly into Node. But *being able* to do so and doing so *easily* are two different things.

When thinking of what's necessary to build a simple but functional static file server, we might come up with the following set of steps:

1. Create an HTTP server and listen for requests.
2. When a request arrives, parse the request URL to determine the location for the file.
3. Check to make sure the file exists.
4. If the file doesn't exist, respond accordingly.

5. If the file does exist, open the file for reading.

6. Prepare a response header.

7. Write the file to the response.

8. Wait for the next request.

Creating an HTTP server and reading files requires the HTTP and File System modules. The Path module will also come in handy, because it has a way of checking to make sure a file exists before trying to open it for reading. In addition, we'll want to define a global variable for the base directory, or use the predefined __dirname (more on this in the upcoming sidebar "Why Not Use __dirname?" on page 110).

The top of the application has the following code at this point:

```
var http = require('http'),
    path = require('path'),
      fs = require('fs'),
    base = '/home/examples/public_html';
```

Creating a server using the HTTP module isn't anything new. And the application can get the document requested by directly accessing the HTTP request object's url property. To double-check the response compared to requests, we'll also throw in a console.log of the requested file's pathname. This is in addition to the console.log message that's written when the server is first started:

```
http.createServer(function (req, res) {

    pathname = base + req.url;
    console.log(pathname);


}).listen(8124);

console.log('Server running at 8124/');
```

Before attempting to open the file for reading and writing to the HTTP response, the application needs to check that it exists. The path.exists function is a good choice at this point. If the file doesn't exist, write a brief message to this effect and set the status code to 404: document not found.

```
path.exists(pathname, function(exists) {
    if (exists) {
       // insert code to process request
    } else {
        res.writeHead(404);
        res.write('Bad request 404\n');
        res.end();
    }
}
```

Now we're getting into the meat of the new application. In examples in previous chapters, we used fs.readFile to read in a file. The problem with fs.readFile, though, is that it wants to read the file completely into memory before making it available.

Documents served over the Web can be quite large. In addition, there can be many requests for a document at any given time. Something like fs.readFile just won't scale.

 The path.exists method has been deprecated in Node 0.8. Instead, use fs.exists. The examples file referenced in the preface include applications that support both environments.

Instead of using fs.readFile, the application creates a read stream via the fs.createR eadStream method, using the default settings. Then it's a simple matter to just *pipe* the file contents directly to the HTTP response object. Since the stream sends an end signal when it's finished, we don't need to use the end method call with the read stream:

```
res.setHeader('Content-Type', 'test/html');

// 200 status - found, no errors
res.statusCode = 200;

// create and pipe readable stream
var file = fs.createReadStream(pathname);
file.on("open", function() {
    file.pipe(res);
});
file.on("error", function(err) {
  console.log(err);
});
```

The read stream has two events of interest: open and error. The open event is sent when the stream is ready, and the error if a problem occurs. The application calls the pipe method in the callback function for the open event.

At this point, the static file server looks like the application in Example 6-1.

Example 6-1. A simple static file web server

```
var http = require('http'),
    path = require('path'),
    fs   = require('fs'),
    base = '/home/examples/public_html';

http.createServer(function (req, res) {

  pathname = base + req.url;
  console.log(pathname);

  path.exists(pathname, function(exists) {
     if (!exists) {
       res.writeHead(404);
       res.write('Bad request 404\n');
       res.end();
     } else {
        res.setHeader('Content-Type', 'text/html');

        // 200 status - found, no errors
```

```
      res.statusCode = 200;

      // create and pipe readable stream
      var file = fs.createReadStream(pathname);
      file.on("open", function() {
        file.pipe(res);
      });
      file.on("error", function(err) {
        console.log(err);
      });
    }
  });
}).listen(8124);

console.log('Server running at 8124/');
```

I tested it with a simple HTML file, which has nothing more than an img element, and the file loaded and displayed properly:

```
<!DOCTYPE html>
<head>
   <title>Test</title>
   <meta charset="utf-8" />
</head>
<body>
<img src="./phoenix5a.png" />
</body>
```

I then tried it with another example file I had, which contained an HTML5 video element:

```
<!DOCTYPE html>
<head>
   <title>Video</title>
   <meta charset="utf-8" />
</head>
<body>
   <video id="meadow" controls>
      <source src="videofile.mp4" />
      <source src="videofile.ogv" />
      <source src="videofile.webm" />
   </video>
</body>
```

Though the file would open and the video displayed when I tried the page with Chrome, the video element did not work when I tested the page with Internet Explorer 10. Looking at the console output provided the reason why:

```
Server running at 8124/
/home/examples/public_html/html5media/chapter1/example2.html
/home/examples/public_html/html5media/chapter1/videofile.mp4
/home/examples/public_html/html5media/chapter1/videofile.ogv
/home/examples/public_html/html5media/chapter1/videofile.webm
```

Though IE10 is capable of playing the MP4 video, it tests all three of the videos because the content type of the response header is `text/html` for each. Though other browsers will ignore the incorrect content type and display the media correctly, IE does not—appropriately, in my opinion, because I may not have quickly found the error in the application otherwise.

This application is a perfect example of why we have to test our server-side applications in all target browsers, even though, seemingly, we should be able to test the application with just one since the functionality we're testing is on the server.

The application has to be modified to test for the file extension for each file and then return the appropriate MIME type in the response header. We could code this functionality ourselves, but I'd rather make use of an existing module: node-mime.

You can install node-mime using npm: `npm install mime`. The GitHub site is at *https://github.com/broofa/node-mime*.

The node-mime module can return the proper MIME type given a filename (with or without path), and can also return file extensions given a content type. The node-mime module is added to the requirements list like so:

```
mime = require('mime');
```

The returned content type is used in the response header, and also output to the console, so we can check the value as we test the application:

```
// content type
var type = mime.lookup(pathname);
console.log(type);
res.setHeader('Content-Type', type);
```

Now when we access the file with the video element in IE10, the video file works.

What doesn't work, though, is when we access a directory instead of a file. When this happens, an error is output to the console, and the web page remains blank for the user:

```
{ [Error: EISDIR, illegal operation on a directory] errno: 28, code: 'EISDIR' }
```

We not only need to check if the resource being accessed exists, but we also need to check whether it's a file or a directory. If it's a directory being accessed, we can either display its contents, or we can output an error—it's the developer's choice.

The final version of a minimal static file server, in Example 6-2, uses `fs.stats` to check for the existence of the requested object and whether it's a file. If the resource doesn't exist, an HTTP status of 404 is returned. If the resource exists, but it's a directory, an HTTP error status code of 403—forbidden—is returned. In all cases, the request is handled properly.

Example 6-2. Final version of minimal static file server

```
var http = require('http'),
    url =  require('url'),
    fs  = require('fs'),
    mime = require('mime');
    base = '/home/examples/public_html';

http.createServer(function (req, res) {

    pathname = base + req.url;
    console.log(pathname);

    fs.stat(pathname, function(err, stats) {
        if (err) {
            res.writeHead(404);
            res.write('Bad request 404\n');
            res.end();
        } else if (stats.isFile()) {
            // content type
            var type = mime.lookup(pathname);
            console.log(type);
            res.setHeader('Content-Type', type);

            // 200 status - found, no errors
            res.statusCode = 200;

            // create and pipe readable stream
            var file = fs.createReadStream(pathname);
            file.on("open", function() {

                file.pipe(res);
            });
            file.on("error", function(err) {
                console.log(err);
            });
        } else {
            res.writeHead(403);
            res.write('Directory access is forbidden');
            res.end();
        }
    });
}).listen(8124);
console.log('Server running at 8124/');
```

The following is the console output for accessing one web page that contains both image and video file links:

```
/home/examples/public_html/html5media/chapter2/example16.html
text/html
/home/examples/public_html/html5media/chapter2/bigbuckposter.jpg
image/jpeg
/home/examples/public_html/html5media/chapter2/butterfly.png
image/png
/home/examples/public_html/favicon.ico
image/x-icon
/home/examples/public_html/html5media/chapter2/videofile.mp4
video/mp4
/home/examples/public_html/html5media/chapter2/videofile.mp4
video/mp4
```

Note the proper handling of the content types. Figure 6-1 shows one web page that contains a video element loaded into Chrome, and the network access displayed in the browser's console.

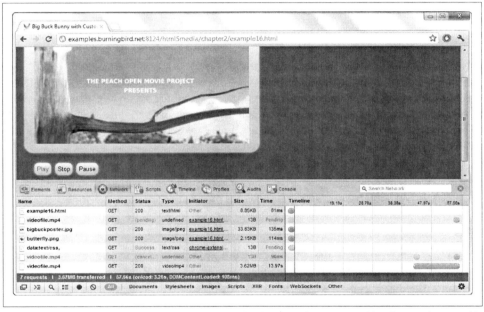

Figure 6-1. Displaying the browser console while loading a web page served by the simple static file server from Example 6-2

You get a better feel for how the read stream works when you load a page that has a video element and begin to play it. The browser grabs the read stream output at a speed it can manage, filling its own internal buffer, and then pauses the output. If you close the server while the video content is playing, the video continues to play...up to the point where it exhausts its current video buffer. The video element then goes blank because the read stream is no longer available. It's actually a little fascinating to see how well everything works with so little effort on our part.

Though the application works when tested with several different documents, it's not perfect. It doesn't handle many other types of web requests, it doesn't handle security or caching, and it doesn't properly handle the video requests. One web page application I tested that uses HTML video also makes use of the HTML5 video element API to output the state of the video load process. This application didn't get the information it needs to work as designed.

Chapter 12 revisits this application and covers what additional effort is needed to create a fully functional HTML5 video server.

There are many little gotchas that can trip us when it comes to creating a static file server. Another approach is to use an existing static file server. In the next section, we'll look at one included in the Connect middleware.

Middleware

What is *middleware*? That's a good question, and one that, unfortunately, doesn't have a definitive answer.

Generally, middleware is software that exists between you, as the developer, and the underlying system. By *system*, we can mean either the operating system, or the underlying technology, such as we get from Node. More specifically, middleware inserts itself into the communication chain between your application and the underlying system—hence its rather descriptive name.

For instance, rather than have to provide all the functionality necessary for serving static files via a web server, you can use middleware to handle most of it. The middleware then takes care of all the tedious bits, so you can focus on those aspects of your application that are unique to your needs and requirements. However, middleware doesn't stop with just serving up static files. Some middleware provides authorization components, proxies, routers, cookie and session management, and other necessary web technologies.

Middleware isn't a utility library or simple set of functions. What middleware you choose defines how your application is both designed and developed. You have to be comfortable with your choice of middleware before you begin incorporating it, because you'd have a difficult time switching mid-development.

Currently, there are two major middleware applications used in Node applications: JSGI (JavaScript Gateway Interface) and Connect. JSGI is a middleware technology for JavaScript generally, not Node specifically. Its use is facilitated for Node with the JSGI-node module. Connect, on the other hand, was developed for use with Node.

 The JSGI site is at *http://wiki.commonjs.org/wiki/JSGI/Level0/A/Draft2*. The JSGI-node GitHub site is at *https://github.com/persvr/jsgi-node*.

I'm covering only Connect in this book, for three reasons. One, it's simpler to use. JSGI would require us to spend too much time trying to understand how it works in general (independent of its use with Node), whereas with Connect, we can jump right in. Two, Connect provides middleware support for Express, a very popular framework (covered in Chapter 7). Three, and perhaps most importantly, over time Connect has seemingly floated to the top as best in breed. It's the most used middleware if the npm registry is any indication.

 You will find an introduction to Connect 2.0 at *http://tjholowaychuk .com/post/18418627138/connect-2-0*. The Connect source is at *https:// github.com/senchalabs/Connect*. (For more information on installation, see the sidebar "Working with Alpha Modules" on page 112).

Connect Basics

You can install Connect using npm:

```
npm install connect
```

Connect is, in actuality, a framework in which you can use one or more middleware applications. The documentation for Connect is sparse. However, it is relatively simple to use once you've seen a couple of working examples.

Working with Alpha Modules

At the time I wrote the first draft of this chapter, the npm registry had the stable version (1.8.5) of Connect, but I wanted to cover the development version, 2.x, since it will most likely be the version you'll be using.

I downloaded the source code for Connect 2.x directly from GitHub, and moved into my development environment's *node_modules* directory. I then changed to the Connect directory and installed it using npm, but without specifying the module's name, and using the -d flag to install the dependencies:

```
npm install -d
```

You can use npm to install directly from the Git repository. You can also use Git directly to clone the version and then use the technique I just described to install it.

Be aware that if you install a module directly from source, and you perform an npm update, npm will overwrite the module with what it considers to be the "latest" module —even if you are using a newer version of the module.

In Example 6-3, I created a simple server application using Connect, and using two of the middleware[1] bundled with Connect: connect.logger and connect.favicon. The logger middleware logs all requests to a stream—in this case, the default STDIO.out put stream—and the favicon middleware serves up the *favicon.ico* file. The application includes the middleware using the use method on the Connect request listener, which is then passed as a parameter to the HTTP object's createServer method.

Example 6-3. Incorporating the logger and favicon middleware into a Connect-based application

```
var connect = require('connect');
var http = require('http');

var app = connect()
   .use(connect.favicon())
   .use(connect.logger())
   .use(function(req,res) {
      res.end('Hello World\n');
   });

http.createServer(app).listen(8124);
```

You can use any number of middleware—either built in with Connect or provided by a third party—by just including additional use states.

Rather than create the Connect request listener first, we can also incorporate the Connect middleware directly into the createServer method, as shown in Example 6-4.

---

1. Connect refers to the individual middleware options as just "middleware." I follow its convention in this chapter.

Example 6-4. Incorporating Connect bundled middleware into an application directly

```
var connect = require('connect');
var http = require('http');

http.createServer(connect()
   .use(connect.favicon())
   .use(connect.logger())
   .use(function(req,res) {
      res.end('Hello World\n');
   })).listen(8124);
```

Connect Middleware

Connect comes bundled with at least 20 middleware. I'm not going to cover them all in this section, but I am going to demonstrate enough of them so that you have a good understanding of how they work together.

 Other examples of the Connect middleware are utilized in the Express applications created in Chapter 7.

connect.static

Earlier, we created a simplified static file server from scratch. Connect provides middleware that implements the functionality of that server, and more. It is extremely easy to use—you just specify the `connect.static` middleware option, passing in the root directory for all requests. The following implements most of what we created in Example 6-2, but with far less code:

```
var connect = require('connect'),
    http = require('http'),
    __dirname = '/home/examples';

http.createServer(connect()
   .use(connect.logger())
   .use(connect.static(_dirname + '/public_html'), {redirect: true})
   ).listen(8124);
```

The `connect.static` middleware takes the root path as the first parameter, and an optional object as the second. Among the options supported in the second object are:

maxAge
   Browser cache in milliseconds: defaults to 0

hidden
   Set to true to allow transfer of hidden files; default is `false`

redirect
   Set to `true` to redirect to trailing / when the pathname is a directory

This short Connect middleware application represents a big difference in behavior from the earlier scratch application. The Connect solution handles the browser cache, protects against malformed URLs, and more properly handles HTTP HTML5 video, which the server built from scratch could not. Its only shortcoming when compared to the scratch server is that we have more control over error handling with the scratch server. However, the connect.static middleware does provide the appropriate response and status code to the browser.

The code just shown, and the earlier examples in the section, also demonstrate another Connect middleware: connect.logger. We'll discuss it next.

connect.logger

The logger middleware module logs incoming requests to a stream, set to stdout by default. You can change the stream, as well as other options including buffer duration, format, and an immediate flag that signals whether to write the log immediately or on response.

There are several tokens with which you can build the format string, in addition to four predefined formats you can use:

default
    ':remote-addr - - [:date] ":method :url HTTP/:http-version" :status :res[con
    tent-length] ":referrer" ":user-agent"'

short
    ':remote-addr - :method :url HTTP/:http-version :status :res[content-
    length] - :response-time ms'

tiny
    ':method :url :status :res[content-length] - :response-time ms'

dev
    Concise output colored by response status for development use

The default format generates log entries like the following:

```
99.28.217.189 - - [Sat, 25 Feb 2012 02:18:22 GMT] "GET /example1.html HTTP/1.1" 304
- "-" "Mozilla/5.0 (Windows NT 6.1; WOW64) AppleWebKit/535.11 (KHTML, like Gecko)
 Chrome/17.0.963.56 Safari/535.11"
99.28.217.189 - - [Sat, 25 Feb 2012 02:18:22 GMT] "GET /phoenix5a.png HTTP/1.1" 304
 - "http://examples.burningbird.net:8124/example1.html"
"Mozilla/5.0 (Windows NT 6.1; WOW64) AppleWebKit/535.11 (KHTML, like Gecko)
Chrome/17.0.963.56 Safari/535.11"
99.28.217.189 - - [Sat, 25 Feb 2012 02:18:22 GMT] "GET /favicon.ico HTTP/1.1"
304 - "-" "Mozilla/5.0 (Windows NT 6.1; WOW64) AppleWebKit/535.11 (KHTML, like Gecko)
 Chrome/17.0.963.56 Safari/535.11"
99.28.217.189 - - [Sat, 25 Feb 2012 02:18:28 GMT]
"GET /html5media/chapter2/example16.html HTTP/1.1" 304 - "-"
"Mozilla/5.0 (Windows NT 6.1; WOW64) AppleWebKit/535.11 (KHTML, like Gecko)
Chrome/17.0.963.56 Safari/535.11"
```

This is very informative, but also very verbose. It's also very familiar, resembling the default log format we get with a server such as Apache. You can change the format, and you can also direct the output to a file. Example 6-5 makes use of connect.log ger, directing the log entries to a file and setting the format to the dev predefined format.

Example 6-5. Setting logging to a file and changing logger format

```
var connect = require('connect'),
    http = require('http'),
    fs = require('fs'),
    __dirname = '/home/examples';

var writeStream = fs.createWriteStream('./log.txt',
      {'flags' : 'a',
       'encoding' : 'utf8',
       'mode' : 0666});

http.createServer(connect()
  .use(connect.logger({format : 'dev', stream : writeStream }))
  .use(connect.static(__dirname + '/public_html'))
  ).listen(8124);
```

Now the logging output looks like:

```
GET /example1.html 304 4ms
GET /phoenix5a.png 304 1ms
GET /favicon.ico 304 1ms
GET /html5media/chapter2/example16.html 304 2ms
GET /html5media/chapter2/bigbuckposter.jpg 304 1ms
GET /html5media/chapter2/butterfly.png 304 1ms
GET /html5media/chapter2/example1.html 304 1ms
GET /html5media/chapter2/bigbuckposter.png 304 0ms
GET /html5media/chapter2/videofile.mp4 304 0ms
```

While not as informative, this is a handy way of checking request state and load times.

connect.parseCookie and connect.cookieSession

The scratch file server didn't provide any functionality to work with HTTP cookies, nor did it handle session state. Luckily for us, both are handled with Connect middleware.

Chances are, one of your first JavaScript client applications was to create an HTTP request cookie. The connect.parseCookie middleware provides the functionality that allows us to access the cookie data on the server. It parses the cookie header, populating req.cookies with the cookie/data pairs. Example 6-6 shows a simple web server that extracts the cookie for a key value of username and writes a somewhat creepy but relevant message to stdout.

Example 6-6. Accessing an HTTP request cookie, and using it for a console message

```
var connect = require('connect')
  , http = require('http');
```

```
var app = connect()
  .use(connect.logger('dev'))
  .use(connect.cookieParser())
  .use(function(req, res, next) {
      console.log('tracking ' + req.cookies.username);
      next();
  })
  .use(connect.static('/home/examples/public_html'));

http.createServer(app).listen(8124);
console.log('Server listening on port 8124');
```

I'll get into the use of the anonymous function, and especially the purpose of `next`, in the section "Custom Connect Middleware" on page 118. Focusing for now on `con nect.cookieParser`, we see that this middleware intercepts the incoming request, pulls the cookie data out of the header, and stores the data in the request object. The anonymous function then accesses the `username` data from the `cookies` object, outputting it to the console.

To create an HTTP response cookie, we pair `connect.parseCookie` with `connect.cook ieSession`, which provides secure session persistence. Text is passed as a string to the `connect.cookieParser` function, providing a secret key for session data. The data is added directly to the session object. To clear the session data, set the session object to `null`.

Example 6-7 creates two functions—one to clear the session data, and one to output a tracking message—that are used as middleware for incoming requests. They're added as middleware in addition to `logger`, `parseCookie`, `cookieSession`, and `static`. The user is prompted for his or her username in the client page, which is then used to set a request cookie. On the server, the username and the number of resources the person has accessed in the current session are persisted via an encrypted response cookie.

Example 6-7. Using a session cookie to track resource accesses

```
var connect = require('connect')
  , http = require('http');

// clear all session data
function clearSession(req, res, next) {
  if ('/clear' == req.url) {
    req.session = null;
    res.statusCode = 302;
    res.setHeader('Location', '/');
    res.end();
  } else {
    next();
  }
}

// track user
function trackUser(req, res, next) {
```

```
  req.session.ct = req.session.ct || 0;
  req.session.username = req.session.username || req.cookies.username;
  console.log(req.cookies.username + ' requested ' +
                      req.session.ct++ + ' resources this session');
  next();
}

// cookie and session
var app = connect()
  .use(connect.logger('dev'))
  .use(connect.cookieParser('mumble'))
  .use(connect.cookieSession({key : 'tracking'}))
  .use(clearSession)
  .use(trackUser);

// static server
app.use(connect.static('/home/examples/public_html'));
// start server and listen
http.createServer(app).listen(8124);
console.log('Server listening on port 8124');
```

Figure 6-2 shows a web page accessed through the server application in Example 6-8.
The JavaScript console is open to display both cookies. Note that the response cookie,
unlike the request, is encrypted.

Figure 6-2. JavaScript console open in Chrome, displaying request and response cookies

The number of documents the user accesses is tracked, either until the user accesses the /clear URL (in which case the session object is set to null) or closes the browser, ending the session.

Example 6-7 also made use of a couple of custom middleware functions. In the next (and final) section on Connect, we'll discuss how these work with Connect, and how to create a third-party middleware.

Custom Connect Middleware

In Example 6-7 in the previous section, we created two functions as Connect middleware in order to process incoming requests before the final static server. The three parameters passed to the functions are the HTTP request and response objects, and next, a callback function. These three form the signature for a Connect middleware function.

To get a closer look at how Connect middleware works, let's examine one used in earlier code, connect.favicon. This is nothing more than a simple function to either serve the default *favicon.ico* or provide a custom path:

```
connect()
.use (connect.favicon('someotherloc/favicon.ico'))
```

The reason I cover connect.favicon, other than its usefulness, is that it's one of the simplest middleware, and therefore easy to reverse engineer.

The source code for connect.favicon, especially when compared with other source codes, shows that all exported middleware return a function with the following minimum signature or profile:

```
return function(req, res, next)
```

The next callback, passed as the last parameter to the function, is called if the middleware does not process the current request, or doesn't process it completely. The next callback is also called if the middleware has an error, and an error object is returned as the parameter, as shown in Example 6-8.

Example 6-8. The favicon Connect middleware

```
module.exports = function favicon(path, options){
  var options = options || {}
    , path = path || __dirname + '/../public/favicon.ico'
    , maxAge = options.maxAge || 86400000;

  return function favicon(req, res, next){
    if ('/favicon.ico' == req.url) {
      if (icon) {
        res.writeHead(200, icon.headers);
        res.end(icon.body);
      } else {
        fs.readFile(path, function(err, buf){
          if (err) return next(err);
```

```
        icon = {
          headers: {
              'Content-Type': 'image/x-icon'
            , 'Content-Length': buf.length
            , 'ETag': '"' + utils.md5(buf) + '"'
            , 'Cache-Control': 'public, max-age=' + (maxAge / 1000)
          },
          body: buf
        };
        res.writeHead(200, icon.headers);
        res.end(icon.body);
      });
    }
  } else {
    next();
  }
 };
};
```

The next callback is, of course, how the chained functions are called, in sequence. In
an incoming request, if the middleware can completely handle the request, such as the
request *favicon.ico* request, no further middleware are invoked. This is why you would
include the connect.favicon middleware before connect.logger in your applications—
to prevent requests for *favicon.ico* from cluttering up the logs:

```
http.createServer(connect()
    .use(connect.favicon('/public_html/favicon.ico'))
    .use(connect.logger())
    .use(connect.static(_dirname + '/public_html'))
    ).listen(8124);
```

You've seen how you can create a custom Connect middleware directly in the application, and how a bundled Connect middleware looks, but how would you create a
third-party middleware that's not going to be embedded directly in the application?

To create an external Connect middleware, create the module as you would any other
module, but make sure it has all the pieces that Connect requires—specifying the three
parameters (req, res, and next), and that it calls next if it doesn't completely handle
the request.

Example 6-9 creates a Connect middleware that checks to see if the requested file exists
and that it is a file (not a directory). If the request is a directory, it returns a 403 status
code and a custom message. If the file doesn't exist, it returns a 404 status code and,
again, a custom message. If neither happens, then it calls next to trigger the Connect
middleware into invoking the next function (in this case, connect.static).

Example 6-9. Creating a custom error handler middleware module

```
var fs = require('fs');

module.exports = function customHandler(path, missingmsg, directorymsg) {
    if (arguments.length < 3) throw new Error('missing parameter in customHandler');
```

```
    return function customHandler(req, res, next) {
        var pathname = path + req.url;
        console.log(pathname);
        fs.stat(pathname, function(err, stats) {
            if (err) {
                res.writeHead(404);
                res.write(missingmsg);
                res.end();
            } else if (!stats.isFile()) {
                res.writeHead(403);
                res.write(directorymsg);
                res.end();
            } else {
                next();
            }
        });
    }
}
```

The custom Connect middleware throws an error when one occurs, but if an error occurs within the returned function, next is called with an error object:

```
next(err);
```

The following code shows how we can use this custom middleware in an application:

```
var connect = require('connect'),
    http = require('http'),
    fs = require('fs'),
    custom = require('./custom'),
    base = '/home/examples/public_html';

http.createServer(connect()
    .use(connect.favicon(base + '/favicon.ico'))
    .use(connect.logger())
    .use(custom(base + '/public_html', '404 File Not Found',
            '403 Directory Access Forbidden'))
    .use(connect.static(base))
).listen(8124);
```

Connect does have an errorHandler function, but it doesn't serve the purpose we're trying to achieve. Rather, its purpose is to provide a formatted output of an exception. You'll see it in use with an Express application in Chapter 7.

There are several other bundled middleware, as well as a significant number of third-party middleware you can use with Connect. In addition, Connect forms the middleware layer for the Express application framework, discussed in Chapter 7. First, though, let's take a quick look at two other types of services necessary for many Node applications: routers and proxies.

Routers

Routers accept something from one source and forward it to another. Typically what's forwarded is a data packet, but at the application level, it can also be a resource request.

If you've used Drupal or WordPress, you've seen a router in action. Without any URL redirection, rather than your readers accessing an article with a URL like:

http://yourplace.org/article/your-title

they'd use:

http://yourplace.org/node/174

The latter URL is an example of a router in action. The URL provides information about what the web application should do, in this case:

* Access the node database (*node* in this case being a Drupal node).
* Find and display the node identified by 174.

Another variation is:

http://yourplace.org/user/3

Again, access the user database, and find and display the user identified by 3.

In Node, the primary use for a router is to extract the information we need from a URI —usually using some pattern—and to use that information to trigger the right process, passing the extracted information to the process.

There are several routers available for Node developers, including one built into Express, but I'm going to demonstrate one of the more popular: Crossroads.

 The primary Crossroads site is at *http://millermedeiros.github.com/cross roads.js/*.

We can install the Crossroad router module with npm:

```
npm install crossroads
```

The module provides an extensive and well-documented API, but I'm going to focus only on three different methods:

addRoute
: Defines a new route pattern listener

parse
: Parses a string and dispatches a match to the appropriate route

matched.add
: Maps a route handler to a route match

We define a route using a regular expression that can contain curly brackets ({}) delimiting named variables that will be passed to the route handler function. For instance, both of the following route patterns:

```
{type}/{id}
node/{id}
```

will match:

http://something.org/node/174

The difference is that a type parameter is passed to the route handler for the first pattern, but not the second.

You can also use a colon (:) to denote optional segments. The following:

```
category/:type:/:id:
```

will match:

category/
category/tech/
category/history/143

To trigger the route handler, you parse the request:

```
parse(request);
```

If the request matches any of the existing route handler functions, that function is called.

In Example 6-10, I created a simple application that looks for any given category, and an optional publication and publication item. It prints out to the console, the action specified in the request.

Example 6-10. Using Crossroads to route URL request into specific actions

```
var crossroads = require('crossroads'),
    http = require('http');

crossroads.addRoute('/category/{type}/:pub:/:id:', function(type,pub,id) {
  if (!id && !pub) {
    console.log('Accessing all entries of category ' + type);
    return;
  } else if (!id) {
    console.log('Accessing all entries of category ' + type +
                ' and pub ' + pub);
    return;
  } else {
    console.log('Accessing item ' + id + ' of pub ' + pub +
                ' of category ' + type);
  }
});
http.createServer(function(req,res) {

  crossroads.parse(req.url);
```

```
    res.end('and that\'s all\n');
}).listen(8124);
```

The following requests:

```
http://examples.burningbird.net:8124/category/history
http://examples.burningbird.net:8124/category/history/journal
http://examples.burningbird.net:8124/category/history/journal/174
```

Generate the following console messages:

```
Accessing all entries of category history
Accessing all entries of category history and pub journal
Accessing item 174 of pub journal of category history
```

To match how something like Drupal works, with its combination of type of object and identifier, Example 6-11 uses another Crossroads method, matched.add, to map a route handler to a specific route.

Example 6-11. Mapping a route handler to a given route

```
var crossroads = require('crossroads'),
    http = require('http');

var typeRoute = crossroads.addRoute('/{type}/{id}');

function onTypeAccess(type,id) {
   console.log('access ' + type + ' ' + id);
};

typeRoute.matched.add(onTypeAccess);

http.createServer(function(req,res) {

  crossroads.parse(req.url);
  res.end('processing');
}).listen(8124);
```

This application would match either of the following:

/node/174
/user/3

Routing is typically used with database access to generate the returned page content. It can also be used with middleware or framework modules in order to process incoming requests, though these applications may also provide their own routing software. I'll demonstrate using Crossroads with Connect and a proxy in the next section.

Proxies

A *proxy* is a way of routing requests from several different sources through one server for whatever reason: caching, security, even obscuring the originator of the request. As an example, publicly accessible proxies have been used to restrict some people's access to certain web content by making it seem that a request originates from someplace other than its actual origin. This type of proxy is also called a *forward proxy*.

A *reverse proxy* is a way of controlling how requests are sent to a server. As an example, you may have five servers, but you don't want people directly accessing four of them. Instead, you direct all traffic through the fifth server, which proxies the requests to the other servers. Reverse proxies can also be used for load balancing, and to improve the overall performance of a system by caching requests as they are made.

Another proxy use is to expose a local service to a cloud-based service. An example of this type of proxy is reddish-proxy, which exposes a local Redis instance to the new Reddish service at *https://reddi.sh/*.

In Node, the most popular proxy module is http-proxy. This module provides all of the proxy uses I could think of, and some I couldn't. It provides forward and reverse proxying, can be used with WebSockets, supports HTTPS, and can incorporate latency. It's used at the popular nodejitsu.com (*http://nodejitsu.com*) website, so, as the creators claim, it's *battle hardened*.

The http-proxy GitHub page is at *https://github.com/nodejitsu/node-http-proxy*.

Install http-proxy using npm:

```
npm install http-proxy
```

The simplest use of http-proxy is to create a standalone proxy server that listens for incoming requests on one port, and proxies them to a web server listening on another:

```
var http = require('http'),
    httpProxy = require('http-proxy');

httpProxy.createServer(8124, 'localhost').listen(8000);

http.createServer(function (req, res) {
  res.writeHead(200, { 'Content-Type': 'text/plain' });
  res.write('request successfully proxied!' + '\n' + JSON.stringify(req.headers, true,
  2));
  res.end();
}).listen(8124);
```

All this simple application does is listen for requests on port 8000 and proxy them to the HTTP server listening on port 8124.

The output to the browser from running this application on my system was:

```
request successfully proxied!
{
  "host": "examples.burningbird.net:8000",
  "connection": "keep-alive",
  "user-agent": "Mozilla/5.0 (Windows NT 6.1; WOW64) AppleWebKit/535.11
  (KHTML, like Gecko) Chrome/17.0.963.56 Safari/535.11",
  "accept": "text/html,application/xhtml+xml,application/xml;q=0.9,*/*;q=0.8",
  "accept-encoding": "gzip,deflate,sdch",
  "accept-language": "en-US,en;q=0.8",
  "accept-charset": "ISO-8859-1,utf-8;q=0.7,*;q=0.3",
  "cookie": "username=Shelley",
  "x-forwarded-for": "99.190.71.234",
  "x-forwarded-port": "54344",
  "x-forwarded-proto": "http"
}
```

The bits related to the use of the proxy are in bold text in the output. Notice the request cookie still hanging around from an earlier example?

You can also use http-proxy from the command line. In the *bin* directory, there is a command-line application, which takes `port`, `target`, a configuration file, a flag to indicate silencing the proxy log output, or -h (for *help*). To listen for requests in port 8000 and proxy to port 8124 on the `localhost`, use:

```
./node-http-proxy --port 8000 --target localhost:8124
```

It can't get much simpler than this. If you want to run the proxy in the background, attach the ampersand (&) to the end.

I'll demonstrate some of the http-proxy capabilities with WebSockets and HTTPS later in the book, but for now, we'll pull together the technologies demonstrated in this chapter—a static file server, the Connect middleware, the Crossroads router, and the http-proxy proxy—to create one last example, so you can try a working application that combines all these pieces.

In Example 6-12, I'm using the http-proxy to test for a dynamic incoming request (the request URL starts with /node/). If a match is found, the router proxies the request to one server, which uses the Crossroads router to parse out the relevant data. If the request isn't for a dynamic resource, the proxy then routes the request to a static file server that's utilizing several Connect middleware, including `logger`, `favicon`, and `static`.

Example 6-12. Combining Connect, Crossroads, and http-proxy to handle dynamic and static content requests

```
var connect = require('connect'),
    http = require('http'),
    fs = require('fs'),
    crossroads = require('crossroads'),
    httpProxy = require('http-proxy'),
    base = '/home/examples/public_html';

// create the proxy that listens for all requests
```

```
httpProxy.createServer(function(req,res,proxy) {

  if (req.url.match(/^\/node\//))
    proxy.proxyRequest(req, res, {
      host: 'localhost',
      port: 8000
    });
  else
    proxy.proxyRequest(req,res, {
      host: 'localhost',
      port: 8124
    });
}).listen(9000);

// add route for request for dynamic resource
crossroads.addRoute('/node/{id}/', function(id) {
  console.log('accessed node ' + id);
});

// dynamic file server
http.createServer(function(req,res) {
  crossroads.parse(req.url);
  res.end('that\'s all!');
}).listen(8000);

// static file server
http.createServer(connect()
  .use(connect.favicon())
  .use(connect.logger('dev'))
  .use(connect.static(base))
  ).listen(8124);
```

Trying the server out with the following URL requests:

```
/node/345
/example1.html
/node/800
/html5media/chapter2/example14.html
```

results in the following console entries, as well as the proper response being returned to the browser:

```
accessed node 345
GET /example1.html 304 3ms
GET /phoenix5a.png 304 1ms
accessed node 800
GET /html5media/chapter2/example14.html 304 1ms
GET /html5media/chapter2/bigbuckposter.jpg 304 1ms
```

I wouldn't say we're halfway to our own CMS (content management system), but we're getting the tools we need if we wanted to build one. But then, why build our own when we can use Node-enabled frameworks (covered in the next chapter)?

CHAPTER 7
The Express Framework

Framework software provides infrastructure support that allows us to create websites and applications more quickly. It provides a skeleton on which to build, handling many of the mundane and ubiquitous aspects of development so we can focus on creating the functionality unique to our application or site. It also provides cohesiveness to our code, which can make the code easier to manage and maintain.

The terms *frameworks* and *libraries* have been used interchangeably, because both provide reusable functionality that can be utilized by developers in a variety of applications. They both offer discrete capabilities as well, but they differ in that frameworks usually also provide an infrastructure that can impact the overall design of your application.

There are some very sound frameworks in Node.js, including Connect (covered in Chapter 6), though I see Connect more as middleware than a framework. Two Node frameworks that stand out—because of support, capability, and popularity—are Express and Geddy. If you ask people about the differences between the two, they'll say Express is more Sinatra-like, while Geddy is more like Rails. What this means in non-Ruby terms is that Geddy is MVC (Model-View-Controller)–based, while Express is, well, more RESTful (more on what that means later in the chapter).

There's also a new kid in town, Flatiron, which previously existed as independent components but is now pulled together into a comprehensive product. Another framework popular at the node-toolbox website is Ember.js, formerly known as SproutCore 2.0. This in addition to CoreJS, which is also MVC-based.

I debated how much to cover of each in this chapter, and knew I'd have a hard time covering one framework in a single chapter, much less several, so I decided to focus on Express. Though the other frameworks are excellent, I like the openness and extensibility of Express, and it is, currently, the most popular of the frameworks.

The Geddy.js site is at *http://geddyjs.org/*. Flatiron can be found at *http://flatironjs.org/*, the Ember.js Github page is at *https://github.com/emberjs/ember.js*, and the primary CoreJS site is at *http://echo.nextapp.com/site/corejs*. The Express GitHub page is at *https://github.com/visionmedia/express*. You can find the Express documentation at *http://expressjs.com/*.

Express: Up and Running

We can easily install Express with npm:

```
npm install express
```

To get a feel for Express, the best first step is to use the command-line version of the tool to generate an application. Since you're never sure what an application will do, you'll want to run this application in a clean directory—not a directory where you have all sorts of valuable stuff.

I named my new application `site`, which is simple enough:

```
express site
```

The application generates several directories:

```
create : site
   create : site/package.json
   create : site/app.js
   create : site/public
   create : site/public/javascripts
   create : site/public/images
   create : site/routes
   create : site/routes/index.js
   create : site/public/stylesheets
   create : site/public/stylesheets/style.css
   create : site/views
   create : site/views/layout.jade
   create : site/views/index.jade
```

It also provides a helpful message to change to the site directory and run `npm install`:

```
npm install -d
```

Once the new application is installed, run the generated *app.js* file with `node`:

```
node app.js
```

It starts a server at port 3000. Accessing the application shows a web page with the words:

```
Express

Welcome to Express
```

You've created your first Express application. Now let's see what we need to do to make it do something more interesting.

The app.js File in More Detail

Example 7-1 shows the source code for the *app.js* file we just ran.

Example 7-1. Source code for the app.js file

```
/*
 * Module dependencies.
 */

var express = require('express')
  , routes = require('./routes')
  , http = require('http');

var app = express();

app.configure(function(){
  app.set('views', __dirname + '/views');
  app.set('view engine', 'jade');
  app.use(express.favicon());
  app.use(express.logger('dev'));
  app.use(express.static(__dirname + '/public'));
  app.use(express.bodyParser());
  app.use(express.methodOverride());
  app.use(app.router);
});


app.configure('development', function(){
  app.use(express.errorHandler());
});

app.get('/', routes.index);

http.createServer(app).listen(3000);

console.log("Express server listening on port 3000");
```

From the top, the application includes three modules: Express, Node's HTTP, and a module just generated, routes. In the *routes* subdirectory, an *index.js* file has the following code:

```
/*
 * GET home page.
 */

exports.index = function(req, res){
  res.render('index', { title: 'Express' });
};
```

A little digging in the code shows us that the Express response object's render method renders a given view with a set of options—in this case, a title of "Express." I'll cover this more later in this chapter, in the section "Routing" on page 134.

Now let's return to *app.js*. After we've included all the necessary modules, we create an Express object instance, and then configure it with a set of options via the `configure` method. (For more information on `configure`, see the upcoming sidebar "Setting the Application Mode" on page 130.) An optional first parameter to `configure` is a string identifying whether the application is of a specific environment (such as `development` or `production`). When an environment is not provided, the application is run in every environment. A second call to `configure` in *app.js* is specific only for the development environment. You can call `configure` for every possible environment, if you wish. The one that matches the environment is the one that will be processed.

Setting the Application Mode

In Express applications, we can define which middleware, settings, and options to apply for any given mode using the `configure` method. In the following example, the method applies the enclosed settings and options to all modes:

```
app.config(function() { ... }
```

while the next `configure` call ensures that the settings apply only in a development environment:

```
app.config('development', function() { ... }
```

This mode can be any that you designate, and is controlled by an environmental variable, `NODE_ENV`:

```
$ export NODE_ENV=production
```

or:

```
$ export NODE_ENV=ourproduction
```

You can use any term you want. By default, the environment is `development`.

To ensure that your application always runs in a specific mode, add a `NODE_ENV` export to the user profile file.

The second function to `configure` is an anonymous function enclosing several middleware references. Some of this is familiar (for instance, the `use` method) from our work with the Connect middleware in Chapter 6; this is not unexpected, since the same person, TJ Holowaychuk, is the primary author of both applications. What isn't familiar are the two `app.set` method calls.

The `app.set` method is used to define various settings, such as the location for application views:

```
app.set('views', __dirname + '/views');
```

and the view engine (in this case, Jade):

```
app.set('view engine', 'jade');
```

What follows in *app.js* is a call to the Express encapsulated `favicon`, `logger`, and `static` file server middleware, which should need no further explanation:

```
app.use(express.favicon());
app.use(express.logger('dev'));
app.use(express.static(__dirname + '/public'));
```

We can also call the middleware as methods when we create the server:

```
var app = express.createServer(
  express.logger(),
  express.bodyParts()
);
```

It doesn't matter which approach you use.

The next three middleware/framework components included in the generated application are:

```
app.use(express.bodyParser());
app.use(express.methodOverride());
app.use(app.router);
```

The `bodyParser` middleware, like the other middleware, comes directly from Connect. All Express does is re-export it.

I covered `logger`, `favicon`, and `static` in the previous chapter, but not `bodyParse`. This middleware parses the incoming request body, converting it into request object properties. The `methodOverride` option also comes to Express via Connect, and allows Express applications to emulate full REST capability via a hidden form field named `_method`.

Full REST (Representational State Transfer) support means support for HTTP `PUT` and `DELETE`, as well as `GET` and `POST`. We'll discuss this more in the upcoming section "Routing and HTTP Verbs" on page 139.

The last configuration item is `app.router`. This optional middleware contains all the defined routes and performs the lookup for any given route. If omitted, the first call to `app.get`—`app.post`, etc.—mounts the routes instead.

Just as with Connect, the order of middleware is important. The `favicon` middleware is called before `logger`, because we don't want *favicon.ico* accesses cluttering the log. The `static` middleware is included before `bodyParser` and `methodOverride`, because neither of these is useful with the static pages—form processing occurs dynamically in the Express application, not via a static page.

There's more on Express/Connect in the section "A Closer Look at the Express/Connect Partnership" on page 133, later in the chapter.

The second call to configure, specific to development mode, adds support for the Express errorHandler. I'll cover it and other error handling techniques next.

Error Handling

Express provides its own error handling, as well as access to the Connect errorHandler.

The Connect errorHandler provides a way of handling exceptions. It's a development tool that gives us a better idea of what's happening when an exception occurs. You can include it like you'd include other middleware:

```
app.use(express.errorHandler());
```

You can direct exceptions to stderr using the dumpExceptions flag:

```
app.use(express.errorHandler({dumpExceptions : true }));
```

You can also generate HTML for an exception using the showStack flag:

```
app.use(express.errorHandler({showStack : true; dumpExceptions : true}));
```

To reiterate: this type of error handling is for development only—we definitely don't want our users to see exceptions. We do, however, want to provide more effective handling for when pages aren't found, or when a user tries to access a restricted subdirectory.

One approach we can use is to add a custom anonymous function as the last middleware in the middleware list. If none of the other middleware can process the request, it should fall gracefully to this last function:

```
app.configure(function(){
  app.use(express.favicon());
  app.use(express.logger('dev'));
  app.use(express.static(__dirname + '/public'));
  app.use(express.bodyParser());
  app.use(express.methodOverride());
  app.use(app.router);
  app.use(function(req, res, next){
    res.send('Sorry ' + req.url + ' does not exist');
  });
});
```

In the next chapter, we'll fine-tune the response by using a template to generate a nice 404 page.

We can use another form of error handling to capture thrown errors and process them accordingly. In the Express documentation, this type of error handler is named app.error, but it didn't seem to exist at the time this book was written. However, the function signature does work—a function with four parameters: error, request, response, and next.

I added a second error handler middleware function and adjusted the 404 middleware function to throw an error rather than process the error directly:

```
app.configure(function(){
  app.use(express.favicon());
  app.use(express.logger('dev'));
  app.use(express.static(__dirname + '/public'));
  app.use(express.bodyParser());
  app.use(express.methodOverride());
  app.use(app.router);
  app.use(function(req, res, next){
    throw new Error(req.url + ' not found');
  });
  app.use(function(err, req, res, next) {
    console.log(err);
    res.send(err.message);
  });
});
```

Now I can process the 404 error, as well as other errors, within the same function. And again, I can use templates to generate a more attractive page.

A Closer Look at the Express/Connect Partnership

Throughout this chapter so far, we've seen the Express/Connect partnership in action. It's through Connect that Express gets much of its basic functionality.

For instance, you can use Connect's session support middleware—cookieParser, cookieSession, and session—to provide session support. You just have to remember to use the Express version of the middleware:

```
app.use(express.cookieParser('mumble'))
app.use(express.cookieSession({key : 'tracking'}))
```

You can also enable static caching with the staticCache middleware:

```
app.use(express.favicon());
app.use(express.logger('dev'));
app.use(express.staticCache());
app.use(express.static(__dirname + '/public'));
```

By default, the cache maintains a maximum of 128 objects, with a maximum of 256 KB each, for a total of about 32 MB. You can adjust these with the options maxObjects and maxLength:

```
app.use(express.staticCache({maxObjects: 100, maxLength: 512}));
```

Prettify a directory listing with directory:

```
app.use(express.favicon());
app.use(express.logger('dev'));
app.use(express.staticCache({maxObjects: 100, maxLength: 512}));
app.use(express.directory(__dirname + '/public'));
app.use(express.static(__dirname + '/public'));
```

If you're using express.directory with routing, though, make sure that the directory middleware follows the app.router middleware, or it could conflict with the routing.

A good rule of thumb: place `express.directory` after the other middleware, but before any error handling.

The `express.directory` options include whether to display hidden files (`false` by default), whether to display icons (`false` by default), and a filter.

 You can also use third-party Connect middleware with Express. Use caution, though, when combining it with routing.

Now it's time to return to the key component of Express: routing.

Routing

The core of all the Node frameworks—in fact, many modern frameworks—is the concept of routing. I covered a standalone routing module in Chapter 6, and demonstrated how you can use it to extract a service request from a URL.

Express routing is managed using the HTTP verbs GET, PUT, DELETE, and POST. The methods are named accordingly, such as `app.get` for GET and `app.post` for POST. In the generated application, shown in Example 7-1, `app.get` is used to access the application root (`'/'`), and is passed a request listener—in this instance, the `routes index` function —to process the data request.

The `routes.index` function is simple:

```
exports.index = function(req, res){
  res.render('index', { title: 'Express' });
};
```

It makes a call to the `render` method on the resource object. The `render` method takes the name of file that provides the template. Since the application has already identified the view engine:

```
app.set('view engine', 'jade');
```

it's not necessary to provide an extension for the file. However, you could also use:

```
res.render('index.jade', { title: 'Express' });
```

You can find the template file in another generated directory named *views*. It has two files: *index.jade* and *layout.jade*. *index.jade* is the file the template file referenced in the `render` method, and has the following contents:

```
extends layout

block content
  h1= title
  p Welcome to #{title}
```

The content of the document is an H1 element with the title, and a paragraph element with a greeting to the title value. The *layout.jade* template provides the overall layout for the document, including a title and link in the head element, and the body contents in the body element:

```
!!!
html
  head
    title= title
    link(rel='stylesheet', href='/stylesheets/style.css')
  body
    block content
```

The *index.jade* file is what provides the content for the body defined in *layout.jade*.

 I cover the use of Jade templates and CSS with Express applications in Chapter 8.

To recap what's happening in this application:

1. The main Express application uses app.get to associate a request listener function (routes.index) with an HTTP GET request.

2. The routes.index function calls res.render to render the response to the GET request.

3. The res.render function invokes the application object's render function.

4. The application render function renders the specified view, with whatever options—in this case, the title.

5. The rendered content is then written to the response object and back to the user's browser.

The last step in the process is when the generated content is written back to the response to the browser. Snooping around the source code shows us that the render method takes a third argument, a callback function that's called with any error and the generated text.

Wanting to take a closer look at the generated content, I modified the route.index file to add in the function and intercept the generated text. I output the text to the console. Since I'm overriding the default functionality, I also sent the generated text back to the browser using res.write—just like we have with other applications in previous chapters—and then called res.end to signal the finish:

```
exports.index = function(req, res){
  res.render('index', { title: 'Express' }, function(err, stuff) {
    if (!err) {
      console.log(stuff);
      res.write(stuff);
```

```
        res.end();
      }
    });
  };
```

Just as we hoped, the application now writes the content to the console as well as the browser. This just demonstrates that, though we're using an unfamiliar framework, it's all based on Node and functionality we've used previously. Of course, since this is a framework, we know there has to be a better method than using `res.write` and `res.end`. There is, and it's discussed in the next section, which looks a little more closely at routing paths.

Routing Path

The route, or route path, given in Example 7-1 is just a simple / (forward slash) signifying the root address. Express compiles all routes to a regular expression object internally, so you can use strings with special characters, or just use regular expressions directly in the path strings.

To demonstrate, I created a bare-bones routing path application in Example 7-2 that listens for three different routes. If a request is made to the server for one of these routes, the parameters from the request are returned to the sender using the Express response object's send method.

Example 7-2. Simple application to test different routing path patterns

```
var express = require('express')
  , http = require('http');

var app = express();

app.configure(function(){
});

app.get(/^\/node?(?:\/(\d+)(?:\.\.(\d+))?)?/, function(req, res){
   console.log(req.params);
   res.send(req.params);
});

app.get('/content/*',function(req,res) {
   res.send(req.params);
});

app.get("/products/:id/:operation?", function(req,res) {
   console.log(req);
   res.send(req.params.operation + ' ' + req.params.id);
});

http.createServer(app).listen(3000);

console.log("Express server listening on port 3000");
```

We're not doing any routing to views or handling any static content, so we didn't need to provide middleware in the app.configure method. However, we do need to call the app.configure method if we want to gracefully handle requests that don't match any of the routes. The application is also using the default environment (development).

The first of the app.get method calls is using a regular expression for the path. This regular expression is adapted from one provided in the Express Guide, and listens for any request for a node. If the request also provides a unique identifier or range of identifiers, this is captured in the request object's params array, which is sent back as a response. The following requests:

```
node
nodes
 /node/566
/node/1..10
/node/50..100/something
```

return the following params array values:

```
[null, null]
[null, null]
["566", null]
["1", "10"]
["50", "100"]
```

The regular expression is looking for a single identifier or a range of identifiers, given as two values with a range indicator (..) between them. Anything after the identifier or range is ignored. If no identifier or range is provided, the parameters are null.

The code to process the request doesn't use the underlying HTTP response object's write and end methods to send the parameters back to the requester; instead, it uses the Express send method. The send method determines the proper headers for the response (given the data type of what's being sent) and then sends the content using the underlying HTTP end method.

The next app.get is using a string to define the routing path pattern. In this case, we're looking for any content item. This pattern will match anything that begins with /content/. The following requests:

```
/content/156
/content/this_is_a_story
/content/apples/oranges
```

result in the following params values:

```
["156"]
["this_is_a_story"]
["apples/oranges"]
```

The asterisk (*) is liberal in what it accepts, and everything after content/ is returned.

The last app.get method is looking for a product request. If a product identifier is given, it can be accessed directly via params.id. If an operation is given, it can be accessed directly via `params.operation`. Any combination of the two values is allowed, *except* not providing at least one identifier or one operation.

The following URLs:

```
/products/laptopJK3444445/edit
/products/fordfocus/add
/products/add
/products/tablet89/delete
/products/
```

result in the following returned values:

```
edit laptopJK3444445
add fordfocus
undefined add
delete tablet89
Cannot GET /products/
```

The application outputs the request object to the console. When running the application, I directed the output to an *output.txt* file so I could examine the request object more closely:

```
node app.js > output.txt
```

The request object is a socket, of course, and we'll recognize much of the object from our previous work exploring the Node HTTP request object. What we're mainly interested in is the `route` object added via Express. Following is the output for the `route` object for one of the requests:

```
route:
 { path: '/products/:id/:operation?',
   method: 'get',
   callbacks: [ [Function] ],
   keys: [ [Object], [Object] ],
   regexp: /^\/products\/(?:([^\/]+?))(?:\/([^\/]+?))?\/?$/i,
   params: [ id: 'laptopJK3444445', operation: 'edit' ] },
```

Note the generated regular expression object, which converts my use of the optional indicator (:) in the path string into something meaningful for the underlying JavaScript engine (thankfully, too, since I'm lousy at regular expressions).

Now that we have a better idea of how the routing paths work, let's look more closely at the use of the HTTP verbs.

 Any request that doesn't match one of the three given path patterns just generates a generic 404 response: `Cannot GET /whatever`.

Routing and HTTP Verbs

In the previous examples, we used `app.get` to process incoming requests. This method is based on the HTTP GET method and is useful if we're looking for data, but not if we want to process new incoming data or edit or delete existing data. We need to make use of the other HTTP verbs to create an application that maintains as well as retrieves data. In other words, we need to make our application *RESTful*.

 As noted earlier, REST means Representational State Transfer. *RESTful* is a term used to describe any web application that applies HTTP and REST principles: directory-structured URLs, statelessness, data transferred in an Internet media type (such as JSON), and the use of HTTP methods (GET, POST, DELETE, and PUT).

Let's say our application is managing that most infamous of products, the widget. To create a new widget, we'll need to create a web page providing a form that gets the information about the new widget. We can generate this form with the application, and I'll demonstrate this approach in Chapter 8, but for now we'll use a static web page, shown in Example 7-3.

Example 7-3. Sample HTML form to post widget data to the Express application

```
<!doctype html>
<html lang="en">
<head>
 <meta charset="utf-8" />
 <title>Widgets</title>
</head>
<body>
<form method="POST" action="/widgets/add"
enctype="application/x-www-form-urlencoded">

 <p>Widget name: <input type="text" name="widgetname" id="widgetname"
size="25" required/></p>

 <p>Widget Price: <input type="text"
pattern="^\$?([0-9]{1,3},([0-9]{3},)*[0-9]{3}|[0-9]+)(.[0-9][0-9])?$"
name="widgetprice" id="widgetprice" size="25" required/></p>

 <p>Widget Description: <br /><textarea name="widgetdesc" id="widgetdesc"
cols="20" rows="5">No Description</textarea>
 <p>

 <input type="submit" name="submit" id="submit" value="Submit"/>
 <input type="reset" name="reset" id="reset" value="Reset"/>
 </p>
 </form>
</body>
```

The page takes advantage of the new HTML5 attributes **required** and **pattern** to provide validation of data. Of course, this works only with browsers that support HTML5, but for now, I'll assume you're using a modern HTML5-capable browser.

The widget form requires a widget name, price (with an associated regular expression to validate the data structure in the pattern attribute), and description. Browser-based validation should ensure we get the three values, and that the price is properly formatted as US currency.

In the Express application, we're just going to persist new widgets in memory, as we want to focus purely on the Express technology at this time. As each new widget is posted to the application, it's added to an array of widgets via the **app.post** method. Each widget can be accessed by its application-generated identifier via the **app.get** method. Example 7-4 shows the entire application.

Example 7-4. Express application to add and display widgets

```
var express = require('express')
  , http = require('http')
  , app = express();

app.configure(function(){
  app.use(express.favicon());
  app.use(express.logger('dev'));
  app.use(express.static(__dirname + '/public'));
  app.use(express.bodyParser());
  app.use(app.router);
});

app.configure('development', function(){
  app.use(express.errorHandler());
});

// in memory data store
var widgets = [
  { id : 1,
    name : 'My Special Widget',
    price : 100.00,
    descr : 'A widget beyond price'
  }
]

// add widget
app.post('/widgets/add', function(req, res) {
  var indx = widgets.length + 1;
  widgets[widgets.length] =
  { id : indx,
    name : req.body.widgetname,
    price : parseFloat(req.body.widgetprice),
    descr : req.body.widgetdesc };
  console.log('added ' + widgets[indx-1]);
  res.send('Widget ' + req.body.widgetname + ' added with id ' + indx);
});
```

```
// show widget
app.get('/widgets/:id', function(req, res) {
   var indx = parseInt(req.params.id) - 1;
   if (!widgets[indx])
      res.send('There is no widget with id of ' + req.params.id);
   else
      res.send(widgets[indx]);
});

http.createServer(app).listen(3000);

console.log("Express server listening on port 3000");
```

The first widget is seeded into the widget array, so we have existing data if we want to immediately query for a widget without adding one first. Note the conditional test in `app.get` to respond to a request for a nonexistent or removed widget.

Running the application (*example4.js* in the examples), and accessing the application using / or */index.html* (or */example3.html*, in the examples) serves up the static HTML page with the form. Submitting the form generates a page displaying a message about the widget being added, as well as its identifier. We can then use the identifier to display the widget—in effect, a dump of the widget object instance:

```
http://whateverdomain.com:3000/widgets/2
```

It works...but there's a problem with this simple application.

First, it's easy to make a typo in the widget fields. You can't put in data formatted as anything other than currency in the price field, but you can put in the wrong price. You can also easily type in the wrong name or description. What we need is a way to update a widget, as well as a way to remove a widget we no longer need.

The application needs to incorporate support for two other RESTful verbs: PUT and DELETE. PUT is used to update the widget, while DELETE is used to remove it.

To update the widget, we'll need a form that comes prepopulated with the widget data in order to edit it. To delete the widget, we'll need a form that confirms whether we truly want to delete the widget. In an application, these are generated dynamically using a template, but for now, since we're focusing on the HTTP verbs, I created static web pages that edit and then delete the already created widget, widget 1.

The form for updating widget 1 is shown in the following code. Other than being populated with the information for widget 1, there is just one other difference between this form and the form to add a new widget: the addition of a hidden field named _method, shown in bold text:

```
<form method="POST" action="/widgets/1/update"
enctype="application/x-www-form-urlencoded">

<p>Widget name: <input type="text" name="widgetname"
id="widgetname" size="25" value="My Special Widget" required/></p>
```

```
<p>Widget Price: <input type="text"
pattern="^\$?([0-9]{1,3},([0-9]{3},)*[0-9]{3}|[0-9]+)(.[0-9][0-9])?$"
name="widgetprice" id="widgetprice" size="25" value="100.00" required/></p>

<p>Widget Description: <br />
<textarea name="widgetdesc" id="widgetdesc" cols="20"
rows="5">A widget beyond price</textarea>
<p>

<input type="hidden" value="put" name="_method" />

<input type="submit" name="submit" id="submit" value="Submit"/>
<input type="reset" name="reset" id="reset" value="Reset"/>
</p>
</form>
```

Since PUT and DELETE are not supported in the form method attribute, we have to add them using a hidden field with a specific name, _method, and give them a value of either put, for PUT, or delete for DELETE.

The form to delete the widget is simple: it contains the hidden _method field, and a button to confirm the deletion of widget 1:

```
<p>Are you sure you want to delete Widget 1?</p>
<form method="POST" action="/widgets/1/delete"
enctype="application/x-www-form-urlencoded">

<input type="hidden" value="delete" name="_method" />

<p>
<input type="submit" name="submit" id="submit" value="Delete Widget 1"/>
</p>
</form>
```

To ensure that the HTTP verbs are handled properly, we need to add another middleware, express.methodOverride, following express.bodyParser in the app.configure method call. The express.methodOverride middleware alters the HTTP method to whatever is given as value in this hidden field:

```
app.configure(function(){
  app.use(express.favicon());
  app.use(express.logger('dev'));
  app.use(express.static(__dirname + '/public'));
  app.use(express.bodyParser());
  app.use(express.methodOverride());
  app.use(app.router);
});
```

Next, we'll need to add functionality to process these two new verbs. The update request replaces the widget object's contents with the new contents, while the delete request deletes the widget array entry *in place*, deliberately leaving a null value since we do not want to reorder the array because of the widget removal.

To complete our widget application, we'll also add in an index page for accessing widgets without any identifier or operation. All the index page does is list all the widgets currently in the memory store.

Example 7-5 shows the complete widget application with all the new functionality shown in bold text.

Example 7-5. Widget application, modified to include the ability to edit and delete a widget and list all widgets

```
var express = require('express')
  , http = require('http')
  , app = express();

app.configure(function(){
  app.use(express.favicon());
  app.use(express.logger('dev'));
  app.use(express.static(__dirname + '/public'));
  app.use(express.bodyParser());
  app.use(express.methodOverride());
  app.use(app.router);
});

app.configure('development', function(){
  app.use(express.errorHandler());
});
// in memory data store
var widgets = [
  { id : 1,
    name : 'My Special Widget',
    price : 100.00,
    descr : 'A widget beyond price'
  }
]

// index for /widgets/
app.get('/widgets', function(req, res) {
   res.send(widgets);
});

// show a specific widget
app.get('/widgets/:id', function(req, res) {
   var indx = parseInt(req.params.id) - 1;
   if (!widgets[indx])
      res.send('There is no widget with id of ' + req.params.id);
   else
      res.send(widgets[indx]);
});

// add a widget
app.post('/widgets/add', function(req, res) {
  var indx = widgets.length + 1;
  widgets[widgets.length] =
   { id : indx,
     name : req.body.widgetname,
```

```
      price : parseFloat(req.body.widgetprice),
      descr : req.body.widgetdesc };
  console.log(widgets[indx-1]);
  res.send('Widget ' + req.body.widgetname + ' added with id ' + indx);
});

// delete a widget
app.del('/widgets/:id/delete', function(req,res) {
  var indx = req.params.id - 1;
  delete widgets[indx];

  console.log('deleted ' + req.params.id);
  res.send('deleted ' + req.params.id);
});

// update/edit a widget
app.put('/widgets/:id/update', function(req,res) {
  var indx = parseInt(req.params.id) - 1;
  widgets[indx] =
   { id : indx,
     name : req.body.widgetname,
     price : parseFloat(req.body.widgetprice),
     descr : req.body.widgetdesc };
  console.log(widgets[indx]);
  res.send ('Updated ' + req.params.id);
});

http.createServer(app).listen(3000);

console.log("Express server listening on port 3000");
```

After running the application, I add a new widget, list the widgets out, update `widget` 1's price, delete the widget, and then list the widgets out again. The `console.log` messages for this activity are:

```
Express server listening on port 3000
{ id: 2,
  name: 'This is my Baby',
  price: 4.55,
  descr: 'baby widget' }
POST /widgets/add 200 4ms
GET /widgets 200 2ms
GET /edit.html 304 2ms
{ id: 0,
  name: 'My Special Widget',
  price: 200,
  descr: 'A widget beyond price' }
PUT /widgets/1/update 200 2ms
GET /del.html 304 2ms
deleted 1
DELETE /widgets/1/delete 200 3ms
GET /widgets 200 2ms
```

Notice the HTTP PUT and DELETE verbs in bold text in the output. When I list the widgets out the second time, the values returned are:

```
[
  null,
  {
    "id": 2,
    "name": "This is my Baby",
    "price": 4.55,
    "descr": "baby widget"
  }
]
```

We now have a RESTful Express application. But we also have another problem.

If our application managed only one object, it might be OK to cram all the functionality into one file. Most applications, however, manage more than one object, and the functionality for all of those applications isn't as simple as our little example. What we need is to convert this RESTful Express application into a RESTful MVC Express application.

Cue the MVC

Handling all the functionality your application needs in one file would work for a very tiny application, but most applications need better organization. MVC is a popular software architecture, and we want to be able to incorporate the advantages of this architecture and still be able to use Express. This effort isn't as intimidating as it seems, because we have existing functionality we can emulate: Ruby on Rails.

Ruby on Rails has inspired much of the fundamental nature of Node, providing an underlying design we can use to incorporate support for MVC into our Express application. Express has already incorporated the use of routes (fundamental to Rails), so we're halfway there. Now we need to provide the second component—the separation of model, view, and controller. For the controller component, we're going to need a set of defined actions for each object we maintain.

Rails supports several different actions that map a route (verb and path) to a data action. The mapping is based on another concept, CRUD (create, read, update, and delete—the four fundamental persistent storage functions). The Rails website provides a guide that supplies an excellent table showing the mapping we need to create in our application. I extrapolated from the Rails table to create Table 7-1, which shows the mapping for maintaining widgets.

Table 7-1. REST/route/CRUD mapping for maintaining widgets

HTTP verb	Path	Action	Used for
GET	/widgets	index	Displaying widgets
GET	/widgets/new	new	Returning the HTML form for creating a new widget
POST	/widgets	create	Creating a new widget
GET	/widgets/:id	show	Displaying a specific widget
GET	/widgets/:id/edit	edit	Returning the HTML for editing a specific widget

HTTP verb	Path	Action	Used for
PUT	*/widgets/:id*	update	Updating a specific widget
DELETE	*/widgets/:id*	destroy	Deleting a specific widget

We're already there for most of the functionality—we just need to clean it up a bit.

 Just a reminder: you also might have issues with existing middleware when implementing the MVC change. For instance, the use of the `direc tory` middleware, which provides a pretty directory printout, conflicts with the `create` action, since they work on the same route. Solution? Place the `express.directory` middleware after the `app.router` in the configure method call.

First, we're going to create a *controllers* subdirectory and create a new file in it named *widgets.js*. Then we're going to copy all of our `apt.get` and `apt.put` method calls into this new file.

Next, we need to convert the method calls into the appropriate MVC format. This means converting the routing method call into a function for each, which is then exported. For instance, the function to create a new widget:

```
// add a widget
app.post('/widgets/add', function(req, res) {
  var indx = widgets.length + 1;
  widgets[widgets.length] =
   { id : indx,
     name : req.body.widgetname,
     price : parseFloat(req.body.widgetprice)};
  console.log(widgets[indx-1]);
  res.send('Widget ' + req.body.widgetname + ' added with id ' + indx);
});
```

is converted into `widgets.create`:

```
// add a widget
exports.create = function(req, res) {
  var indx = widgets.length + 1;
  widgets[widgets.length] =
   { id : indx,
     name : req.body.widgetname,
     price : parseFloat(req.body.widgetprice)},
  console.log(widgets[indx-1]);
  res.send('Widget ' + req.body.widgetname + ' added with id ' + indx);
};
```

Each function still receives the request and resource object. The only difference is that there isn't a direct route-to-function mapping.

Example 7-6 shows the new *widgets.js* file in the *controllers* subdirectory. Two of the methods, `new` and `edit`, are placeholders for now, to be addressed in Chapter 8. We're still using an in-memory data store, and I simplified the widget object, removing the description field to make the application easier for testing.

Example 7-6. The widgets controller

```
var widgets = [
   { id : 1,
     name : "The Great Widget",
     price : 1000.00
   }
]

// index listing of widgets at /widgets/
exports.index = function(req, res) {
   res.send(widgets);
};

// display new widget form
exports.new = function(req, res) {
   res.send('displaying new widget form');
};

// add a widget
exports.create = function(req, res) {
  var indx = widgets.length + 1;
  widgets[widgets.length] =
  { id : indx,
    name : req.body.widgetname,
    price : parseFloat(req.body.widgetprice) };
  console.log(widgets[indx-1]);
  res.send('Widget ' + req.body.widgetname + ' added with id ' + indx);
};

// show a widget
exports.show = function(req, res) {
   var indx = parseInt(req.params.id) - 1;
   if (!widgets[indx])
      res.send('There is no widget with id of ' + req.params.id);
   else
      res.send(widgets[indx]);
};

// delete a widget
exports.destroy = function(req, res) {
   var indx = req.params.id - 1;
   delete widgets[indx];

   console.log('deleted ' + req.params.id);
   res.send('deleted ' + req.params.id);
};

// display edit form
exports.edit = function(req, res) {
   res.send('displaying edit form');
};
```

```
// update a widget
exports.update = function(req, res) {
  var indx = parseInt(req.params.id) - 1;
  widgets[indx] =
  { id : indx,
    name : req.body.widgetname,
    price : parseFloat(req.body.widgetprice)}
  console.log(widgets[indx]);
  res.send ('Updated ' + req.params.id);
};
```

Notice that edit and new are both GET methods, as their only purpose is to serve a form. It's the associated create and update methods that actually change the data: the former is served as POST, the latter as PUT.

To map the routes to the new functions, I created a second module, maproutecontroller, with one exported function, mapRoute. It has two parameters—the Express app object and a prefix representing the mapped controller object (in this case, widgets). It uses the prefix to access the widgets controller object, and then maps the methods it knows are in this object (because the object is a controller and has a fixed set of required methods) to the appropriate route. Example 7-7 has the code for this new module.

Example 7-7. Function to map routes to controller object methods

```
exports.mapRoute = function(app, prefix) {

  prefix = '/' + prefix;

  var prefixObj = require('./controllers/' + prefix);

  // index
  app.get(prefix, prefixObj.index);

  // add
  app.get(prefix + '/new', prefixObj.new);

  // show
  app.get(prefix + '/:id', prefixObj.show);

  // create
  app.post(prefix + '/create', prefixObj.create);

  // edit
  app.get(prefix + '/:id/edit', prefixObj.edit);

  // update
  app.put(prefix + '/:id', prefixObj.update);

  // destroy
  app.del(prefix + '/:id', prefixObj.destroy);

};
```

The mapRoute method is a very simple function, and should be recognizable when you compare the routes given to those in Table 7-1.

Last, we finish the main application that pulls all these pieces together. Thankfully, it's a lot cleaner now that we don't have all the routing method calls. To handle a possibly growing number of objects, I use an array to contain the prefix name for each. If we add a new object, we add a new prefix to the array.

 Express comes with an MVC application in the *examples* subdirectory. It uses a routine that accesses the *controllers* directory and infers the prefix names from the filenames it finds. With this approach, we don't have to change the application file to add a new object.

Example 7-8 shows the finished application. I added back in the original routes.index view, except I changed the title value in the *routes/index.js* file from "Express" to "Widget Factory."

Example 7-8. Application that makes use of the new MVC infrastructure to maintain widgets

```
var express = require('express')
  , routes = require('./routes')
  , map = require('./maproutecontroller')
  , http = require('http')
  , app = express();

app.configure(function(){
  app.use(express.favicon());
  app.use(express.logger('dev'));
  app.use(express.staticCache({maxObjects: 100, maxLength: 512}));
  app.use(express.static(__dirname + '/public'));
  app.use(express.bodyParser());
  app.use(express.methodOverride());
  app.use(app.router);
  app.use(express.directory(__dirname + '/public'));
  app.use(function(req, res, next){
    throw new Error(req.url + ' not found');
  });
  app.use(function(err, req, res, next) {
    console.log(err);
    res.send(err.message);
  });
});

app.configure('development', function(){
  app.use(express.errorHandler());
});

app.get('/', routes.index);
var prefixes = ['widgets'];

// map route to controller
```

```
prefixes.forEach(function(prefix) {
  map.mapRoute(app, prefix);
});

http.createServer(app).listen(3000);

console.log("Express server listening on port 3000");
```

Cleaner, simpler, extensible. We still don't have the *view* part of the MVC, but I'll cover that in the next chapter.

Testing the Express Application with cURL

Instead of testing with a browser, we'll test the application with cURL. This Unix utility is extremely helpful when it comes to testing a RESTful application without having to create all the forms.

To test the widgets index, use the following cURL command (based on running the application from my examples site, and on port 3000—adjust the command accordingly for your setup):

```
curl --request GET http://examples.burningbird.net:3000/widgets
```

Following the request option, specify the method (in this case, GET), and then the request URL. You should get back a dump of all widgets currently in the data store.

To test creating a new widget, first issue a request for the new object:

```
curl --request GET http://examples.burningbird.net:3000/widgets/new
```

A message is returned about retrieving the new widget form. Next, test adding a new widget, passing the data for the widget in the cURL request, and changing the method to POST:

```
curl --request POST http://examples.burningbird.net:3000/widgets/create
  --data 'widgetname=Smallwidget&widgetprice=10.00'
```

Run the index test again to make sure the new widget is displayed:

```
curl --request GET http://examples.burningbird.net:3000/widgets
```

The result should be:

```
[
  {
    "id": 1,
    "name": "The Great Widget",
    "price": 1000
  },
  {
    "id": 2,
    "name": "Smallwidget",
    "price": 10
  }
```

Next, update the new widget, setting its price to 75.00. The method is now PUT:

```
curl --request  PUT http://examples.burningbird.net:3000/widgets/2
--data 'widgetname=Smallwidget&widgetprice=75.00'
```

Once you've verified the data was changed, go ahead and delete the new record, changing the HTTP method to DELETE:

```
curl --request DELETE http://examples.burningbird.net:3000/widgets/2
```

Now that we have the controller component of the MVC, we need to add the view components, which I cover in Chapter 8. Before moving on, though, read the sidebar "Beyond Basic Express" on page 151 for some final tips.

Beyond Basic Express

Express is a framework, but it's a very basic framework. If you want to do something like creating a content management system, you'll have quite a bit of work to do.

There are third-party applications that are built on Express and that provide both types of functionality. One, Calipso, is a full content management system (CMS) built on Express and using MongoDB for persistent storage.

Express-Resource is a lower-level framework that provides simplified MVC functionality to Express so you don't have to create your own.

Tower.js is another web framework that provides a higher level of abstraction and is modeled after Ruby on Rails, with full MVC support. RailwayJS is also a MVC framework, built on Express and modeled after Ruby on Rails.

Another higher-level framework is Strata, which takes a different tack from Tower.js and RailwayJS. Rather than a Rails model, it follows the module established by WSGI (Python) and Rack (Ruby). It's a lower-level abstraction, which can be simpler to work with if you've not programmed in Ruby and Rails.

CHAPTER 8

Express, Template Systems, and CSS

Frameworks such as Express provide a great deal of useful functionality, but one thing they don't provide is a way of separating the data from the presentation. You can use JavaScript to generate HTML to process the result of a query or update, but the effort can quickly become tedious—especially if you have to generate every part of the page, including sidebars, headers, and footers. Sure, you can use functions, but the work can still verge on overwhelming.

Luckily for us, as framework systems have developed, so have template systems, and the same holds true for Node and Express. In Chapter 7, we briefly used Jade, the template system installed by default with Express, to generate an index page. Express also supports other compatible template systems, including another popular choice, EJS (embedded JavaScript). Jade and EJS take a completely different approach, but both deliver the expected results.

In addition, though you can manually create CSS files for your website or application, you can also use a *CSS engine* that can simplify this aspect of your web design and development. Rather than having to remember to add in all of the curly braces and semicolons, you use a simplified structure that can be cleaner to maintain. One such CSS engine that works quite nicely with Express and other Node applications is Stylus.

In this chapter I'll primarily focus on Jade, since it is installed by default with Express. However, I'm going to briefly cover EJS, so you can see two different types of template systems and how they work. I'll also introduce the use of Stylus to manage the CSS to ensure that the pages display nicely.

The Embedded JavaScript (EJS) Template System

Embedded JavaScript is a good name for EJS, because it best describes how it works: JavaScript embedded into HTML markup handles the melding of data and document structure. It's a very simple template system based on Ruby's ERB (embedded Ruby).

The EJS GitHub page can be found at *https://github.com/visionmedia/ejs*.

Learning the Basic Syntax

If you've worked with most content management systems (CMS), you'll quickly grasp the fundamentals of EJS. The following is an example of an EJS template:

```
<% if (names.length) { %>
  <ul>
    <% names.forEach(function(name){ %>
      <li><%= name %></li>
    <% }) %>
  </ul>
<% } %>
```

In the code, the EJS is embedded directly into HTML, in this example providing the data for the individual list items for an unordered list. The angle brackets and percentage sign pairs (`<%`, `%>`) are used to delimit EJS instructions: a conditional test ensures that an array has been provided, and then the JavaScript processes the array, outputting the individual array values.

 EJS is based on the Ruby ERB templating system, which is why you'll frequently see "erb-like" used to describe its format.

The values themselves are output with the equals sign (=), which is a shortcut for "print this value here":

```
<%= name %>
```

The value is escaped when it's printed out. To print out an unescaped value, use a dash (-), like so:

```
<%- name %>
```

If for some reason you don't want to use the standard open and closing EJS tags (`<%`, `%>`), you can define custom ones using the EJS object's **open** and **close** methods:

```
ejs.open('<<');
ejs.close('>>');
```

You can then use these custom tags instead of the default ones:

```
<h1><<=title >></h1>
```

Unless you have a solid reason for doing so, though, I'd stick with the default.

Though blended with HTML, EJS is JavaScript, so you have to provide the open and closing curly braces, as well as the proper format when using the array object's forEach method.

For the finished product, the HTML is then rendered via an EJS function call, either returning a JavaScript function that generates a result, or generating the finished result. I'll demonstrate this once we get EJS for Node installed. Let's do that now.

Using EJS with Node

The module that's installed is a version of EJS capable of being used with Node. It's not the same thing you'll get if you go to the EJS site and directly download EJS. EJS for Node can be used with client-side JavaScript, but I'm going to focus on its use with Node applications.

Install the template system using npm:

```
npm install ejs
```

Once EJS is installed, you can use it directly in a simple Node application—you don't have to use it with a framework like Express. As a demonstration, render HTML from a given template file as follows:

```
<html>
<head>
<title><%= title %></title>
</head>
<body>
<% if (names.length) { %>
  <ul>
    <% names.forEach(function(name){ %>
      <li><%= name %></li>
    <% }) %>
  </ul>
<% } %>
</body>
```

Call the EJS object's renderFile method directly. Doing so opens the template and uses the data provided as an option to generate the HTML.

Example 8-1 uses the standard HTTP server that comes with Node to listen for a request on port 8124. When a request is received, the application calls the EJS renderFile method, passing in the path for the template file, as well as a names array and a document title. The last parameter is a callback function that either provides an error (and a fairly readable error, at that) or the resulting generated HTML. In the example, the result is sent back via the response object if there's no error. If there *is* an error, an error message is sent in the result, and the error object is output to the console.

Example 8-1. Generating HTML from data and an EJS template

```
var   http = require('http')
    , ejs = require('ejs')
;

// create http server
http.createServer(function (req, res) {

  res.writeHead(200, {'content-type': 'text/html'});

  // data to render
  var names = ['Joe', 'Mary', 'Sue', 'Mark'];
  var title = 'Testing EJS';

  // render or error
  ejs.renderFile(__dirname + '/views/test.ejs',
                 {title : 'testing', names : names},
                   function(err, result) {
      if (!err) {
         res.end(result);
      } else {
         res.end('An error occurred accessing page');
         console.log(err);
      }
  });

}).listen(8124);

console.log('Server running on 8124/');
```

One variation of the rendering method is render, which takes the EJS template as a string and then returns the formatted HTML:

```
var str = fs.readFileSync(__dirname + '/views/test.ejs', 'utf8');

var html = ejs.render(str, {names : names, title: title });

res.end(html);
```

A third rendering method, which I won't demonstrate, is compile, which takes an EJS template string and returns a JavaScript function that can be invoked to render HTML each time it's called. You can also use this method to enable EJS for Node in client-side applications.

The use of compile is demonstrated in Chapter 9, in the section "Building a Game Leaderboard" on page 190.

Using the EJS for Node Filters

In addition to support for rendering EJS templates, EJS for Node also provides a set of predefined filters, which can further simplify the HTML generation. One filter, `first`, extracts out the first value in a supplied array of values. Another filter, `downcase`, takes the result of the first filter and lowercases the text:

```
var names = ['Joe Brown', 'Mary Smith', 'Tom Thumb', 'Cinder Ella'];

var str = '<p><%=: users | first | downcase %></p>';

var html = ejs.render(str, {users : names });
```

The result is the following:

```
<p>joe brown</p>
```

The filters can be chained together, with the result of one being piped to the next. The use of the filter is triggered by the colon (:) following the equals sign (=), which is then followed by the data object. The following example of the use of filters takes a set of `people` objects, maps a new object consisting solely of their names, sorts the names, and then prints out a concatenated string of the names:

```
var people = [
    {name : 'Joe Brown', age : 32},
    {name : 'Mary Smith', age : 54},
    {name : 'Tom Thumb', age : 21},
    {name : 'Cinder Ella', age : 16}];

var str = "<p><%=: people | map:'name' | sort | join %></p>";
var html = ejs.render(str, {people : people });
```

Here is the result of that filter combination:

```
Cinder Ella, Joe Brown, Mary Smith, Tom Thumb
```

The filters aren't documented in the EJS for Node documentation, and you have to be careful using them interchangeably because some of the filters want a string, not an array of objects. Table 8-1 contains a list of the filters, and a brief description of what type of data they work with and what they do.

Table 8-1. EJS for Node filters

Filter	Type of data	Purpose
first	Accepts and returns array	Returns first element of array
last	Accepts and returns array	Returns last element of array
capitalize	Accepts and returns string	Capitalizes first character in string
downcase	Accepts and returns string	Lowercases all characters in string
upcase	Accepts and returns string	Capitalizes all characters in string
sort	Accepts and returns array	Applies Array.sort to array

Filter	Type of data	Purpose
sort_by:'prop'	Accepts array and property name; returns array	Creates custom sort function to sort array of objects by property
size	Accepts array; returns numeric	Returns Array.length
plus:n	Accepts two numbers or strings; returns number	Returns a + b
minus:n	Accepts two numbers or strings; returns number	Returns b − a
times:n	Accepts two numbers or strings; returns number	Returns a * b
divided_by:n	Accepts two numbers or strings; returns number	Returns a / b
join:'val'	Accepts array; returns string	Applies Array.join with given value, or , by default
truncate:n	Accepts string and length; returns string	Applies String.substr
truncate_words:n	Accepts string and word length; returns string	Applies String.split and then String.splice
replace:pattern, substitution	Accepts string, pattern, and substitution; returns string	Applies String.replace
prepend:value	Accepts string and string value; returns string	Prepends value to string
append:value	Accepts string and string value; returns string	Appends value to string
map:'prop'	Accepts array and property; returns array	Creates new array consisting of given object properties using Array.map
reverse	Accepts array or string	If array, applies Array.reverse; if string, splits words, reverses, rejoins
get	Accepts object and property	Returns property of given object
json	Accepts object	Converts to JSON string

Using a Template System (EJS) with Express

The template system provides the missing piece we need to complete the *views* portion of the MVC (Model-View-Controller) application architecture introduced in Chapter 7.

 The *model* portion of the MVC architecture is added in Chapter 10.

In Chapter 7, I provided a quick introduction for using a template system in Example 7-1. The example used Jade, but we can easily convert it to use EJS. How easily? Example 8-2 is an exact duplicate of the application in Example 7-1, except now using EJS rather than Jade. Exactly one line is changed, shown in bold.

Example 8-2. Using EJS as a template system for an application

```
var express = require('express')
  , routes = require('./routes')
  , http = require('http');

var app = express();

app.configure(function(){
  app.set('views', __dirname + '/views');
  app.set('view engine', 'ejs');
  app.use(express.favicon());
  app.use(express.logger('dev'));
  app.use(express.static(__dirname + '/public'));
  app.use(express.bodyParser());
  app.use(express.methodOverride());
  app.use(app.router);
});

app.configure('development', function(){
  app.use(express.errorHandler());
});

app.get('/', routes.index);

http.createServer(app).listen(3000);

console.log("Express server listening on port 3000");
```

The index.js route doesn't require any change at all, because it's not using anything that's specific to any template system; it's using the Express resource object's render method, which works regardless of template system (as long as the system is compatible with Express):

```
exports.index = function(req, res){
  res.render('index', { title: 'Express' }, function(err, stuff) {
    if (!err) {
      console.log(stuff);
      res.write(stuff);
      res.end();
    }
  });
};
```

In the *views* directory, the *index.ejs* file (note the extension) uses EJS for Node annotation rather than the Jade we saw in Chapter 7:

```
<html>
<head>
```

```
<title><%= title %></title>
</head>
<body>
<h1><%= title %></title>
<p>Welcome to <%= title %></p>
</body>
```

This demonstrates the beauty of working with an application that separates the model from the controller from the view: you can swap technology in and out, such as using a different template system, without impacting the application logic or data access.

To recap what's happening with this application:

1. The main Express application uses `app.get` to associate a request listener function (`routes.index`) with an HTTP GET request.

2. The `routes.index` function calls `res.render` to render the response to the GET request.

3. The `res.render` function invokes the application object's `render` function.

4. The application `render` function renders the specified view, with whatever options —in this case, the `title`.

5. The rendered content is then written to the response object, and back to the user's browser.

In Chapter 7, we focused on the routing aspects of the application, and now we'll focus on the view. We'll take the application we created at the end of Chapter 7, in Example 7-6 through Example 7-8, and add in the views capability. First, though, we need to do a little restructuring of the environment to ensure that the application can grow as needed.

Restructuring for a Multiple Object Environment

Though the application is the Widget Factory, widgets aren't going to be the only objects the system maintains. We need to restructure the environment so that we can add objects as needed.

Currently, the environment is as follows:

```
/application directory
   /routes - home directory controller
   /controllers - object controllers
   /public - static files
   /views - template files
```

The *routes* and the *controllers* directories can stay as they are, but the *views* and the *public* directory need to be modified to allow for different objects. Instead of placing all widget views directly in *views*, we add them to a new subdirectory of *views* named, appropriately enough, *widgets*:

```
/application directory
   / views
      /widgets
```

Instead of placing all widget static files directly in the *public* directory, we also place them in a *widgets* subdirectory:

```
/application directory
   /public
      /widgets
```

Now, we can add new objects by adding new directories, and we'll be able to use filenames of *new.html* and *edit.ejs* for each, without worrying about overwriting existing files.

Note that this structure assumes we may have static files for our application. The next step is to figure out how to integrate the static files into the newly dynamic environment.

Routing to Static Files

The first component of the application to refine is adding a new widget. This consists of two parts: displaying a form to get the new widget's information, and storing the new widget into the existing widget data store.

We can create an EJS template for the form, though it won't have any dynamic components—or at least, it won't at this time with the way the page is designed. However, it makes no sense to serve something through the template system that doesn't need the system's capability.

We could also just change how the form is accessed—instead of accessing the form using */widgets/new*, we'd access it as */widgets/new.html*. However, this introduces an inconsistency into the application routing. In addition, if we add dynamic components later to the form page, then we'll have to change the references to the new form.

A better approach is to handle the routing request and serve the static page as if it were dynamic, but without using the template system.

The Express resource object has a `redirect` method we could use to redirect the request to the *new.html* file, but *new.html* is what's going to show up in the address bar on the browser when finished. It also returns a 302 status code, which we don't want. Instead, we'll use the resource object's `sendfile` method. This method takes as parameters a file path, possible options, and an optional callback function with an error as its only parameter. The widget controller is using only the first parameter.

The filepath is:

```
__dirname + "/../public/widgets/widget.html"
```

We used the relative indicator `..` since the public directory is located off the *controllers* directory's parent. However, we can't use this path in `sendfile` as is, because it generates a 403 forbidden error. Instead, we use the `path` module's `normalize` method to convert the path's use of relative indicators into the equivalent absolute path:

```
// display new widget form
exports.new = function(req, res) {
    var filePath = require('path').normalize(__dirname +
                                        "/../public/widgets/new.html");
    res.sendfile(filePath);
};
```

The HTML page with the form is nothing to get excited about—just a simple form, as shown in Example 8-3. However, we did add the description field back in to make the data a little more interesting.

Example 8-3. HTML new widget form

```
<!doctype html>
<html lang="en">
<head>
 <meta charset="utf-8" />
 <title>Widgets</title>
</head>
<body>
<h1>Add Widget:</h1>

<form method="POST" action="/widgets/create"
enctype="application/x-www-form-urlencoded">

 <p>Widget name: <input type="text" name="widgetname"
id="widgetname" size="25" required/></p>
 <p>Widget Price: <input type="text"
pattern="^\$?([0-9]{1,3},([0-9]{3},)*[0-9]{3}|[0-9]+)(.[0-9][0-9])?$"
name="widgetprice" id="widgetprice" size="25" required/></p>

 <p>Widget Description: <br />
<textarea name="widgetdesc" id="widgetdesc" cols="20"
rows="5"></textarea>
 <p>

 <input type="submit" name="submit" id="submit" value="Submit"/>
 <input type="reset" name="reset" id="reset" value="Reset"/>
</p>
</form>
</body>
```

The form is `POST`ed, of course.

Now that the application can display the new widget form, we need to modify the widget controller to process the form posting.

 There's also an Express extension module, express-rewrite, that provides URL rewrite capability. Install it with npm like so:

```
npm install express-rewrite
```

Processing a New Object Post

Prior to adding in the new template support, we need to make changes to the main application file to incorporate the use of the EJS template system. I won't repeat the *app.js* file completely from Example 7-8 in Chapter 7, because the only change is to the configure method call to include the EJS template engine and *views* directory:

```
app.configure(function(){
  app.set('views', __dirname + '/views');
  app.set('view engine', 'ejs');
  app.use(express.favicon());
  app.use(express.logger('dev'));
  app.use(express.staticCache({maxObjects: 100, maxLength: 512}));
  app.use(express.static(__dirname + '/public'));
  app.use(express.bodyParser());
  app.use(express.methodOverride());
  app.use(app.router);
  app.use(express.directory(__dirname + '/public'));
  app.use(function(req, res, next){
    throw new Error(req.url + ' not found');
  });
  app.use(function(err, req, res, next) {
    console.log(err);
    res.send(err.message);
  });
});
```

Now we're ready to convert the widget controller so it uses templates, starting with the code to add a new widget.

The actual processing of the data in the widget controller for the new widget doesn't change. We still pull the data from the request body, and add it to the in-memory widget store. However, now that we have access to a template system, we're going to change how we respond to the successful addition of a new widget.

I created a new EJS template, named *added.ejs*, shown in Example 8-4. All it does is provide a listing of the widget's properties, and a message consisting of the title sent with the widget object.

Example 8-4. "Widget added" confirmation view template

```
<head>
<title><%= title %></title>
</head>
<body>
<h1><%= title %> | <%= widget.name %></h1>
<ul>
<li>ID: <%= widget.id %></li>
<li>Name: <%= widget.name %></li>
<li>Price: <%= widget.price.toFixed(2) %></li>
<li>Desc: <%= widget.desc %></li>
</ul>
</body>
```

The code to process the update is little different from that shown in Chapter 7, other than the fact that we're now rendering a view rather than sending a message back to the user (the part that changes is in bold text):

```
// add a widget
exports.create = function(req, res) {

  // generate widget id
  var indx = widgets.length + 1;

  // add widget
  widgets[widgets.length] =
   { id : indx,
     name : req.body.widgetname,
     price : parseFloat(req.body.widgetprice),
     desc : req.body.widgetdesc };

  //print out to console and confirm addition to user
  console.log(widgets[indx-1]);
  res.render('widgets/added', {title: 'Widget Added', widget : widgets[indx-1]});
};
```

The two options sent to the view are the page title and the widget object. Figure 8-1 shows the informative, though plain, result.

 The code to process a new widget doesn't do any validation of the data or check for authority or SQL injection hacks. Data validation, security, and authorization are covered in Chapter 15.

Figure 8-1. Confirmation of the added widget

The next two processes to convert to templates, update and deletion, require a way of specifying which widget to perform the action on. In addition, we also need to convert the index display of all widgets. For all three processes, we're going to use a view to create both the widgets index page and a picklist, covered next.

Working with the Widgets Index and Generating a Picklist

A *picklist* is nothing more than a list of choices from which one can choose. For the widget application, a picklist could be a selection or drop-down list incorporated into an update or delete page, using Ajax and client-side scripting, but we're going to incorporate the functionality into the widget application's index page.

Right now, the widget application index page just has a data dump of the widget data store. It's informative, but ugly and not all that useful. To improve the result, we're going to add a view to display all of the widgets in a table—one widget per row, with the widget properties in columns. We're also going to add two more columns: one with a link to edit the widget, and one with a link to delete the widget. These provide the missing piece to the application: a way to edit or delete a widget without having to remember or know its identifier.

Example 8-5 has the contents of the template for this new view, named *index.ejs*. Since the file is located in the *widgets* subdirectory, we don't have to worry that it's the same name as the higher-level *index.ejs* file.

Example 8-5. Widgets index page with links to edit and delete the individual widgets

```
<!doctype html>
<html lang="en">
<head>
 <meta charset="utf-8" />
 <title><%= title %></title>
</head>
<body>
<% if (widgets.length) { %>
  <table>
  <caption>Widgets</caption>
  <tr><th>ID</th><th>Name</th><th>Price</th><th>Description</th></tr>
    <% widgets.forEach(function(widget){ %>
      <tr>
      <td><%= widget.id %></td>
      <td><%= widget.name %></td>
      <td>$<%= widget.price.toFixed(2) %></td>
      <td><%= widget.desc %></td>
      <td><a href="/widgets/<%= widget.id %>/edit">Edit</a></td>
      <td><a href="/widgets/<%= widget.id %>">Delete</a></td>
      </tr>
    <% }) %>
  </table>
<% } %>
</body>
```

The controller code to trigger this new view is extremely simple: a call to render the view, sending the entire array of widgets through as data:

```
// index listing of widgets at /widgets/
exports.index = function(req, res) {
    res.render('widgets/index', {title : 'Widgets', widgets : widgets});
};
```

In Example 8-5, if the object has a `length` property (is an array), its element objects are traversed and their properties are printed out as table data, in addition to the links to edit and delete the object. Figure 8-2 shows the table after several widgets have been added to our in-memory data store.

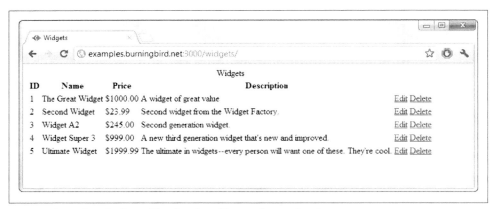

Figure 8-2. Widget display table after the addition of several widgets

The link (route) to delete the object is actually the same as the link (route) to show it: */widgets/:id*. We'll add a mostly hidden form to the Show Widget page that includes a button to delete the widget if it's no longer needed. This allows us to incorporate the necessary trigger for the deletion without having to add a new route. It also provides another level of protection to ensure that users know exactly which widget they're deleting.

 Rather than incorporate the delete request into the Show Widget page, it's also perfectly acceptable to create another route, such as */widgets/:id/delete*, and generate an "Are you sure?" page from the index page link, which then triggers the deletion.

Showing an Individual Object and Confirming an Object Deletion

To display an individual widget is as simple as providing a placeholder for all of its properties, embedded into whatever HTML you want to use. In the widget application, I'm using an unordered list (`ul`) for the widget properties.

Since we're also encompassing into the page the trigger for deleting the object, at the bottom I've added a form that displays a button reading "Delete Widget." In the form is the hidden _method field that is used to generate the HTTP DELETE verb that routes to the application's destroy method. The entire template is shown in Example 8-6.

Example 8-6. View to display a widget's properties and a form to delete the widget

```
<!doctype html>
<html lang="en">
<head>
 <meta charset="utf-8" />
 <title><%= title %></title>
</head>
<body>
<h1><%= widget.name %></h1>
<ul>
<li>ID: <%= widget.id %></li>
<li>Name: <%= widget.name %></li>
<li>Price: $<%= widget.price.toFixed(2) %></li>
<li>Description: <%= widget.desc %></li>
</ul>
<form method="POST" action="/widgets/<%= widget.id %>"
enctype="application/x-www-form-urlencoded">

 <input type="hidden" value="delete" name="_method" />

 <input type="submit" name="submit" id="submit" value="Delete Widget"/>
</form>

</body>
```

Very little modification is required in the controller code for either the show or the destroy methods. I've left the destroy method as is for now. All it does is delete the object from the in-memory store and send a message back to this effect:

```
exports.destroy = function(req, res) {
   var indx = req.params.id - 1;
   delete widgets[indx];

   console.log('deleted ' + req.params.id);
   res.send('deleted ' + req.params.id);
};
```

The show method required little change—simply replacing the send message with a call to render the new view:

```
// show a widget
exports.show = function(req, res) {
   var indx = parseInt(req.params.id) - 1;
   if (!widgets[indx])
      res.send('There is no widget with id of ' + req.params.id);
   else
      res.render('widgets/show', {title : 'Show Widget', widget : widgets[indx]});
};
```

Figure 8-3 demonstrates what the Show Widget page looks like, complete with the Delete Widget button at the bottom.

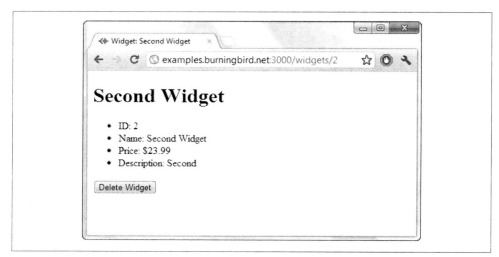

Figure 8-3. The Show Widget page with delete button

By now, you've seen how simple it is to incorporate views into the application. The best thing of all about this system is that you can incorporate changes into the view templates without having to stop the application: it uses the changed template the next time the view is accessed.

One last view for the update widget, and we're done converting the widget application to use the EJS template system.

Providing an Update Form and Processing a PUT Request

The form to edit the widget is exactly the same as the form to add a widget, except for the addition of one field: _method. In addition, the form is prepopulated with the data for the widget being edited, so we need to incorporate the template tags and appropriate values.

Example 8-7 contains the contents for the *edit.ejs* template file. Note the use of the template tags with the value fields in the input elements. Also notice the addition of the _method field.

Example 8-7. The Edit view template file, with data prepopulated

```
<!doctype html>
<html lang="en">
<head>
 <meta charset="utf-8" />
 <title><%= title %></title>
</head>
<body>
<h1>Edit <%= widget.name %></h1>
```

```
<form method="POST" action="/widgets/<%= widget.id %>"
enctype="application/x-www-form-urlencoded">

<p>Widget name: <input type="text" name="widgetname"
id="widgetname" size="25" value="<%=widget.name %>" required /></p>

<p>Widget Price: <input type="text"
pattern="^\$?([0-9]{1,3},([0-9]{3},)*[0-9]{3}|[0-9]+)(.[0-9][0-9])?$"
name="widgetprice" id="widgetprice" size="25" value="<%= widget.price %>" required/></p>
<p>Widget Description: <br />
<textarea name="widgetdesc" id="widgetdesc" cols="20"
rows="5"><%= widget.desc %></textarea>
<p>

<input type="hidden" value="put" name="_method" />

<input type="submit" name="submit" id="submit" value="Submit"/>
<input type="reset" name="reset" id="reset" value="Reset"/>
</p>
</form>
</body>
```

Figure 8-4 shows the page with a widget loaded. All you need to do is edit the field values, and then click Submit to submit the changes.

Figure 8-4. The Edit widget view

The modification to the controller code is as simple as the other modifications have been. The Edit view is accessed using `res.render`, and the widget object is passed as data:

```
// display edit form
exports.edit = function(req, res) {
   var indx = parseInt(req.params.id) - 1;
   res.render('widgets/edit', {title : 'Edit Widget', widget : widgets[indx]});
};
```

The code to process the update is very close to what we had in Chapter 7, except that instead of sending a message that the object is updated, we're using a view. We're not creating a new view, though. Instead, we're using the *widgets/added.ejs* view we used earlier. Since both just display the object's properties and can take a title passed in as data, we can easily repurpose the view just by changing the title:

```
// update a widget
exports.update = function(req, res) {
  var indx = parseInt(req.params.id) - 1;
  widgets[indx] =
   { id : indx + 1,
     name : req.body.widgetname,
     price : parseFloat(req.body.widgetprice),
     desc : req.body.widgetdesc}
  console.log(widgets[indx]);
  res.render('widgets/added', {title: 'Widget Edited', widget : widgets[indx]})
};
```

Again, the view used doesn't impact what route (URL) is shown, so it doesn't matter if we reuse a view. Being able to reuse a view can save us a lot of work as the application increases in difficulty.

You've had a chance to see pieces of the controller code throughout these sections as we convert it to use templates. Example 8-8 is an entire copy of the changed file, which you can compare to Example 7-6 in Chapter 7 to see how easily views incorporate into the code, and how much work they can save us.

Example 8-8. The widget controller implemented with views

```
var widgets = [
   { id : 1,
     name : "The Great Widget",
     price : 1000.00,
     desc: "A widget of great value"
   }
]

// index listing of widgets at /widgets/
exports.index = function(req, res) {
   res.render('widgets/index', {title : 'Widgets', widgets : widgets});
};

// display new widget form
exports.new = function(req, res) {
   var filePath = require('path').normalize(__dirname + "/../public/widgets/new.html");
   res.sendfile(filePath);
};
```

```javascript
// add a widget
exports.create = function(req, res) {

  // generate widget id
  var indx = widgets.length + 1;

  // add widget
  widgets[widgets.length] =
    { id : indx,
      name : req.body.widgetname,
      price : parseFloat(req.body.widgetprice),
      desc : req.body.widgetdesc };

  //print out to console and confirm addition to user
  console.log(widgets[indx-1]);
  res.render('widgets/added', {title: 'Widget Added', widget : widgets[indx-1]});
};

// show a widget
exports.show = function(req, res) {
  var indx = parseInt(req.params.id) - 1;
  if (!widgets[indx])
    res.send('There is no widget with id of ' + req.params.id);
  else
    res.render('widgets/show', {title : 'Show Widget', widget : widgets[indx]});
};

// delete a widget
exports.destroy = function(req, res) {
  var indx = req.params.id - 1;
  delete widgets[indx];

  console.log('deleted ' + req.params.id);
  res.send('deleted ' + req.params.id);
};

// display edit form
exports.edit = function(req, res) {
  var indx = parseInt(req.params.id) - 1;
  res.render('widgets/edit', {title : 'Edit Widget', widget : widgets[indx]});
};

// update a widget
exports.update = function(req, res) {
  var indx = parseInt(req.params.id) - 1;
  widgets[indx] =
    { id : indx + 1,
      name : req.body.widgetname,
      price : parseFloat(req.body.widgetprice),
      desc : req.body.widgetdesc}
  console.log(widgets[indx]);
  res.render('widgets/added', {title: 'Widget Edited', widget : widgets[indx]})
};
```

This is the last time you'll see the controller code for this chapter. Yet we're about to make a profound change to the application: we're going to replace the template system.

The Jade Template System

Jade is the template system installed with Express by default. It is quite different from EJS: rather than embed the template tags directly into HTML, you use a simplified version of HTML.

 The Jade website is at *http://jade-lang.com/*.

Taking the Nickel Tour of the Jade Syntax

In the Jade template system, HTML elements are given by their name, but you don't use any angle brackets. Nesting is indicated by indentation. So, rather than:

```
<html>
<head>
<title>This is the title</title>
</head>
<body>
<p>Say hi World</p>
</body>
</html>
```

You have:

```
html
    head
        title This is it
    body
        p Say Hi to the world
```

The contents of both the title and the paragraph elements are just included after the element name. There are no ending tags—they're assumed—and again, indentation triggers nesting. Another example is the following, which also makes use of both class name and identifier, as well as additional nesting:

```
    html
    head
        title This is it
    body
        div.content
            div#title
                p nested data
```

This generates:

```
<html>
<head>
<title>This is it</title>
</head>
<body>
<div class="content">
<div id="title">
<p>nested data</p>
</div>
</div>
</body>
</html>
```

If you have large bodies of content, such as text for a paragraph, you can use the vertical bar, or pipe (|), to concatenate the text:

```
p
  | some text
  | more text
  | and even more
```

This becomes:

```
<p>some text more text and even more</p>
```

Another approach is to end the paragraph element with a period (.) indicating that the block contains only text and allowing us to omit the vertical bar:

```
p.
  some text
  more text
  and even more
```

If we want to include HTML as the text, we can; it ends up being treated as HTML in the generated source:

```
body.
  <h1>A header</h1>
  <p>A paragraph</p>
```

Form elements generally have attributes, and they're incorporated in Jade in parentheses, including setting their values (if any). The attributes need only be separated by whitespace, but I list them each on a separate line to make the template more readable.

The following Jade template:

```
html
  head
    title This is it
  body
    form(method="POST"
        action="/widgets"
        enctype="application/x-www-form-urlencoded")
      input(type="text"
            name="widgetname"
            id="widgetname"
            size="25")
```

```
input(type="text"
      name="widgetprice"
      id="widgetprice"
      size="25")
input(type="submit"
      name="submit"
      id="submit"
      value="Submit")
```

generates the following HTML:

```
<html>
<head>
<title>This is it</title>
</head>
<body>
<form method="POST" action="/widgets"
 enctype="application/x-www-form-urlencoded">
<input type="text" name="widgetname" id="widgetname" size="25"/>
<input type="text" name="widgetprice" id="widgetprice" size="25"/>
<input type="submit" name="submit" id="submit" value="Submit"/>
</form>
</body>
</html>
```

Using block and extends to Modularize the View Templates

Now we're going to convert the widget application so it uses Jade rather than EJS. The
only change that we need to make to the widget application code is in *app.js*, to change
the template engine:

```
app.set('view engine', 'jade');
```

No other change is necessary to the application. None. Zip.

All of the templates share the same page layout. The layout is rather plain; there are no
sidebars or footers, or any use of CSS. Because of the page's plain nature, we haven't
minded duplicating the same layout markup in each view in the prior examples. However, if we start to add more to the overall page structure—such as sidebars, a header,
and a footer—then having to maintain the same layout information in each file is going
to get cumbersome.

The first thing we're going to do in our conversion, then, is create a layout template
that will be used by all the other templates.

 Express 3.x completely changed its handling of views, including how it
implements partial views and uses layouts. You can use the Jade templates in this section with Express 2.x if you add the following in the
configure method call:

```
app.set('view options', {layout: false});
```

Example 8-9 contains the complete *layout.jade* file. It uses the HTML5 doctype, adds a head element with title and meta elements, adds the body element, and then references a block called content. That's how you include blocks of content defined in other template files.

Example 8-9. Simple layout template in Jade

```
doctype 5
html(lang="en")
  head
    title #{title}
    meta(charset="utf-8")
  body
    block content
```

Notice the use of the pound sign and curly braces (#{}) for the title. This is how we embed data passed to the template in Jade. The use of the identifier doesn't change from EJS, just the syntax.

To use the new layout template, we start off each of the content templates with:

```
extends layout
```

The use of extends lets the template engine know where to find the layout template for the page view, while the use of block instructs the template engine about where to place the generated content.

You don't have to use content for the block name, and you can use more than one block. In addition, you can also include other template files if you want to break up the layout template even further. I modified *layout.jade* to include a header rather than the markup directly in the layout file:

```
doctype 5
html(lang="en")
  include header
  body
    block content
```

I then defined the header content in a file named *header.jade*, with the following:

```
head
  title #{title}
  meta(charset="utf-8")
```

There are two things to note in the new *layout.jade* and *header.jade* code.

First, the include directive is relative. If you split the views into the following subdirectory structure:

```
/views
   /widgets
       layout.jade
      /standard
          header.jade
```

you'd use the following to include the header template in the layout file:

```
include standard/header
```

The file doesn't have to be Jade, either—it could be HTML, in which case you'll need to use the file extension:

```
include standard/header.html
```

Second, do not use indentation in the *header.jade* file. The indentation comes in from the parent file and doesn't need to be duplicated in the included template file. In fact, if you do so, your template will generate an error.

Now that we've defined the layout template, it's time to convert the EJS views into Jade.

 Now is also the time you might consider swapping the static Add Widget form file for a dynamic one so that it can also take advantage of the new layout template.

Converting the Widget Views into Jade Templates

The first view to convert from EJS to Jade is the *added.ejs* template, which provides feedback for the successful addition of a new widget. The template file is named *added.jade* (the name must be the same, though the extension different, to work with the existing controller code), and it makes use of the newly defined *layout.jade* file, as shown in Example 8-10.

Example 8-10. The "Widget added" confirmation page converted to Jade

```
extends layout

block content
  h1 #{title} | #{widget.name}
  ul
    li id: #{widget.id}
    li Name: #{widget.name}
    li Price: $#{widget.price.toFixed()}
    li Desc: #{widget.desc}
```

Notice how we can still use the toFixed method to format the price output.

The block is named content, so it integrates with the expectations of the block name set in the *layout.jade* file. The simplified HTML for an h1 header and an unordered list is integrated with the data passed from the controller—in this case, the widget object.

Running the widget application and adding a new widget generates the same HTML as generated with the EJS: a header and a list of widget properties for the newly added widget—all without our changing any of the controller code.

Converting the main widgets display view

The next template to convert is the index template that lists all of the widgets in a table, with options to edit or delete the widget as table columns. We're going to try something a little different with this template. We're going to separate the table row generation for each widget from the overall table generation.

First, we'll create the *row.jade* template. It assumes that the data is an object named `widget`, with the properties accessible off the object:

```
tr
  td #{widget.id}
  td #{widget.name}
  td $#{widget.price.toFixed(2)}
  td #{widget.desc}
  td
    a(href='/widgets/#{widget.id}/edit') Edit
  td
    a(href='/widgets/#{widget.id}') Delete
```

Each link *must* be included on a separate line; otherwise, we lose the nesting indication with the indentation.

The main *index.jade* file that references the newly created row template is shown in Example 8-11. This template introduces two new Jade constructs: a conditional test and an iteration. The conditional is used to test for the `length` property on the `widgets` object, assuring us we're dealing with an array. The iteration construct uses an abbreviated form of the `Array.forEach` method, where the array is traversed and each instance is assigned to the new variable, `widget`.

Example 8-11. The index template for creating a table of widgets

```
extends layout

block content
  table
    caption Widgets
      if widgets.length
        tr
          th ID
          th Name
          th Price
          th Description
          th
          th
        each widget in widgets
          include row
```

This is a whole lot less work than having to manually enter all those angle brackets, especially with the table headers (th). The results of the Jade template are identical to those from the EJS template: an HTML table with widgets in each row, and the ability to edit or delete each widget.

Converting the edit and deletion forms

The next two conversions are working with forms.

First, we'll convert the edit template into one using Jade. The only really tricky part of the conversion is handling all the various attributes. Though you can separate them by a space, I find it helps to list each on a separate line. This way, you can see that you've properly included all the attributes and can easily double-check their values. Example 8-12 contains the rather long template for the Edit Widget form.

Example 8-12. Jade template for the Edit Widget form

```
extends layout

block content
  h1 Edit #{widget.name}
  form(method="POST"
      action="/widgets/#{widget.id}"
      enctype="application/x-www-form-urlencoded")
    p Widget Name:
      input(type="text"
          name="widgetname"
          id="widgetname"
          size="25"
          value="#{widget.name}"
          required)
    p Widget Price:
      input(type="text"
          name="widgetprice"
          id="widgetprice"
          size="25"
          value="#{widget.price}"
          pattern="="^\$?([0-9]{1,3},([0-9]{3},)*[0-9]{3}|[0-9]+)(.[0-9][0-9])?$"
          required)
    p Widget Description:
      br
      textarea(name="widgetdesc"
          id="widgetdesc"
          cols="20"
          rows="5") #{widget.desc}
    p
      input(type="hidden"
          name="_method"
          id="_method"
          value="put")
      input(type="submit"
          name="submit"
          id="submit"
          value="Submit")
      input(type="reset"
          name="reset"
          id="reset"
          value="reset")
```

During the conversion of the Show Widget page, I noticed that the top of the page is basically a repeat of what is displayed in the *added.jade* template from Example 8-10: an unordered list with all of the widget's properties. Another opportunity to simplify!

I created a new template, *widget.jade*, that just displays the widget information as an unordered list:

```
ul
  li id: #{widget.id}
  li Name: #{widget.name}
  li Price: $#{widget.price.toFixed(2)}
  li Desc: #{widget.desc}
```

I then modified the *added.jade* file from Example 8-10 to use this new template:

```
extends layout

block content
  h1 #{title} | #{widget.name}
  include widget
```

The new Show Widget template also makes use of the new *widget.jade* template, as demonstrated in Example 8-13.

Example 8-13. The new Show Widget template in Jade

```
extends layout

block content
  h1 #{widget.name}
  include widget
  form(method="POST"
      action="/widgets/#{widget.id}"
      enctype="application/x-www-form-urlencoded")
    input(type="hidden"
          name="_method"
          id="_method"
          value="delete")
    input(type="submit"
          name="submit"
          id="submit"
          value="Delete Widget")
```

You can see how modularizing the templates makes each template that much cleaner, and thus easier to maintain.

With the newly modularized template, we can now show and delete a specific widget...and that leads to a quirk where the Jade template differs from the EJS template.

In the widget application, when widgets are deleted, they are deleted *in place*. This means the `array` element is basically set to `null`, so that the widget location in the array is maintained relative to its identifier. This in-place maintenance doesn't cause a problem when we add and delete widgets and display them in the index page in EJS, but it *does* cause a problem with Jade: we get an error about missing properties, because it doesn't filter out `null` array elements like the EJS template processing does.

This is trivially easy to fix. As shown in Example 8-11, just add another conditional test to the Jade markup in the *index.jade* file to make sure the widget object exists (i.e., is not `null`):

```
extends layout

block content
  table
    caption Widgets
      if widgets.length
        tr
          th ID
          th Name
          th Price
          th Description
          th
          th
        each widget in widgets
          if widget
            include row
```

And now, all of the template views have been converted to Jade, and the application is complete. (Well, until we add in the data portion in Chapter 10.)

But while the application is complete, it's not very attractive. Of course, it's easy enough to add a stylesheet into the header to modify the presentation of all the elements, but we'll also briefly take a look at another approach: using Stylus.

Incorporating Stylus for Simplified CSS

It's a simple matter to include a stylesheet into any of the template files. In the Jade template file, we can add one to the *header.jade* file:

```
head
  title #{title}
  meta(charset="utf-8")
  link(type="text/css"
       rel="stylesheet"
       href="/stylesheets/main.css"
       media="all")
```

The stylesheet is now immediately available to all of our application views because they all use the layout template, which uses this header.

 Now you can definitely see the value of converting the static *new.html* file into a template view: making the change to the header doesn't impact it, and it has to be manually edited.

If you've grown fond of the syntax for Jade, though, you can use a variation of this syntax for CSS by incorporating the use of Stylus into your application.

To use Stylus, first install it with npm:

```
npm install stylus
```

Stylus is not like the Jade template system. It doesn't create dynamic CSS views. What it does is generate static stylesheets from a Stylus template the first time the template is accessed, or each time the template is modified.

 Read more about Stylus at *http://learnboost.github.com/stylus/docs/js .html*.

To incorporate Stylus into the widget application, we have to include the module within the main application file's (*app.js*) `require` section. Then we have to include the Stylus middleware along with the others in the `configure` method call, passing in an option with the source for the Stylus templates, and the destination where the compiled stylesheets are to be placed. Example 8-14 shows the newly modified *app.js* file with these changes in bold text.

Example 8-14. Adding Stylus CSS template support to the widget application

```
var express = require('express')
  , routes = require('./routes')
  , map = require('./maproutecontroller')
  , http = require('http')
  , stylus = require('stylus')
  , app = express();

app.configure(function(){
  app.set('views', __dirname + '/views');
  app.set('view engine', 'jade');
  app.use(express.favicon());
  app.use(express.logger('dev'));
  app.use(express.staticCache({maxObjects: 100, maxLength: 512}));
  app.use(stylus.middleware({
      src: __dirname + '/views'
    , dest: __dirname + '/public'
  }));
  app.use(express.static(__dirname + '/public'));
  app.use(express.bodyParser());
  app.use(express.methodOverride());
  app.use(app.router);
  app.use(express.directory(__dirname + '/public'));
  app.use(function(req, res, next){
    throw new Error(req.url + ' not found');
  });
  app.use(function(err, req, res, next) {
    console.log(err);
```

```
    res.send(err.message);
  });
});

app.configure('development', function(){
  app.use(express.errorHandler());
});

app.get('/', routes.index);

var prefixes = ['widgets'];

// map route to controller
prefixes.forEach(function(prefix) {
  map.mapRoute(app, prefix);
});

http.createServer(app).listen(3000);

console.log("Express server listening on port 3000");
```

The first time you access the widget application after making this change, you may notice a very brief hesitation. The reason is that the Stylus module is generating the stylesheet—an event that happens when a new or modified stylesheet template is added and the application is restarted. After the stylesheet has been generated, though, it's the generated copy that's served up—it isn't recompiled with every page access.

 You will need to restart your Express application if you make changes to the stylesheet template.

The Stylus stylesheet templates all have the same extension: *.styl*. The source directory is set to *views*, but it expects the stylesheet templates to be in a *stylesheets* directory under *views*. When it generates the static stylesheets, it places them in a *stylesheets* directory under the destination directory (in this case, */public*).

After working with Jade, you should find the Stylus syntax very familiar. Again, each element that is being styled is listed, followed by the indented stylesheet setting. The syntax strips away the need for curly braces, colons, and semicolons.

For example, to change the background color for the web page to yellow, and the text color to red, use the following for the Stylus template:

```
body
    background-color yellow
    color red
```

If you want elements to share settings, list them on the same line with a comma between them, just like you would with CSS:

```
p, tr
    background-color yellow
    color red
```

Or you can list the elements on separate lines:

```
p
tr
    background-color yellow
    color red
```

If you want to use a pseudoclass, such as :hover or :visited, use the following syntax:

```
textarea
input
    background-color #fff
    &:hover
        background-color cyan
```

The ampersand (&) represents the parent selector. All combined, the following Stylus template:

```
Combined, the following:
p, tr
    background-color yellow
    color red

textarea
input
    background-color #fff
    &:hover
        background-color cyan
```

generates the following static CSS file:

```
p,
tr {
    background-color: #ff0;
    color: #f00;
}
textarea,
input {
    background-color: #fff;
}
textarea:hover,
input:hover {
    background-color: #0ff;
}
```

There's more to working with Stylus, but I'll leave that to you as an off-book exercise. The Stylus website provides a good set of documentation for the syntax. Before leaving this chapter, though, we'll create a Stylus stylesheet that enhances the presentation of the widget application.

Specifically, we'll add a border and spacing to the HTML table element in the index widget listing page. We're also going to change the font for the headers and remove the bullet indicators for the unordered list. These are small changes, but they'll be a start in refining the appearance of the widget application.

The new stylesheet template is shown in Example 8-15. It's not terribly big and doesn't use any involved CSS. It's basic stuff, but it does improve—smooth out a bit—the overall appearance of the application.

Example 8-15. Stylus template for widget application

```
body
  margin 50px
table
  width 90%
  border-collapse collapse
table, td, th, caption
  border 1px solid black
td
  padding 20px
caption
  font-size larger
  background-color yellow
  padding 10px
h1
  font 1.5em Georgia, serif
ul
  list-style-type none
form
  margin 20px
  padding 20px
```

Figure 8-5 shows the index page after several widgets have been added. Again, it's nothing fancy, but the data content is a lot easier to read with the new stylesheet.

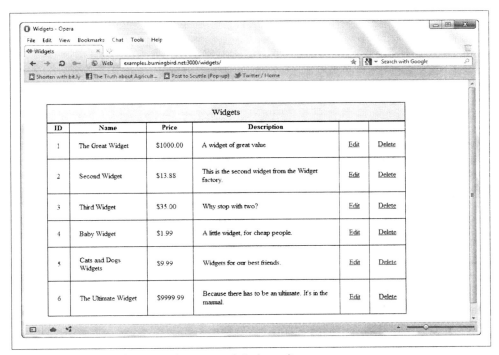

Figure 8-5. Widget application index page with Stylus styling

CHAPTER 9

Structured Data with Node and Redis

When it comes to data, there's relational databases and Everything Else, otherwise known as *NoSQL*. In the NoSQL category, a type of structured data is based on key/value pairs, typically stored in memory for extremely fast access. The three most popular in-memory key/value stores are Memcached, Cassandra, and Redis. Happily for Node developers, there is Node support for all three stores.

Memcached is primarily used as a way of caching data queries for quick access in memory. It's also quite good with distributed computing, but has limited support for more complex data. It's useful for applications that do a lot of queries, but less so for applications doing a lot of data writing and reading. Redis is the superior data store for the latter type of application. In addition, Redis can be persisted, and it provides more flexibility than Memcached—especially in its support for different types of data. However, unlike Memcached, Redis works only on a single machine.

The same factors also come into play when comparing Redis and Cassandra. Like Memcached, Cassandra has support for clusters. However, also like Memcached, it has limited data structure support. It's good for ad hoc queries—a use that does not favor Redis. However, Redis is simple to use, uncomplicated, and typically faster than Cassandra. For these reasons, and others, Redis has gained a greater following among Node developers, which is why I picked it over Memcached and Cassandra to cover in this chapter on key/value in-memory data stores.

I'm going to take a break from the more tutorial style of technology coverage in the previous chapters and demonstrate Node and Redis by implementing three use cases that typify the functionality these two technologies can provide:

- Building a game leaderboard
- Creating a message queue
- Tracking web page statistics

These applications also make use of modules and technologies covered in earlier chapters, such as the Jade template system (covered in Chapter 8), the Async module (covered in Chapter 5), and Express (covered in Chapter 7 and Chapter 8).

The Redis site is at *http://redis.io/*. Read more on Memcached at *http://memcached.org/*, and on Apache Cassandra at *http://cassandra.apache.org/*.

Getting Started with Node and Redis

There are several modules supporting Redis, including Redback, which provides a higher-level interface, but in this chapter we'll focus on just one: node_redis, or just redis (the convention we'll use), by Matt Ranney. I like redis because it provides a simple and elegant interface to directly access Redis commands, so you can leverage what you know about the data store with minimal intervention.

 The redis GitHub page is at *https://github.com/mranney/node_redis*.

You can install the redis module using npm:

```
npm install redis
```

I also recommend using the hiredis library, as it's nonblocking and improves performance. Install it using the following:

```
npm install hiredis redis
```

To use redis in your Node applications, you first include the module:

```
var redis = require('redis');
```

Then you'll need to create a Redis client. The method used is `createClient`:

```
var client = redis.createClient();
```

The `createClient` method can take three optional parameters: `port`, `host`, and options (outlined shortly). By default, the host is set to `127.0.0.1`, and the port is set to `6379`. The port is the one used by default for a Redis server, so these default settings should be fine if the Redis server is hosted on the same machine as the Node application.

The third parameter is an object that supports the following options:

parser
> The Redis protocol reply parser; set by default to `hiredis`. You can also use `java script`.

return_buffers
> Defaults to `false`. If `true`, all replies are sent as Node buffer objects rather than strings.

detect_buffers
> Defaults to `false`. If `true`, replies are sent as buffer objects if any input to the original commands were buffers.

socket_nodelay
> Defaults to `true`; specifies whether to call `setNoDelay` on TCP stream.

no_ready_check
> Defaults to `false`. Set to `true` inhibits the "ready check" sent to server to check if it is ready for more commands.

Use the default settings until you're more comfortable with Node and Redis.

Once you have a client connection to the Redis data store, you can send commands to the server until you call the `client.quit` method call, which closes the connection to the Redis server. If you want to force a closure, you can use the `client.end` method instead. However, the latter method doesn't wait for all replies to be parsed. The `client.end` method is a good one to call if your application is stuck or you want to start over.

Issuing Redis commands through the client connection is a fairly intuitive process. All commands are exposed as methods on the client object, and command arguments are passed as parameters. Since this is Node, the last parameter is a callback function, which returns an error and whatever data or reply is given in response to the Redis command.

In the following code, the `client.hset` method is used to set a hash property:

```
client.hset("hashid", "propname", "propvalue", function(err, reply) {
    // do something with error or reply
});
```

The `hset` command sets a value, so there's no return data, only the Redis acknowledgment. If you call a method that gets multiple values, such as `client.hvals`, the second parameter in the callback function will be an array—either an array of single strings, or an array of objects:

```
client.hvals(obj.member, function (err, replies) {
    if (err) {
        return console.error("error response - " + err);
    }

    console.log(replies.length + " replies:");
    replies.forEach(function (reply, i) {
        console.log("    " + i + ": " + reply);
    });
});
```

Because the Node callback is so ubiquitous, and because so many of the Redis commands are operations that just reply with a confirmation of success, the redis module provides a `redis.print` method you can pass as the last parameter:

```
client.set("somekey", "somevalue", redis.print);
```

The `redis.print` method prints either the error or the reply to the console and returns.

Now that you have an idea how the redis module works, it's time to try it out with actual applications.

Building a Game Leaderboard

One possible use for Redis is to create a game leaderboard. A leaderboard is a score-keeping device for digital games on computers and handheld devices such as smart-phones and tablets. A widely used one is OpenFeint, which allows game players to create an online profile and then store scores for various games. Players can compete among friends, or compete for the top score for any given game.

This is the type of application that can be served by a hybrid data solution. The profiles could be stored in a relational data store, but the scores themselves could be stored in a data store like Redis. The data needs for the scores are simple, and the score data is accessed and modified frequently, and by large numbers of users. One game developer for Facebook estimated it had 10,000 concurrent users, with 200,000 requests per minute during peak game times. However, the system to handle the requests doesn't have to be Herculean in nature, because the data isn't complex, and transactional enforcement really isn't a necessity there. Frankly, a relational or document database is overkill. A key/value data store like Redis is ideal.

The Redis *hash* and the *sorted set* are the most appropriate data structures for this type of application. The hash is ideal because the information about each score is more than just one or two fields. Typically, you'll store a member ID, perhaps the player's name (to limit having to go back to the relational or document store that often), perhaps the game name if the system provides leaderboards for more than one game, the last date played, the score, and any other relevant information.

The sorted set is the best data structure for tracking just the scores and username, and being able to quickly access the highest 10 or 100 scores.

To create the application that updates the Redis database, I converted the TCP client/server application I created in Chapter 3 to send data from the TCP client to the server, which then updates Redis. It wouldn't be unusual for a gaming application to store the data via TCP socket rather than HTTP or other means.

The TCP client takes whatever we type at the command line and sends it to the server. The code is exactly the same as that shown in Example 3-3, so I won't repeat it. When I run the TCP client, unlike previous testing, instead of just sending through plain-text messages, I send JSON representing the information being stored in the Redis database. An example is the following:

```
{"member" : 400, "first_name" : "Ada", "last_name" : "Lovelace", "score" : 53455,
"date" : "10/10/1840"}
```

The server is modified to convert the data string it receives into a JavaScript object, and to access the individual members to store into a hash. The member identifier and score are also added to a sorted set, with the game score used as the set score. Example 9-1 shows the modified TCP server application.

Example 9-1. TCP server that updates the Redis data store

```
var net = require('net');
var redis = require('redis');

var server = net.createServer(function(conn) {
   console.log('connected');

   // create Redis client
   var client = redis.createClient();

   client.on('error', function(err) {
     console.log('Error ' + err);
   });

   // fifth database is game score database
   client.select(5);
   conn.on('data', function(data) {
      console.log(data + ' from ' + conn.remoteAddress + ' ' +
        conn.remotePort);
      try {
         var obj = JSON.parse(data);

         // add or overwrite score
         client.hset(obj.member, "first_name", obj.first_name, redis.print);
         client.hset(obj.member, "last_name", obj.last_name, redis.print);
         client.hset(obj.member, "score", obj.score, redis.print);
         client.hset(obj.member, "date", obj.date, redis.print);

         // add to scores for Zowie!
         client.zadd("Zowie!", parseInt(obj.score), obj.member);
      } catch(err) {
         console.log(err);
      }
   });
   conn.on('close', function() {
      console.log('client closed connection');
      client.quit();
   });
}).listen(8124);

console.log('listening on port 8124');
```

The Redis connection is established when the server is created, and closed when the server is closed. Another approach is to create a static client connection that persists across requests, but this has disadvantages. For more on when to create the Redis client, see the upcoming sidebar "When to Create the Redis Client" on page 200. The object conversion and persistence of the data to Redis is enclosed in exception handling to prevent the server from failing if we fat-finger the input.

As mentioned earlier, two different data stores are being updated: the individual's score information (including name, score, and date) is stored in a hash, and the member ID and score are stored in a sorted set. The member ID is used as the key in the hash, while the game score is used as the score for the member ID in the sorted set. The critical component to making the application work is the member ID appearing in both data stores.

The next part of the application is a way of displaying the top five score holders of our fictional game (named *Zowie!* in this exercise). In a sorted set, you can retrieve a range of data by score using the Redis `zrange` command. However, this function returns the range of values sorted from lowest to highest, which is the opposite of what we want. What we want is to return the five highest scores, sorted by highest number first. The Redis command to use is `zrevrange`.

To display the top five game players, this time we'll create an HTTP server that will return the results as a simple table list. To ensure a relatively decent display, we're going to use the Jade template system, but instead of using it with the Express framework—since the gaming application isn't based on Express—we'll just use Jade by itself.

To use Jade outside of express, you read in the primary template file and then call the `compile` method, passing in the template file string and options. The only option I'm providing is `filename`, because in the template file I'm using the `include` directive, and this requires `filename`. I'm actually using the template filename and location, but you'll want to use any filename that returns a directory location relative to the files included in the Jade template.

As for the template itself, Example 9-2 has the contents of the Jade file. Note that I'm using the `include` directive to embed the CSS directly in the file. Since I'm not utilizing a static file server in this application, the application can't serve up the CSS file if I just embed a link to the CSS file. Also note the use of the pipe (|) with the `style` opening and ending tags, which are in HTML rather than Jade syntax. That's because Jade does not process the include file if it's listed within a `style` tag.

Example 9-2. Jade template file for displaying the five highest scores

```
doctype 5
html(lang="en")
  head
    title Zowie! Top Scores
    meta(charset="utf-8")
    | <style type="text/css">
    include main.css
    | </style>
  body
    table
      caption Zowie! Top Scorers!
        tr
```

```
th Score
th Name
th Date
if scores.length
  each score in scores
    if score
      tr
        td #{score.score}
        td #{score.first_name} #{score.last_name}
        td #{score.date}
```

To render the template, the application reads in the template file (using a synchronous file read, since this occurs only once, when the application is first started) and then uses it to compile a template function:

```
var layout = require('fs').readFileSync(__dirname + '/score.jade', 'utf8');
var fn = jade.compile(layout, {filename: __dirname + '/score.jade'});
```

The compiled Jade function can then be used anytime you want to render the HTML from the template, passing in whatever data the template is expecting:

```
var str = fn({scores : result});
res.end(str);
```

This will all make more sense when we see the complete server application, but for now, let's return to the Redis part of the application.

The top scores application is using two Redis calls: zrevrange to get a range of scores, and hgetall to get all the hash fields for each member listed in the top scores. And this is where things get a little tricky.

You can easily combine results from multiple tables when you're using a relational database, but the same doesn't hold true when you're accessing data from a key/value data store such as Redis. It's doable, but since this is a Node application, we have the extra complexity of each Redis call being asynchronous.

This is where a library such as Async comes in handy. I covered Async in Chapter 5, and demonstrated a couple of the Async methods (waterfall and parallel). One method I didn't demonstrate was series, which is the ideal function for our use here. The Redis functions need to be called in order, so the data is returned in order, but each interim step doesn't need the data from previous steps. The Async parallel functionality would run all the calls at once, which is fine, but then the results from each are returned in a random order—not guaranteed to return highest score first. The waterfall functionality isn't necessary, because again, each step doesn't need data from the previous step. The Async series functionality ensures that each Redis hgetall call is made in sequence and the data is returned in sequence, but takes into account that each functional step doesn't care about the others.

So we now have a way for the Redis commands to get called in order and ensure the data is returned in proper sequence, but the code to do so is clumsy: we have to add a separate step in the Async series for each hgetall Redis call and return the result once for each score returned. Working with 5 values isn't a problem, but what if we want to return 10? Or 100? Having to manually code each Redis call into the Async series is going to become more than tedious—the code is error prone and difficult to maintain.

What the scores application does is loop through the array of values returned from the `zrevrange` Redis call, passing each value as a parameter to a function named `makeCallbackFunc`. All this helper function does is return a callback function that invokes Redis `hgetall`, using the parameter to get the data for a specific member, and then call the callback function as the last line of its callback—an Async requirement for being able to chain results. The callback function returned from `makeCallbackFunc` is pushed onto an array, and it's this array that gets sent as a parameter to the Async `series` method. Additionally, since the redis module returns the `hgetall` result as an object, and the Async `series` function inserts each object into an array as it finishes, when all of this functionality is complete we can just take the final result and pass it into the template engine to generate the text to return to the server.

Example 9-3 is the complete code for the top scores server application. Though it sounds like a lot of work, there isn't that much code, thanks to the elegance and usability of both the Redis and Async modules.

Example 9-3. The game top score service

```
var http = require('http');
var async = require('async');
var redis = require('redis');
var jade = require('jade');

// set up Jade template
var layout = require('fs').readFileSync(__dirname + '/score.jade', 'utf8');
var fn = jade.compile(layout, {filename: __dirname + '/score.jade'});

// start Redis client
var client = redis.createClient();

// select fifth database
client.select(5);

// helper function
function makeCallbackFunc(member) {
   return function(callback) {
      client.hgetall(member, function(err, obj) {
         callback(err,obj);
      });
   };
}
http.createServer(function(req,res) {

   // first filter out icon request
   if (req.url === '/favicon.ico') {
      res.writeHead(200, {'Content-Type': 'image/x-icon'} );
      res.end();
      return;
```

```
    }
    // get scores, reverse order, top five only
    client.zrevrange('Zowie!',0,4, function(err,result) {
        var scores;
        if (err) {
            console.log(err);
            res.end('Top scores not currently available, please check back');
            return;
        }

        // create array of callback functions for Async.series call
        var callFunctions = new Array();

        // process results with makeCallbackFunc, push newly returned
        // callback into array
        for (var i = 0; i < result.length; i++) {
            callFunctions.push(makeCallbackFunc(result[i]));
        }

        // using Async series to process each callback in turn and return
        // end result as array of objects
        async.series(
            callFunctions,
            function (err, result) {
                if (err) {
                    console.log(err);
                    res.end('Scores not available');
                    return;
                }

                // pass object array to template engine
                var str = fn({scores : result});
                res.end(str);
            });
    });
}).listen(3000);

console.log('Server running on 3000/');
```

Before the HTTP server is created, we set up the Jade template function and also establish a running client to the Redis data store. When a new request is made of the server, we filter out all requests for the *favicon.ico* file (no need to call Redis for a *favicon.ico* request), and then access the top five scores using **zrevrange**. Once the application has the scores, it uses the Async **series** method to process the Redis hash requests one at a time and in sequence so it can get an ordered result back. This resulting array is passed to the Jade template engine.

Figure 9-1 shows the application after I've added in several different scores for different folks.

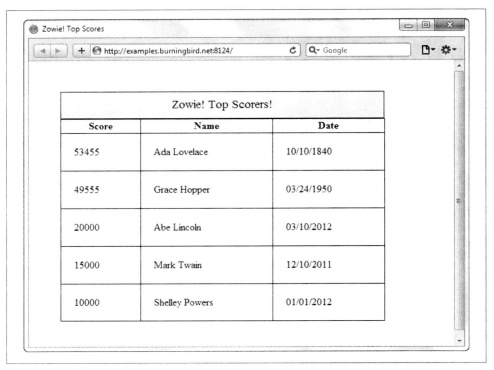

Figure 9-1. The Zowie! game top scorers

Creating a Message Queue

A *message queue* is an application that takes as input some form of communication, which is then stored into a queue. The messages are stored until they're retrieved by the message receiver, when they are popped off the queue and sent to the receiver (either one at a time, or in bulk). The communication is asynchronous, because the application that stores the messages doesn't require that the receiver be connected, and the receiver doesn't require that the message-storing application be connected.

Redis is an ideal storage medium for this type of application. As the messages are received by the application that stores them, they're pushed on to the end of the message queue. When the messages are retrieved by the application that receives them, they're popped off the front of the message queue.

For the message queue demonstration, I created a Node application to access the web logfiles for several different subdomains. The application uses a Node child process and the Unix `tail -f` command to access recent entries for the different logfiles. From these log entries, the application uses two regular expression objects: one to extract the resource accessed, and the second to test whether the resource is an image file. If the accessed resource is an image file, the application sends the resource URL in a TCP message to the message queue application.

All the message queue application does is listen for incoming messages on port 3000, and stores whatever is sent into a Redis data store.

The third part of the demonstration application is a web server that listens for requests on port 8124. With each request, it accesses the Redis database and pops off the front entry in the image data store, returning it via the response object. If the Redis database returns a null for the image resource, it prints out a message that the application has reached the end of the message queue.

The first part of the application, which processes the web log entries, is shown in Example 9-4. The Unix `tail` command is a way of displaying the last few lines of a text file (or piped data). When used with the `-f` flag, the utility displays a few lines of the file and then sits, listening for new file entries. When one occurs, it returns the new line. The `tail -f` command can be used on several different files at the same time, and manages the content by labeling where the data comes from each time it comes from a different source. The application isn't concerned about which access log is generating the latest tail response—it just wants the log entry.

Once the application has the log entry, it performs a couple of regular expression matches on the data to look for image resource access (files with a *.jpg*, *.gif*, *.svg*, or *.png* extension). If a pattern match is found, the application sends the resource URL to the message queue application (a TCP server).

Example 9-4. Node application that processes web log entries, and sends image resource requests to the message queue

```
var spawn = require('child_process').spawn;
var net = require('net');

var client = new net.Socket();
client.setEncoding('utf8');

// connect to TCP server
client.connect ('3000','examples.burningbird.net', function() {
    console.log('connected to server');
});

// start child process
var logs = spawn('tail', ['-f',
        '/home/main/logs/access.log',
        '/home/tech/logs/access.log',
        '/home/shelleypowers/logs/access.log',
        '/home/green/logs/access.log',
        '/home/puppies/logs/access.log']);

// process child process data
logs.stdout.setEncoding('utf8');
logs.stdout.on('data', function(data) {
```

```
    // resource URL
    var re = /GET\s(\S+)\sHTTP/g;

    // graphics test
    var re2 = /\.gif|\.png|\.jpg|\.svg/;

    // extract URL, test for graphics
    // store in Redis if found
    var parts = re.exec(data);
    console.log(parts[1]);
    var tst = re2.test(parts[1]);
    if (tst) {
       client.write(parts[1]);
    }
});
logs.stderr.on('data', function(data) {
   console.log('stderr: ' + data);
});

logs.on('exit', function(code) {
   console.log('child process exited with code ' + code);
   client.end();
});
```

Typical console log entries for this application are given in the following block of code, with the entries of interest (the image file accesses) in bold:

```
/robots.txt
/weblog
/writings/fiction?page=10
/images/kite.jpg
/node/145
/culture/book-reviews/silkworm
/feed/atom/
/images/visitmologo.jpg
/images/canvas.png
/sites/default/files/paws.png
/feeds/atom.xml
```

Example 9-5 contains the code for the message queue. It's a simple application that starts a TCP server and listens for incoming messages. When it receives a message, it extracts the data from the message and stores it in the Redis database. The application uses the Redis **rpush** command to push the data on the end of the images list (bolded in the code).

Example 9-5. Message queue that takes incoming messages and pushes them onto a Redis list

```
var net = require('net');
var redis = require('redis');

var server = net.createServer(function(conn) {
   console.log('connected');

   // create Redis client
   var client = redis.createClient();
```

```
  client.on('error', function(err) {
    console.log('Error ' + err);
  });

  // sixth database is image queue
  client.select(6);
  // listen for incoming data
  conn.on('data', function(data) {
      console.log(data + ' from ' + conn.remoteAddress + ' ' +
        conn.remotePort);

      // store data
      client.rpush('images',data);
  });

}).listen(3000);
server.on('close', function(err) {
   client.quit();
});

console.log('listening on port 3000');
```

The message queue application console log entries would typically look like the following:

```
listening on port 3000
connected
/images/venus.png from 173.255.206.103 39519
/images/kite.jpg from 173.255.206.103 39519
/images/visitmologo.jpg from 173.255.206.103 39519
/images/canvas.png from 173.255.206.103 39519
/sites/default/files/paws.png from 173.255.206.103 39519
```

The last piece of the message queue demonstration application is the HTTP server that listens on port 8124 for requests, shown in Example 9-6. As the HTTP server receives each request, it accesses the Redis database, pops off the next entry in the images list, and prints out the entry in the response. If there are no more entries in the list (i.e., if Redis returns null as a reply), it prints out a message that the message queue is empty.

Example 9-6. HTTP server that pops off messages from the Redis list and returns to the user

```
var redis = require("redis"),
    http = require('http');

var messageServer = http.createServer();

// listen for incoming request
messageServer.on('request', function (req, res) {

   // first filter out icon request
   if (req.url === '/favicon.ico') {
      res.writeHead(200, {'Content-Type': 'image/x-icon'} );
      res.end();
      return;
```

```
  }

  // create Redis client
  var client = redis.createClient();


  client.on('error', function (err) {
    console.log('Error ' + err);
  });

  // set database to 1
  client.select(6);

   client.lpop('images', function(err, reply) {
      if(err) {
        return console.error('error response ' + err);
      }

      // if data
      if (reply) {
         res.write(reply + '\n');
      } else {
         res.write('End of queue\n');
      }
      res.end();
   });
   client.quit();

});

messageServer.listen(8124);

console.log('listening on 8124');
```

Accessing the HTTP server application with a web browser returns a URL for the image
resource on each request (browser refresh) until the message queue is empty.

When to Create the Redis Client

In the chapter examples, sometimes I create a Redis client and persist it for the life of
the application, while other times I create a Redis client and release it as soon as the
Redis command is finished. So when is it better to create a persistent Redis connection
versus create a connection and release it immediately?

Good question.

To test the impact of the two different approaches, I created a TCP server that listened
for requests and stored a simple hash in the Redis database. I then created another
application, as a TCP client, that did nothing more than send an object in a TCP message to the server.

I used the ApacheBench application to run several concurrent iterations of the client
and tested how long it took for each run. I ran the first batch with the Redis client

---

connection persisted for the life of the server, and ran the second batch where the client connection was created for each request and immediately released.

What I expected to find was that the application that persisted the client connection was faster, and I was right...to a point. About halfway through the test with the persistent connection, the application slowed down dramatically for a brief period of time, and then resumed its relatively fast pace.

Of course, what most likely happened is that the queued requests for the Redis database eventually blocked the Node application, at least temporarily, until the queue was freed up. I didn't run into this same situation when opening and closing the connections with each request, because the extra overhead required for this process slowed the application just enough so that it didn't hit the upper end of concurrent users.

I'll have more on this test, as well as other tests with ApacheBench and other performance and debugging tools, in Chapter 14 and Chapter 16.

Adding a Stats Middleware to an Express Application

The creator of Redis originally intended to use the technology to create a statistics application. It's an ideal use for Redis: a simple data store, quickly and frequently written, and providing the ability to summarize an activity.

In this section, we're going to use Redis to add statistics for the widget application we started in earlier chapters. The statistics are limited to two collections: a set of all IP addresses that have accessed pages from the widget application, and the number of times different resources have been accessed. To create this functionality, we make use of a Redis *set* and the ability to increment numeric strings. Our application also uses the Redis transaction control, *multi*, to get the two separate data collections at the same time.

The first step of the application is to add new middleware that records access information to the Redis database. The middleware function uses a Redis set and the `sadd` method to add each IP address, because a set ensures that an existing value isn't recorded twice. We're collecting a set of IP addresses for visitors, but we're not keeping track of each time the visitor accesses a resource. The function is also using one of the Redis incremental functions, but not `incr`, which increments a string; instead, it uses `hincrby`, because the resource URL and its associated access counter are stored as a hash.

Example 9-7 displays the code for the middleware, located in a file named *stats.js*. The second Redis database is used for the application, the IPs are stored in a set identified by `ip`, and the URL/access counter hash is stored in a hash identified by `myurls`.

Example 9-7. The Redis stats middleware

```
var redis = require('redis');
```

```
module.exports = function getStats() {

    return function getStats(req, res, next) {
        // create Redis client
        var client = redis.createClient();

        client.on('error', function (err) {
            console.log('Error ' + err);
        });

        // set database to 2
        client.select(2);

        // add IP to set
        client.sadd('ip',req.socket.remoteAddress);

        // increment resource count
        client.hincrby('myurls',req.url, 1);

      client.quit();
      next();
    }
}
```

The statistics interface is accessed at the top-level domain, so we'll add the code for the router to the *index.js* file in the *routes* subdirectory.

First, we need to add the route to the main application file, just after the route for the top-level index:

```
app.get('/', routes.index);

app.get('/stats',routes.stats);
```

The controller code for the statistic application makes use of the Redis transaction control, accessible via the `multi` function call. Two sets of data are accessed: the set of unique IP addresses, returned by `smembers`, and the URL/count hash, returned with `hgetall`. Both functions are invoked, in sequence, when the `exec` method is called, and both sets of returned data are appended as array elements in the `exec` function's callback method, as shown in Example 9-8. Once the data is retrieved, it's passed in a `render` call to a new view, named `stats`. The new functionality for the *index.js* file appears in bold text.

Example 9-8. The routes index file with the new controller code for the statistics application

```
var redis = require('redis');

// home page
exports.index = function(req, res){
  res.render('index', { title: 'Express' });
};


// stats
```

```
exports.stats = function(req, res){

    var client = redis.createClient();

    client.select(2);

    // Redis transaction to gather data
    client.multi()
    .smembers('ip')
    .hgetall('myurls')
    .exec(function(err, results) {
        var ips = results[0];
        var urls = results[1];
        res.render('stats',{ title: 'Stats', ips : ips, urls : urls});
        client.quit();
    });
};
```

I mentioned that `multi` and `exec` are Redis transaction control commands. These aren't the same type of transaction controls you're probably used to with a relational database. All the `multi` command does is collect a set of Redis commands that are then processed sequentially when the `exec` command is given. This type of functionality is useful in the Node world because it provides a way of getting multiple collections of data that are all returned at the exact same time—no need for nested callback functions or having to use something like Step or Async to get all the data at once.

Having said that, don't let the fact that the Redis commands are seemingly chained together fool you into thinking that the data from one command is then available in the next, as can happen with JavaScript functions that are chained together. Each Redis command is processed in isolation, and the data is just added as an array element in the result, and everything is returned at once.

There's no locking the data down during the transaction, either, as you'd also expect with a relational database transaction. So any changes to the Redis database during the query can impact the results.

The last piece of the application is the view, created as a Jade template. The template is very simple: the IP addresses displayed in an unordered list, and the URL/counter statistics displayed in a table. The Jade `for...in` syntax is used to loop through the IP array, while the `each...in` syntax is used to access the property names and values of the object that's returned with the Redis `hgetall`. The template is shown in Example 9-9.

Example 9-9. The Jade template for the stats application

```
extends layout

block content
  h1= title

  h2 Visitor IP Addresses
  ul
    for ip in ips
      li=ip

  table
    caption Page Visits
    each val, key in urls
      tr
        td #{key}
        td #{val}
```

Figure 9-2 shows the statistics page after several widget application resource pages have been accessed from a couple of different IP addresses.

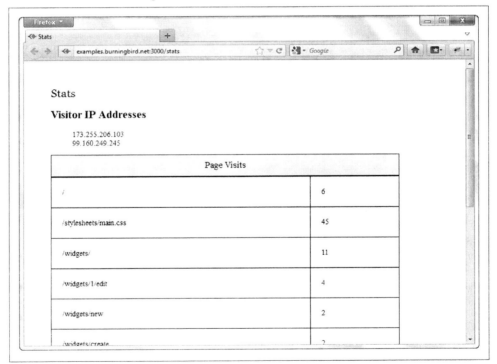

Figure 9-2. The statistics page enabled by Redis

We don't have to first create the hash when using `hincrby`. If the hash key doesn't exist, Redis creates it automatically and sets the value to `0` before the value is incremented.

The only time the functionality fails is if the field already exists and the value in the field isn't a numeric string (i.e., can't be incremented).

Another approach to incrementing a counter for each resource is to use Redis strings, and set the resource URL to be the key:

```
client.incr(url);
```

However, this approach means we would have to get all the keys (the URLs), and then get the counters for each URL. We can't necessarily accomplish all of this using `multi`, and because of the asynchronous nature of accessing the data, we'd end up having to use nested callbacks or some other approach to pull all this data together.

There's no need to go through all of that extra effort when we have built-in functionality via the Redis hash and the `hincrby` command.

CHAPTER 10

Node and MongoDB: Document-Centric Data

Chapter 9 covered one popular NoSQL database structure (key/value pairs via Redis), and this chapter covers another: document-centric data stores via MongoDB.

Where MongoDB differs from relational database systems, such as MySQL, is in its support for storing structured data as documents, rather than implementing the more traditional tables. These documents are encoded as BSON, a binary form of JSON, which probably explains its popularity among JavaScript developers. Instead of a table row, you have a BSON document; instead of a table, you have a collection.

MongoDB isn't the only document-centric database. Other popular versions of this type of data store are CouchDB by Apache, SimpleDB by Amazon, RavenDB, and even the venerable Lotus Notes. There is some Node support of varying degrees for most modern document data stores, but MongoDB and CouchDB have the most. I decided to cover MongoDB rather CouchDB for the same reasons I picked Express over other frameworks: I feel it's easier for a person with no exposure to the secondary technology (in this case, the data store) to be able to grasp the Node examples without having to focus overmuch on the non-Node technology. With MongoDB, we can query the data directly, whereas with CouchDB, we work with the concept of views. This higher level of abstraction does require more up-front time. In my opinion, you can hit the ground running faster with MongoDB than CouchDB.

There are several modules that work with MongoDB, but I'm going to focus on two: the MongoDB Native Node.js Driver (a driver written in JavaScript), and Mongoose, an object modeling tool providing ORM (object-relational mapping) support.

 Though I won't get into too many details in this chapter about how MongoDB works, you should be able to follow the examples even if you have not worked with the database system previously. There's more on MongoDB, including installation help, at *http://www.mongodb.org/*.

The MongoDB Native Node.js Driver

The MongoDB Native Node.js Driver module is a native MongoDB driver for Node. Using it to issue MongoDB instructions is little different from issuing these same instructions into the MongoDB client interface.

 The node-mongodb-native GitHub page is at *https://github.com/mongodb/node-mongodb-native*, and documentation is at *http://mongodb.github.com/node-mongodb-native/*.

After you have installed MongoDB (following the instructions outlined at the MongoDB website) and started a database, install the MongoDB Native Node.js Driver with npm:

```
npm install mongodb
```

Before trying out any of the examples in the next several sections, make sure MongoDB is installed locally, and is running.

 If you're already using MongoDB, make sure to back up your data before trying out the examples in this chapter.

Getting Started with MongoDB

To use the MongoDB driver, you first have to require the module:

```
var mongodb = require('mongodb');
```

To establish a connection to MongoDB, use the `mongodb.Server` object constructor:

```
var server = new mongodb.Server('localhost',:27017, {auto_reconnect: true});
```

All communication with the MongoDB occurs over TCP. The server constructor accepts the host and port as the first two parameters—in this case, the default `localhost` and port `27017`. The third parameter is a set of options. In the code, the `auto_reconnect` option is set to `true`, which means the driver attempts to reestablish a connection if it's lost. Another option is `poolSize`, which determines how many TCP connections are maintained in parallel.

 MongoDB uses one thread per connection, which is why the database creators recommend that developers use connection pooling.

Once you have a connection to MongoDB, you can create a database or connect to an existing one. To create a database, use the `mongodb.Db` object constructor:

```
var db = new mongdb.Db('mydb', server);
```

The first parameter is the database name, and the second is the MongoDB server connection. A third parameter is an object with a set of options. The default option values are sufficient for the work we're doing in this chapter, and the MongoDB driver documentation covers the different values, so I'll skip repeating them in this chapter.

If you've not worked with MongoDB in the past, you may notice that the code doesn't have to provide username and password authentication. By default, MongoDB runs without authentication. When authentication isn't enabled, the database has to run in a trusted environment. This means that MongoDB allows connections only from trusted hosts, typically only the localhost address.

Defining, Creating, and Dropping a MongoDB Collection

MongoDB collections are fundamentally equivalent to relational database tables, but without anything that even closely resembles a relational database table.

When you define a MongoDB collection, you can specify if you want a collection object to actually be created at that time, or only after the first row is added. Using the MongoDB driver, the following code demonstrates the difference between the two; the first statement doesn't create the actual collection, and the second does:

```
db.collection('mycollection', function(err, collection{});
db.createCollection('mycollection', function(err, collection{});
```

You can pass an optional second parameter to both methods, `{safe : true}`, which instructs the driver to issue an error if the collection does not exist when used with `db.collection`, and an error if the collection already exists if used with `db.createCollection`:

```
db.collection('mycollection', {safe : true}, function (err, collection{});
db.createCollection('mycollection', {safe : true}, function(err, collection{});
```

If you use `db.createCollection` on an existing collection, you'll just get access to the collection—the driver won't overwrite it. Both methods return a collection object in the callback function, which you can then use to add, modify, or retrieve document data.

If you want to completely drop the collection, use `db.dropCollection`:

```
db.dropCollection('mycollection', function(err, result){});
```

Note that all of these methods are asynchronous, and are dependent on nested callbacks if you want to process the commands sequentially. This is demonstrated more fully in the next section, where we'll add data to a collection.

Adding Data to a Collection

Before getting into the mechanics of adding data to a collection, and looking at fully operational examples, I want to take a moment to discuss data types. More specifically, I want to repeat what the MongoDB driver mentions about data types, because the use of JavaScript has led to some interesting negotiations between the driver and the MongoDB.

Table 10-1 shows the conversions between the data types supported by MongoDB and their JavaScript equivalents. Note that most conversions occur cleanly—no potentially unexpected effects. Some, though, do require some behind-the-scenes finagling that you should be aware of. Additionally, some data types are provided by the MongoDB Native Node.js Driver, but don't have an equivalent value in MongoDB. The driver converts the data we provide into data the MongoDB can accept.

Table 10-1. Node.js MongoDB driver to MongoDB data type mapping

MongoDB type	JavaScript type	Notes/examples
JSON array	Array [1,2,3]	[1,2,3].
string	String	utf8 encoded.
boolean	Boolean	true or false.
integer	Number	MongoDB supports 32- and 64-bit numbers; JavaScript numbers are 64-bit floats. The MongoDB driver attempts to fit the value into 32 bits; if it fails, it promotes to 64 bits; if this fails, it promotes to the Long class.
integer	Long class	The Long class provides full 64-bit integer support.
float	Number	
float	Double class	Special class representing a float value.
Date	Date	
Regular expression	RegExp	
null	null	
Object	Object	
Object id	ObjectID class	Special class that holds a MongoDB document identifier.
Binary data	Binary class	Class to store binary data.
	Code class	Class to store the JavaScript function and score for the method to run in.
	DbRef class	Class to store reference to another document.
	Symbol class	Specify a symbol (not specific to JavaScript, for languages that use symbols).

Once you have a reference to a collection, you can add documents to it. The data is structured as JSON, so you can create a JSON object and then insert it directly into the collection.

To demonstrate all of the code to this point, in addition to adding data to a collection, Example 10-1 creates a first collection (named `Widgets`) in MongoDB and then adds two documents. Since you might want to run the example a couple of times, it first removes the collection documents using the `remove` method. The `remove` method takes three optional parameters:

- Selector for the document(s); if none is provided, all documents are removed
- An optional safe mode indicator, `safe {true | {w:n, wtimeout:n} | {fsync:true}, default:false}`
- A callback function (required if safe mode indicator is set to `true`)

In the example, the application is using a safe remove, passing in `null` for the first parameter (as a parameter placeholder, ensuring that all documents are removed) and providing a callback function. Once the documents are removed, the application inserts two new documents, with the second insert using safe mode. The application prints to the console the result of the second insert.

The `insert` method also takes three parameters: the document or documents being inserted, an options parameter, and the callback function. You can insert multiple documents by enclosing them in an array. The options for `insert` are:

Safe mode
> `safe {true | {w:n, wtimeout:n} | {fsync:true}, default:false}`

`keepGoing`
> Set to `true` to have application continue if one of the documents generates an error

`serializeFunctions`
> Serialize functions on the document

The method calls are asynchronous, which means there's no guarantee that the first document is inserted before the second. However, it shouldn't be a problem with the widget application—at least not in this example. Later in the chapter, we'll look more closely at some of the challenges of working asynchronously with database applications.

Example 10-1. Creating/opening a database, removing all documents, and adding two new documents

```
var mongodb = require('mongodb');

var server = new mongodb.Server('localhost', 27017, {auto_reconnect: true});
var db = new mongodb.Db('exampleDb', server);

// open database connection
db.open(function(err, db) {
  if(!err) {

    // access or create widgets collection
    db.collection('widgets', function(err, collection) {

      // remove all widgets documents
```

```
collection.remove(null,{safe : true}, function(err, result) {
    if (!err) {
      console.log('result of remove ' + result);

      // create two records
      var widget1 = {title : 'First Great widget',
                     desc : 'greatest widget of all',
                     price : 14.99};
      var widget2 = {title : 'Second Great widget',
                     desc : 'second greatest widget of all',
                     price : 29.99};

      collection.insert(widget1);

      collection.insert(widget2, {safe : true}, function(err, result) {
        if(err) {
           console.log(err);
        } else {
           console.log(result);

           //close database
           db.close();
        }
      });
    }
  });
 });
  }
});
```

The output to the console after the second insert is a variation on:

```
[ { title: 'Second Great widget',
    desc: 'second greatest widget of all',
    price: 29.99,
    _id: 4fc108e2f6b7a3e252000002 } ]
```

The MongoDB generates a unique system identifier for each document. You can access documents with this identifier at a future time, but you're better off adding a more meaningful identifier—one that can be determined easily by context of use—for each document.

As mentioned earlier, we can insert multiple documents at the same time by providing an array of documents rather than a single document. The following code demonstrates how both widget records can be inserted in the same command. The code also incorporates an application identifier with the id field:

```
// create two records
var widget1 = {id: 1, title : 'First Great widget',
               desc : 'greatest widget of all',
               price : 14.99};
var widget2 = {id: 2, title : 'Second Great widget',
               desc : 'second greatest widget of all',
               price : 29.99};
```

```
       collection.insert([widget1,widget2], {safe : true},
                                          function(err, result) {
           if(err) {
             console.log(err);
           } else {
             console.log(result);

             // close database
             db.close();
           }
       });
```

If you do batch your document inserts, you'll need to set the keepGoing option to true to be able to keep inserting documents even if one of the insertions fails. By default, the application stops if an insert fails.

Querying the Data

There are four methods of finding data in the MongoDB Native Node.js Driver:

find
> Returns a cursor with all the documents returned by the query

findOne
> Returns a cursor with the first document found that matches the query

findAndRemove
> Finds a document and then removes it

findAndModify
> Finds a document and then performs an action (such as remove or upsert)

In this section, I'll demonstrate collection.find and collection.findOne, and reserve the other two methods for the next section, "Using Updates, Upserts, and Find and Remove" on page 217.

Both collection.find and collection.findOne support three arguments: the query, options, and a callback. The options object and the callback are optional, and the list of possible options to use with both methods is quite extensive. Table 10-2 shows all the options, their default setting, and a description of each.

Table 10-2. Find options

Option	Default value	Description
limit	Number, default of 0	Limits the number of documents returned (0 is no limit).
sort	Array of indexes	Set to sort the documents returning from query.
fields	Object	Fields to return in the query. Use the property name and a value of 1 to include, or 0 to exclude; that is, { 'prop' : 1} or { 'prop' : 0}, but not both.
skip	Number, default of 0	Skip *n* documents (useful for pagination).
hint	Object	Tell the database to use specific indexes, {'_id' : 1}.

Option	Default value	Description
explain	Boolean, default is false	Explain the query instead of returning data.
snapshot	Boolean, default is false	Snapshot query (MongoDB *journaling* must be enabled).
timeout	Boolean, default is false	Cursor can time out.
tailable	Boolean, default is false	Cursor is *tailable* (only on capped collections, allowing resumption of retrieval, similar to Unix tail command).
batchSize	Number, default is 0	batchSize for the getMoreCommand when iterating over results.
returnKey	Boolean, default is false	Only return the index key.
maxScan	Number	Limit the number of items that can be scanned.
min	Number	Set index bounds.
max	Number	Set index bounds.
showDiskLoc	Boolean, default is false	Show the disk location of results.
comment	String	Add a comment to the query for profiler logs.
raw	Boolean, default is false	Return BSON results as raw buffer documents.
read	Boolean, default is false	Direct the query to a secondary server.

The options allow for a great deal of flexibility with queries, though most queries will most likely need only a few of them. I'll cover some of the options in the examples, but I recommend you try the others with your example MongoDB installation.

The simplest query for all documents in the collection is to use the find method without any parameters. You immediately convert the results to an array using **toArray**, passing in a callback function that takes an error and an array of documents. Example 10-2 shows the application that performs this functionality.

Example 10-2. Inserting four documents and then retrieving them with the find method

```
var mongodb = require('mongodb');

var server = new mongodb.Server('localhost', 27017, {auto_reconnect: true});
var db = new mongodb.Db('exampleDb', server);

// open database connection
db.open(function(err, db) {
  if(!err) {

    // access or create widgets collection
    db.collection('widgets', function(err, collection) {

      // remove all widgets documents
      collection.remove(null,{safe : true}, function(err, result) {
        if (!err) {
          // create four records
          var widget1 = {id: 1, title : 'First Great widget',
                    desc : 'greatest widget of all',
                    price : 14.99, type: 'A'};
```

```
        var widget2 = {id: 2, title : 'Second Great widget',
                    desc : 'second greatest widget of all',
                    price : 29.99, type: 'A'};
        var widget3 = {id: 3, title: 'third widget', desc: 'third widget',
                    price : 45.00, type: 'B'};
        var widget4 = {id: 4, title: 'fourth widget', desc: 'fourth widget',
                    price: 60.00, type: 'B'};

        collection.insert([widget1,widget2,widget3,widget4], {safe : true},
                                            function(err, result) {
            if(err) {
              console.log(err);
            } else {

              // return all documents
              collection.find().toArray(function(err, docs) {
                console.log(docs);

                //close database
                db.close();
              });
            }
          });
        }
      });
    });
  }
});
```

The result printed out to the console shows all four newly added documents, with their system-generated identifiers:

```
[ { id: 1,
    title: 'First Great widget',
    desc: 'greatest widget of all',
    price: 14.99,
    type: 'A',
    _id: 4fc109ab0481b9f652000001 },
  { id: 2,
    title: 'Second Great widget',
    desc: 'second greatest widget of all',
    price: 29.99,
    type: 'A',
    _id: 4fc109ab0481b9f652000002 },
  { id: 3,
    title: 'third widget',
    desc: 'third widget',
    price: 45,
    type: 'B',
    _id: 4fc109ab0481b9f652000003 },
  { id: 4,
    title: 'fourth widget',
    desc: 'fourth widget',
    price: 60,
```

```
        type: 'B',
        _id: 4fc109ab0481b9f652000004 } ]
```

Rather than return all of the documents, we can provide a selector. In the following code, we're querying all documents that have a type of A, and returning all the fields but the type field:

```
// return all documents
collection.find({type:'A'},{fields:{type:0}}).toArray(function(err, docs) {
    if(err) {
      console.log(err);
    } else {
      console.log(docs);

      //close database
      db.close();
    }
});
```

The result of this query is:

```
[ { id: 1,
    title: 'First Great widget',
    desc: 'greatest widget of all',
    price: 14.99,
    _id: 4f7ba035c4d2204c49000001 },
  { id: 2,
    title: 'Second Great widget',
    desc: 'second greatest widget of all',
    price: 29.99,
    _id: 4f7ba035c4d2204c49000002 } ]
```

We can also access only one document using findOne. The result of this query does not have to be converted to an array, and can be accessed directly. In the following, the document with an ID of 1 is queried, and only the title is returned:

```
// return one document
collection.findOne({id:1},{fields:{title:1}}, function(err, doc) {
    if (err) {
      console.log(err);
    } else {
      console.log(doc);

      //close database
      db.close();
    }
});
```

The result from this query is:

```
{ title: 'First Great widget', _id: 4f7ba0fcbfede06649000001 }
```

The system-generated identifier is always returned with the query results.

Even if I modified the query to return all documents with a type of A (there are two), only one is returned with the collection.findOne method. Changing the limit in the options object won't make a difference: the method always returns one document if the query is successful.

Using Updates, Upserts, and Find and Remove

The MongoDB Native Node.js Driver supports several different methods that either modify or remove an existing document—or both, in the case of one method:

update
: Either updates or *upserts* (adds if doesn't exist) a document

remove
: Removes a document

findAndModify
: Finds and modifies or removes a document (returning the modified or removed document)

findAndRemove
: Finds and removes a document (returning the removed document)

The basic difference between update/remove and findAndModify/findAndRemove is that the latter set of methods returns the affected document.

The functionality to use these methods is not very different from what we saw with the inserts. You'll have to open a database connection, get a reference to the collection you're interested in, and then perform the operations.

If the MongoDB currently contains the following document:

```
{ id : 4,
   title: 'fourth widget',
   desc: 'fourth widget'.
   price: 60.00,
   type: 'B'}
```

and you want to modify the title, you can use the update method to do so, as shown in Example 10-3. You can supply all of the fields, and MongoDB does a replacement of the document, but you're better off using one of the MongoDB modifiers, such as $set. The $set modifier instructs the database to just modify whatever fields are passed as properties to the modifier.

Example 10-3. Updating a MongoDB document

```
var mongodb = require('mongodb');

var server = new mongodb.Server('localhost', 27017, {auto_reconnect: true});
var db = new mongodb.Db('exampleDb', server);

// open database connection
db.open(function(err, db) {
  if(!err) {
```

```
    // access or create widgets collection
    db.collection('widgets',function(err, collection) {

        //update
        collection.update({id:4},
          {$set : {title: 'Super Bad Widget'}},
            {safe: true}, function(err, result) {
          if (err) {
            console.log(err);
          } else {
            console.log(result);
            // query for updated record
            collection.findOne({id:4}, function(err, doc) {
                if(!err) {
                    console.log(doc);

                    //close database
                    db.close();
                }
            });
          }
        });
    });
});
```

The resulting document now displays the modified fields.

 You can use $set with multiple fields.

There are additional modifiers that provide other atomic data updates of interest:

$inc
    Increments a field's value by a specified amount

$set
    Sets a field, as demonstrated

$unset
    Deletes a field

$push
    Appends a value to the array if the field is an array (converts it to an array if it wasn't)

$pushAll
    Appends several values to an array

$addToSet
    Adds to an array only if the field is an array

$pull
Removes a value from an array

$pullAll
Removes several values from an array

$rename
Renames a field

$bit
Performs a bitwise operation

So why don't we just remove the document and insert a new one, rather than use a modifier? Because although we had to provide all of the user-defined fields, we don't have to provide the system-generated identifier. This value remains constant with the update. If the system-generated identifier is stored as a field in another document, say a parent document, removing the document will leave the reference to the original document orphaned in the parent.

 Though I don't cover the concept of trees (complex parent/child data structures) in this chapter, the MongoDB website has documentation on them.

More importantly, the use of modifiers ensures that the action is performed *in place*, providing some assurance that one person's update won't overwrite another's.

Though we used none in the example, the `update` method takes four options:

- `safe` for a safe update
- `upsert`, a Boolean set to `true` if an insert should be made if the document doesn't exist (default is `false`)
- `multi`, a Boolean set to `true` if all documents that match the selection criteria should be updated
- `serializeFunction` to serialize functions on the document

If you're unsure whether a document already exists in the database, set the `upsert` option to `true`.

Example 10-3 did a find on the modified record to ensure that the changes took effect. A better approach would be to use `findAndModify`. The parameters are close to what's used with the update, with the addition of a sort array as the second parameter. If multiple documents are returned, updates are performed in sort order:

```
//update
collection.findAndModify({id:4}, [[ti]],
  {$set : {title: 'Super Widget', desc: 'A really great widget'}},
    {new: true}, function(err, doc) {
    if (err) {
```

```
      console.log(err);
    } else {
      console.log(doc);DB
    }
    db.close();
});
```

You can use the `findAndModify` method to remove a document if you use the `remove` option. If you do, no document is returned in the callback function. You can also use the `remove` and the `findAndRemove` methods to remove the document. Earlier examples have used `remove`, without a selector, to remove all the documents before doing an insert. To remove an individual document, provide a selector:

```
collection.remove({id:4},
    {safe: true}, function(err, result) {
  if (err) {
    console.log(err);
  } else {
    console.log(result);
  }
}
```

The result is the number of documents removed (in this case, 1). To see the document being removed, use `findAndRemove`:

```
collection.findAndRemove({id:3}, [['id',1]],
    function(err, doc) {
  if (err) {
    console.log(err);
  } else {
    console.log(doc);
  }
}
```

I've covered the basic CRUD (create, read, update, delete) operations you can perform from a Node application with the Native driver, but there are considerably more capabilities, including working with capped collections, indexes, and the other MongoDB modifiers; sharding (partitioning data across machines); and more. The Native driver documentation covers all of these and provides good examples.

The examples demonstrate some of the challenges associated with handling data access in an asynchronous environment, discussed more fully in the sidebar "Challenges of Asynchronous Data Access" on page 220.

Challenges of Asynchronous Data Access

One of the challenges with asynchronous development and data access is the level of nesting necessary to ensure that one operation is finished before another is started. In the last several sections, you had a chance to see how quickly the callback functions nest, just by performing a few simple operations—access the MongoDB, get a reference to a collection, perform an operation, and verify that it took place.

The MongoDB Native Node.js Driver documentation contains instances where the example developers used a timer to make sure a previous function was finished before performing the next. You're not going to want to use this approach. To avoid the problems with heavily nested callback functions, you can use either named functions, or one of the asynchronous modules, such as Step and Async.

The best approach of all is to ensure that you're doing the minimum functionality necessary in each method that's updating the MongoDB database. If you're having a hard time preventing nested callbacks and the application is difficult to convert using a module like Async, chances are, you are doing too much. In that case, you need to look for opportunities to break down a complex multiple database operation function into manageable units.

Asynchronous programming rewards simplicity.

Implementing a Widget Model with Mongoose

The MongoDB Native Node.js Driver provides a binding to the MongoDB, but doesn't provide a higher-level abstraction. For this, you'll need to use an ODM (object-document mapping) like Mongoose.

 The Mongoose website is at *http://mongoosejs.com/*.

To use Mongoose, install it with npm:

```
npm install mongoose
```

Instead of issuing commands directly against a MongoDB database, you define objects using the Mongoose `Schema` object, and then sync it with the database using the Mongoose `model` object:

```
var Widget = new Schema({
  sn : {type: String, require: true, trim: true, unique: true},
  name : {type: String, required: true, trim: true},
  desc : String,
  price : Number
});

var widget = mongoose.model('Widget', Widget);
```

When we define the object, we provide information that controls what happens to that document field at a later time. In the code just provided, we define a `Widget` object with four explicit fields: three of type `String`, and one of type `Number`. The `sn` and `name` fields are both required and trimmed, and the `sn` field must be unique in the document database.

The collection isn't made at this point, and won't be until at least one document is created. When we do create it, though, it's named `widgets`—the widget object name is lowercased and pluralized.

Anytime you need to access the collection, you make the same call to the `mongoose.model`.

This code is the first step in adding the final component to the Model-View-Controller (MVC) widget implementation started in earlier chapters. In the next couple of sections, we'll finish the conversion from an in-memory data store to MongoDB. First, though, we need to do a little refactoring on the widget application.

Refactoring the Widget Factory

Refactoring is the process of restructuring existing code in such a way as to clean up the cruft behind the scenes with minimal or no impact on the user interface. Since we're converting the widget application over to a MongoDB database, now is a good time to see what other changes we want to make.

Currently, the filesystem structure for the widget application is:

```
/application directory
    /routes - home directory controller
    /controllers - object controllers
    /public - static files
        /widgets
    /views - template files
        /widgets
```

The *routes* subdirectory provides top-level (non-business-object) functionality. The name isn't very meaningful, so I renamed it to *main*. This necessitated some minor modifications to the primary *app.js* file as follows:

```
// top level
app.get('/', main.index);

app.get('/stats', main.stats);
```

Next, I added a new subdirectory named *models*. The MongoDB model definitions are stored in this subdirectory, as the controller code is in the *controllers* subdirectory. The directory structure now looks like the following:

```
/application directory
    /main - home directory controller
    /controllers - object controllers
    /public - static files
        /widgets
    /views - template files
        /widgets
```

The next change to the application is related to the structure of the data. Currently, the application's primary key is an ID field, system-generated but accessible by the user via the routing system. To show a widget, you'd use a URL like the following:

http://localhost:3000/widgets/1

This isn't an uncommon approach. Drupal, a popular content management system (CMS), uses this approach for accessing Drupal nodes (stories) and users, unless a person uses a URL redirection module:

http://burningbird.net/node/78

The problem is that MongoDB generates an identifier for each object, and uses a format that makes it unattractive for routing. There is a workaround—which requires creating a third collection that contains an identifier, and then using it to take the place of the identifier—but the approach is ugly, counter to MongoDB's underlying structure, and not especially doable with Mongoose.

The widget `title` field is unique, but has spaces and characters that make it unattractive as a routing URL. Instead, we define a new field, `sn`, which is the new serial number for the product. When a new widget object is created, the user assigns whatever serial number she wants for the product, and the serial number is used when we access the widget at a later time. If the widget serial number is `1A1A`, for example, it's accessed with:

http://localhost:3000/widgets/1A1A

The new data structure, from an application point of view, is:

```
sn: string
title: string
desc: string
price: number
```

This modification necessitates some changes to the user interface, but they're worthwhile. The Jade templates also need to be changed, but the change is minor: basically replacing references to `id` with references to `sn`, and adding a field for serial number to any form.

 Rather than duplicate all the code again to show minor changes, I've made the examples available at O'Reilly's catalog page for this book (*http://oreilly.com/catalog/9781449323073*); you'll find all of the new widget application files in the *chap12* subdirectory.

The more significant change is to the controller code in the *widget.js* file. The changes to this file, and others related to adding a MongoDB backend, are covered in the next section.

Adding the MongoDB Backend

The first necessary change is to add a connection to the MongoDB database. It's added to the primary *app.js* file, so the connection persists for the life of the application.

First, Mongoose is included into the file:

```
var mongoose = require('mongoose');
```

Then the database connection is made:

```
// MongoDB
mongoose.connect('mongodb://127.0.0.1/WidgetDB');

mongoose.connection.on('open', function() {
    console.log('Connected to Mongoose');
});
```

Notice the URI for the MongoDB. The specific database is passed as the last part of the URI.

This change and the aforementioned change converting *routes* to *main* are all the changes necessary for *app.js*.

The next change is to *maproutecontroller.js*. The routes that reference id must be changed to now reference sn. The modified routes are shown in the following code block:

```
// show
app.get(prefix + '/:sn', prefixObj.show);

// edit
app.get(prefix + '/:sn/edit', prefixObj.edit);

// update
app.put(prefix + '/:sn', prefixObj.update);

// destroy
app.del(prefix + '/:sn', prefixObj.destroy);
```

If we don't make this change, the controller code expects sn as a parameter but gets id instead.

The next code is an addition, not a modification. In the *models* subdirectory, a new file is created, named *widgets.js*. This is where the widget model is defined. To make the model accessible outside the file, it's exported, as shown in Example 10-4.

Example 10-4. The new widget model definition

```
var mongoose = require('mongoose');

var Schema = mongoose.Schema
    ,ObjectId = Schema.ObjectId;

// create Widget model
var Widget = new Schema({
  sn : {type: String, require: true, trim: true, unique: true},
  name : {type: String, required: true, trim: true},
  desc : String,
  price : Number
});

module.exports = mongoose.model('Widget', Widget);
```

The last change is to the widget controller code. We're swapping out the in-memory data store for MongoDB, using a Mongoose model. Though the change is significant from a processing perspective, the code modification isn't very extensive—just a few tweaks, having as much to do with changing id to sn as anything else. Example 10-5 contains the complete code for the widget controller code.

Example 10-5. The newly modified widget controller code

```
var Widget = require('../models/widget.js');

// index listing of widgets at /widgets/
exports.index = function(req, res) {
   Widget.find({}, function(err, docs) {
      console.log(docs);
      res.render('widgets/index', {title : 'Widgets', widgets : docs});
   });
};

// display new widget form
exports.new = function(req, res) {
    console.log(req.url);
    var filePath = require('path').normalize(__dirname +
                                    "/../public/widgets/new.html");
    res.sendfile(filePath);
};

// add a widget
exports.create = function(req, res) {

   var widget = {
     sn : req.body.widgetsn,
     name : req.body.widgetname,
     price : parseFloat(req.body.widgetprice),
     desc: req.body.widgetdesc};

   var widgetObj = new Widget(widget);

   widgetObj.save(function(err, data) {
      if (err) {
         res.send(err);
      } else {
         console.log(data);
         res.render('widgets/added', {title: 'Widget Added', widget: widget});
      }
   });
};

// show a widget
exports.show = function(req, res) {
   var sn = req.params.sn;
   Widget.findOne({sn : sn}, function(err, doc) {
      if (err)
         res.send('There is no widget with sn of ' + sn);
      else
```

```
      res.render('widgets/show', {title : 'Show Widget', widget : doc});
   });
};

// delete a widget
exports.destroy = function(req, res) {
   var sn = req.params.sn;

   Widget.remove({sn : sn}, function(err) {
      if (err) {
         res.send('There is no widget with sn of ' + sn);
      } else {
         console.log('deleted ' + sn);
         res.send('deleted ' + sn);
      }
   });
};

// display edit form
exports.edit = function(req, res) {
   var sn = req.params.sn;
   Widget.findOne({sn : sn}, function(err, doc) {
      console.log(doc);
      if(err)
         res.send('There is no widget with sn of ' + sn);
      else
         res.render('widgets/edit', {title : 'Edit Widget', widget : doc});
   });
};

// update a widget
exports.update = function(req, res) {
  var sn = req.params.sn;
  var widget = {
     sn : req.body.widgetsn,
     name : req.body.widgetname,
     price : parseFloat(req.body.widgetprice),
     desc : req.body.widgetdesc};

  Widget.update({sn : sn}, widget, function(err) {
     if (err)
        res.send('Problem occured with update' + err)
     else
        res.render('widgets/added', {title: 'Widget Edited', widget : widget})
  });
};
```

Now the widget application's data is persisted to a database, rather than disappearing every time the application is shut down. And the entire application is set up in such a way that we can add support for new data entities with minimal impact on the stable components of the application.

The widget application in the examples for this chapter builds on previous chapter work. This means you'll need to start a Redis server, in addition to MongoDB, for the application to work correctly.

CHAPTER 11

The Node Relational Database Bindings

In traditional web development, relational databases are the most popular means of data storage. Node, perhaps because of the type of applications it attracts, or perhaps because it attracts uses that fit outside the traditional development box, doesn't follow this pattern: there is a lot more support for data applications such as Redis and MongoDB than there is for relational databases.

There are some relational database modules you can use in your Node applications, but they may not be as complete as you're used to with database bindings in languages such as PHP and Python. In my opinion, the Node modules for relational databases are not yet production ready.

On the positive side, though, the modules that do support relational databases are quite simple to use. In this chapter I'm going to demonstrate two different approaches to integrating a relational database, MySQL, into Node applications. One approach uses mysql (node-mysql), a popular JavaScript MySQL client. The other approach uses db-mysql, which is part of the new node-db initiative to create a common framework for database engines from Node applications. The db-mysql module is written in C++.

Neither of the modules mentioned currently supports transactions, but mysql-series has added this type of functionality to node-mysql. I'll provide a quick demonstration on this, and also offer a brief introduction to Sequelize, an ORM (object-relational mapping) library that works with MySQL.

There are a variety of relational databases, including SQL Server, Oracle, and SQLite. I'm focusing on MySQL because there are installations available for Windows and Unix environments, it's free for noncommercial use, and it's the most commonly used database with applications most of us have used. It's also the relational database with the most support in Node.

The test database used in the chapter is named nodetest2, and it contains one table with the following structure:

```
id - int(11), primary key, not null, autoincrement
title - varchar(255), unique key, not null
text - text, nulls allowed
created - datetime, nulls allowed
```

Getting Started with db-mysql

The db-mysql Node module is a native module, and requires installation of the MySQL client libraries on your system. Check with *http://nodejsdb.org/db-mysql/* for installation and setup instructions.

Once your environment is set up, you can install db-mysql with npm:

```
npm install db-mysql
```

The db-mysql module provides two classes to interact with the MySQL database. The first is the `database` class, which you use to `connect` and `disconnect` from the database and do a query. The `query` class is what's returned from the database `query` method. You can use the `query` class to create a query either through chained methods representing each component of the query, or directly using a query string; db-mysql is very flexible.

Results, including any error, are passed in the last callback function for any method. You can use nested callbacks to chain actions together, or use the `EventEmitter` event handling in order to process both errors and database command results.

When creating the database connection to a MySQL database, you can pass several options that influence the created database. You'll need to provide, at minimum, a hostname or a port or a socket, and a user, password, and database name:

```
var db = new mysql.Database({
   hostname: 'localhost',
   user: 'username',
   password: 'userpass',
   database: 'databasenm'
});
```

The options are detailed in the db-mysql documentation, as well as in the MySQL documentation.

Using Query String or Chained Methods

To demonstrate db-mysql's flexibility, the application in Example 11-1 connects to a database and runs the same query twice: the first using the `query` class chained methods, the second using a string query. The first query processes the result in a nested callback function, while the second listens for the success and error events and responds accordingly. In both cases, the result is returned in the `rows` object, which returns an array of objects representing each row of data.

Example 11-1. Demonstrating db-mysql's flexibility by showing two different query styles

```
var mysql = require('db-mysql');

// define database connection
var db = new mysql.Database({
    hostname: 'localhost',
    user: 'username',
    password: 'userpass',
    database: 'databasenm'
});

// connect
db.connect();

db.on('error', function(error) {
  console.log("CONNECTION ERROR: " + error);
});

// database connected
db.on('ready', function(server) {

  // query using chained methods and nested callback
  this.query()
      .select('*')
      .from('nodetest2')
      .where('id = 1')
      .execute(function(error, rows, columns) {
        if (error) {
            return console.log('ERROR: ' + error);
        }
        console.log(rows);
        console.log(columns);
  });

  // query using direct query string and event
  var qry = this.query();

  qry.execute('select * from nodetest2 where id = 1');

  qry.on('success', function(rows, columns) {
    console.log(rows); // print out returned rows
    console.log(columns); // print out returns columns
  });
  qry.on('error', function(error) {
    console.log('Error: ' + error);
  });
});
```

The **database** object emits a **ready** event once the database is connected, or **error** if there's a problem with making the connection. The **server** object passed as a parameter for the callback function to the **ready** event contains the following properties:

hostname
      The database hostname

user
: The user used for the database connection

database
: The database connected to

version
: Server software version

The first query in the examples makes use of the query class chained methods that form each component of the query. The chained methods you can use for a SQL query are:

select
: Contains the query's selection criteria—such as a list of column names or asterisk (*) for all columns—or the select string

from
: Contains an array of table names, or the string used in the from statement

join
: A join clause consisting of an options object looking for a type of join, a table to join with, an alias for table (if any), joining conditions (if any), and whether to escape the table and alias names (defaults to true)

where
: Conditional statement, which may contain placeholders and other chained methods representing the and and or conditions

order
: Appends an ORDER BY clause

limit
: Appends a LIMIT clause

add
: Adds a generic clause, such as a UNION

The chained methods provide a more database-neutral approach to performing the same SQL statements. Right now, the Node.js database drivers support MySQL (db-mysql), and Drizzle (db-drizzle). The chained methods handle any variations between the two. The chained methods also automatically handle any escaping of the data in the SQL statement that's necessary for safe usage. Otherwise, if using a straight query, you'll have to use the query.escape method to properly escape the SQL.

The query object emits a success event if the query is successful, or an error. It also emits an each event for each row returned from the query. If the success event is for a query that returns rows, the callback function gets both a rows and a columns object. Each row is an array, with each array element containing an object made up of column name/value pairs. The columns object represents the columns that are part of the result, and each column object contains the column name and type. If the test table in the example has a table with columns of id, title, text, and created, the rows object would look like:

```
{ id: 1,
    title: 'this is a nice title',
    text: 'this is a nice text',
    created: Mon, 16 Aug 2010 09:00:23 GMT }
```

The columns object would look like:

```
[ { name: 'id', type: 2 },
  { name: 'title', type: 0 },
  { name: 'text', type: 1 },
  { name: 'created', type: 6 } ]
```

If the success event is for a query that performs an update, delete, or insert, the success event callback function receives a result object as a parameter. I'll cover this object in more detail in the next section.

Though the queries are each handled using different approaches, both have to be implemented within the database's success event callback function. Since db-mysql is Node functionality, the methods are asynchronous. If you tried to do one of the queries outside of the database connect callback function, it wouldn't succeed because the database connection won't be established at that point.

Updating the Database with Direct Queries

As noted, the db-mysql module provides two different ways to update the data in the relational database: a direct query, or using chained methods. We'll first look at just using a direct query.

When using a direct query, you can use the same SQL you'd use in a MySQL client:

```
qry.execute('update nodetest2 set title = "This is a better title" where id = 1');
```

Or you can make use of placeholders:

```
qry.execute('update nodetest2 set title = ? where id = ?',
                                  ["This was a better title", 1]);
```

Placeholders can be used either with a direct query string or with the chained methods. Placeholders are a way of creating the query string ahead of time and then just passing in whatever values are needed. The placeholders are represented by question marks (?) in the string, and each value is given as an array element in the second parameter to the method.

The result of the operation being performed on the database is reflected in the parameter returned in the callback for the success event. In Example 11-2, a new row is inserted into the test database. Note that it makes use of the MySQL NOW function to set the created field with the current date and time. When using a MySQL function, you'll need to place it directly into the query string—you can't use a placeholder.

Example 11-2. Using placeholders in the query string

```
var mysql = require('db-mysql');

// define database connection
var db = new mysql.Database({
    hostname: 'localhost',
    user: 'username',
    password: 'userpass',
    database: 'databasenm'
});

// connect
db.connect();

db.on('error', function(error) {
   console.log("CONNECTION ERROR: " + error);
});

// database connected
db.on('ready', function(server) {

  // query using direct query string and event
  var qry = this.query();

  qry.execute('insert into nodetest2 (title, text, created) values(?,?,NOW())',
              ['Third Entry','Third entry in series']);

  qry.on('success', function(result) {
    console.log(result);
  });

  qry.on('error', function(error) {
    console.log('Error: ' + error);
  });
});
```

If the operation is successful, the following result is returned as a parameter in the callback function:

```
{ id: 3, affected: 1, warning: 0 }
```

The id is the generated identifier for the table row; the affected property shows the number of rows affected by the change (1), and the warning displays how many warnings the query generated for the rows (in this case, 0).

Database table row updates and deletions are handled in the same manner: either use the exact syntax you'd use in a MySQL client, or use placeholders. Example 11-3 adds a new record to the test database, updates the title, and then deletes the same record. You'll notice I created a different query object for each query. Though you can run the same query multiple times, each query does have its own arguments—including the number of arguments it expects each time the query is run. I used four replacement values in the insert, but if I tried to use only two in the update, I'd get an error. The application also makes use of nested callbacks rather than event capturing.

Example 11-3. Inserting, updating, and deleting a record using nested callbacks

```
var mysql = require('db-mysql');

// define database connection
var db = new mysql.Database({
    hostname: 'localhost',
    user: 'username',
    password: 'password',
    database: 'databasenm'
});

// connect
db.connect();

db.on('error', function(error) {
   console.log("CONNECTION ERROR: " + error);
});

// database connected
db.on('ready', function(server) {

  // query using direct query string and nested callbacks
  var qry = this.query();

  qry.execute('insert into nodetest2 (title, text,created) values(?,?,NOW())',
              ['Fourth Entry','Fourth entry in series'], function(err,result) {
      if (err) {
        console.log(err);
      } else {
        console.log(result);

        var qry2 = db.query();
        qry2.execute('update nodetest2 set title = ? where id = ?',
                 ['Better title',4], function(err,result) {
          if(err) {
            console.log(err);
          } else {
            console.log(result);
            var qry3 = db.query();
            qry3.execute('delete from nodetest2 where id = ?',[4],
                function(err, result) {
              if(err) {
                console.log(err);
              } else {
                console.log(result);
              }
            });
          }
        });
      }
```

```
    });
});
```

One thing you might notice from the example is there's no way to roll back previous SQL statements if an error occurs in any of them. At this time, there is no transaction management in db-mysql. If you need to ensure database consistency, you'll have to provide it yourself in your application. You can do this by checking for an error after each SQL statement is executed, and then reversing previous successful operation(s) if a failure occurs. It's not an ideal situation, and you'll have to be careful about the use of any autoincrementing.

 Transaction support of a kind is supported in another module, mysql-queues, which is covered a little later in the chapter.

Updating the Database with Chained Methods

The db-mysql methods to insert, update, and delete a record are insert, update, and delete, respectively. Both the update and delete chained methods can also make use of the where method, which can in turn make use of the conditional chained methods of and and or. The update method can also use another chained method, set, to set values for the SQL statement.

Example 11-4 duplicates the functionality from Example 11-3, but uses chained methods for the insert and update methods. It does not use the chained method for the delete, because at the time this book was written, the delete method did not work correctly.

Example 11-4. Using chained methods to insert a new record and then update it

```
var mysql = require('db-mysql');

// define database connection
var db = new mysql.Database({
    hostname: 'localhost',
    user: 'username',
    password: 'password',
    database: 'databasenm'
});

// connect
db.connect();

db.on('error', function(error) {
    console.log("CONNECTION ERROR: " + error);
});

// database connected
db.on('ready', function(server) {
```

```
// query using direct query string and nested callbacks
var qry = this.query();
qry.insert('nodetest2',['title','text','created'],
        ['Fourth Entry', 'Fourth entry in series', 'NOW()'])
  .execute(function(err,result) {
    if (err) {
      console.log(err);
    } else {
      console.log(result);

      var qry2 = db.query();
      qry2.update('nodetest2')
        .set({title: 'Better title'})
        .where('id = ?',[4])
        .execute(function(err, result) {
        if(err) {
          console.log(err);
        } else {
          console.log(result);
        }
      });
    }
  });
});
```

I'm not overfond of the chained methods, though I think they're handy if you're bring-
ing in data from an application, or if your application may support multiple databases.

Native JavaScript MySQL Access with node-mysql

Unlike with db-mysql, you don't need to install specialized MySQL client software to
work with node-mysql. You just need to install the module, and you're good to go:

```
npm install mysql
```

The native driver is quite simple to use. You create a client connection to the MySQL
database, select the database to use, and use this same client to do all database operations via the query method. A callback function can be passed as the last parameter in
the query method, and provides information related to the last operation. If no callback
function is used, you can listen for events to determine when processes are finished.

Basic CRUD with node-mysql

As just stated, the node-mysql API is extremely simple: create the client, set the database, and send SQL statements as queries on the client. The callback functions are
optional, and there is some minimal event support. When you're using a callback, the
parameters are typically an error and a result, though in the case of a SELECT query, the
callback also has a fields parameter.

Example 11-5 demonstrates how to use node-mysql to connect to the widget database, create a new record, update it, and delete it. This example, as simple as it is, demonstrates all the functionality that node-mysql supports.

Example 11-5. Demonstration of CRUD with node-mysql

```
var mysql = require('mysql');

var client = mysql.createClient({
  user: 'username',
  password: 'password'
});

client.query('USE databasenm');

// create
client.query('INSERT INTO nodetest2 ' +
  'SET title = ?, text = ?, created = NOW()',
  ['A seventh item', 'This is a seventh item'], function(err, result) {
  if (err) {
    console.log(err);
  } else {
    var id = result.insertId;
    console.log(result.insertId);

    // update
    client.query('UPDATE nodetest2 SET ' +
      'title = ? WHERE ID = ?', ['New title', id], function (err, result) {
      if (err) {
        console.log(err);
      } else {
        console.log(result.affectedRows);

        // delete
        client.query('DELETE FROM nodetest2 WHERE id = ?',
          [id], function(err, result) {
          if(err) {
            console.log(err);
          } else {

            console.log(result.affectedRows);

            // named function rather than nested callback
            getData();
          }
        });
      }
    });
  }
});

// retrieve data
function getData() {
  client.query('SELECT * FROM nodetest2 ORDER BY id', function(err, result,fields) {
    if(err) {
```

```
        console.log(err);
    } else {
      console.log(result);
      console.log(fields);
    }
    client.end();
  });
}
```

The query results are what we'd expect: an array of objects, each representing one row
from the table. The following is an example of the output, representing the first returned
row:

```
[ { id: 1,
    title: 'This was a better title',
    text: 'this is a nice text',
    created: Mon, 16 Aug 2010 15:00:23 GMT },
  ... ]
```

The `fields` parameter also matches our expectations, though the format can differ from
other modules. Rather than an array of objects, what's returned is an object where each
table field is an object property, and its value is an object representing information
about the field. I won't duplicate the entire output, but the following is the information
returned for the first field, `id`:

```
{ id:
  { length: 53,
    received: 53,
    number: 2,
    type: 4,
    catalog: 'def',
    db: 'nodetest2',
    table: 'nodetest2',
    originalTable: 'nodetest2',
    name: 'id',
    originalName: 'id',
    charsetNumber: 63,
    fieldLength: 11,
    fieldType: 3,
    flags: 16899,
    decimals: 0 }, ...
```

The module doesn't support multiple SQL statements concatenated onto each other,
and it doesn't support transactions. The only way to get a close approximation to
transaction support is with mysql-queues, discussed next.

MySQL Transactions with mysql-queues

The mysql-queues module wraps the node-mysql module and provides support for
multiple queries as well as database transaction support. Its use may be a little odd,
especially since it provides asynchronous support without seeming to do so.

Typically, to ensure that asynchronous functions have finished, you'd use nested callbacks, named functions, or a module like Async. In Example 11-6, though, mysql-queues controls the flow of execution, ensuring that the SQL statements that are queued —via the use of the *queue*—are finished before the final SELECT is processed. The SQL statements are completed in order: insert, update, and then the final retrieve.

Example 11-6. Using a queue to control the flow of SQL statement execution

```
var mysql = require('mysql');
var queues = require('mysql-queues');

// connect to database
var client = mysql.createClient({
   user: 'username',
   password: 'password'
   });

client.query('USE databasenm');

//associated queues with query
// using debug
queues(client, true);

// create queue
q = client.createQueue();

// do insert
q.query('INSERT INTO nodetest2 (title, text, created) ' +
        'values(?,?,NOW())',
        ['Title for 8', 'Text for 8']);

// update
q.query('UPDATE nodetest2 SET title = ? WHERE title = ?',
         ['New Title for 8','Title for 8']);

q.execute();

// select won't work until previous queries finished
client.query('SELECT * FROM nodetest2 ORDER BY ID', function(err, result, fields) {
    if (err) {
      console.log(err);
    } else {

      // should show all records, including newest
      console.log(result);
      client.end();
    }
});
```

If you want transactional support, you'll need to start a transaction rather than a queue. And you'll need to use a rollback when an error occurs, as well as a commit when you're finished with the transaction. Again, once you call execute on the transaction, any queries following the method call are queued until the transaction is finished. Example 11-7 contains the same application as in Example 11-6, but this time using a transaction.

Example 11-7. Using a transaction to provide greater control over SQL updates

```
var mysql = require('mysql');
var queues = require('mysql-queues');

// connect to database
var client = mysql.createClient({
   user: 'username',
   password: 'password'
   });

client.query('USE databasenm');

//associated queues with query
// using debug
queues(client, true);

// create transaction
var trans = client.startTransaction();
// do insert
trans.query('INSERT INTO nodetest2 (title, text, created) ' +
         'values(?,?,NOW())',
         ['Title for 8', 'Text for 8'], function(err,info) {

   if (err) {
     trans.rollback();
   } else {
     console.log(info);

     // update
     trans.query('UPDATE nodetest2 SET title = ? WHERE title = ?',
           ['Better Title for 8','Title for 8'], function(err,info) {
       if(err) {
          trans.rollback();
       } else {
          console.log(info);
          trans.commit();
       }
     });
   }
});
trans.execute();

// select won't work until transaction finished
client.query('SELECT * FROM nodetest2 ORDER BY ID', function(err, result, fields) {
   if (err) {
     console.log(err);
   } else {

     // should show all records, including newest
     console.log(result);
     client.end();
```

```
    }
});
```

The mysql-queues adds two important components to the node-mysql module:

- Support for multiple queries without having to use a nested callback
- Transaction support

If you're going to use node-mysql, I strongly recommend you incorporate the use of mysql-queues.

ORM Support with Sequelize

The modules in the previous sections provide a database binding for MySQL, but they don't provide a higher level of abstraction. The Sequelize module does just that with an ORM, though it doesn't currently support transactions.

Defining a Model

To use Sequelize, you define the model, which is a mapping between the database table(s) and JavaScript objects. In our previous examples, we worked with a simple table, nodetest2, with the following structure:

```
id - int(11), primary key, not null
title - varchar(255), unique key, not null
text - text, nulls allowed,
created - datetime, nulls allowed
```

You create the model for this database table using the appropriate database and flags for each field:

```
// define model
var Nodetest2 = sequelize.define('nodetest2',
  {id : {type: Sequelize.INTEGER, primaryKey: true},
   title : {type: Sequelize.STRING, allowNull: false, unique: true},
   text : Sequelize.TEXT,
   created : Sequelize.DATE
  });
```

The supported data types and their mappings are:

- Sequelize.STRING => VARCHAR(255)
- Sequelize.TEXT => TEXT
- Sequelize.INTEGER => INTEGER
- Sequelize.DATE => DATETIME
- Sequelize.FLOAT => FLOAT
- Sequelize.BOOLEAN => TINYINT(1)

The options you can use to further refine the fields are:

type
> Data type of field

allowNull
> `false` to allow `null`s; `true` by default

unique
> `true` to prevent duplicate values; `false` by default

primaryKey
> `true` to set primary key

autoIncrement
> `true` to automatically increment field

The likelihood is that your application and database are new, so once you define the model, you need to sync it with the database to create the database table:

```
// sync
Nodetest2.sync().error(function(err) {
    console.log(err);
});
```

When you do so, and examine the table in the database, you'll find that the table and the model are different because of changes Sequelize makes to the table. For one, it's now called nodetest2s, and for another, there are two new table fields:

```
id - int(11), primary key, autoincrement
title - varchar(255), unique key, nulls not allowed
text - text, nulls allowed
created - datetime, nulls allowed
createdAt - datetime, nulls not allowed
updatedAt - datetime, nulls not allowed
```

These are changes that Sequelize makes, and there's no way to prevent it from making them. You'll want to adjust your expectations accordingly. For starters, you'll want to drop the column `created`, since you no longer need it. You can do this using Sequelize by deleting the field from the class and then running the sync again:

```
// define model
var Nodetest2 = sequelize.define('nodetest2',
  {id : {type: Sequelize.INTEGER, primaryKey: true},
   title : {type: Sequelize.STRING, allowNull: false, unique: true},
   text : Sequelize.TEXT,
   });

// sync
Nodetest2.sync().error(function(err) {
    console.log(err);
});
```

Now you have a JavaScript object representing the model that also maps to a relational database table. Next, you need to add some data to the table.

Using CRUD, ORM Style

The differences between using a MySQL database binding and using an ORM continue. You don't insert a database row when using an ORM; rather, you build a new object instance and save it. The same is true when you update: you don't update via SQL; you either modify a property directly or you use updateAttributes, passing in an object with the changed properties. You also don't delete a row from a database; you access an object instance and then destroy it.

To demonstrate how all these work together, Example 11-8 creates the model, syncs with the database (which creates the table if it doesn't already exist), and then creates a new instance and saves it. After the new instance is created, it's updated twice. All the objects are retrieved and the contents displayed before the recently added object instance is destroyed.

Example 11-8. CRUD using Sequelize

```
var Sequelize = require('sequelize');

var sequelize = new Sequelize('databasenm',
                'username', 'password',
                { logging: false});

// define model
var Nodetest2 = sequelize.define('nodetest2',
  {id : {type: Sequelize.INTEGER, primaryKey: true},
   title : {type: Sequelize.STRING, allowNull: false, unique: true},
   text : Sequelize.TEXT,
   });

// sync
Nodetest2.sync().error(function(err) {
   console.log(err);
});

var test = Nodetest2.build(
   { title: 'New object',
     text: 'Newest object in the data store'});
// save record
test.save().success(function() {

  // first update
  Nodetest2.find({where : {title: 'New object'}}).success(function(test) {
     test.title = 'New object title';
     test.save().error(function(err) {
       console.log(err);
     });
     test.save().success(function() {

        // second update
        Nodetest2.find(
            {where : {title: 'New object title'}}).success(function(test) {
           test.updateAttributes(
```

```
    {title: 'An even better title'}).success(function() {});
    test.save().success(function() {

        // find all
        Nodetest2.findAll().success(function(tests) {
          console.log(tests);


        // find new object and destroy
        Nodetest2.find({ where: {title: 'An even better title'}}).
            success(function(test) {
            test.destroy().on('success', function(info) {
              console.log(info);
              });
          });
        });
      });
    })
  });
  });
});
```

When printing out the results of the findAll, you might be surprised at how much data you're getting back. Yes, you can access the properties directly from the returned value, first by accessing the array entry, and then accessing the value:

```
tests[0].id; // returns identifier
```

But the other data associated with this new object completes the demonstrations showing that you're not in the world of relational database bindings anymore. Here's an example of one returned object:

```
[ { attributes: [ 'id', 'title', 'text', 'createdAt', 'updatedAt' ],
    validators: {},
    _factory:
    { options: [Object],
      name: 'nodetest2',
      tableName: 'nodetest2s',
      rawAttributes: [Object],
      daoFactoryManager: [Object],
      associations: {},
      validate: {},
      autoIncrementField: 'id' },
    _options:
    { underscored: false,
      hasPrimaryKeys: false,
      timestamps: true,
      paranoid: false,
      instanceMethods: {},
      classMethods: {},
      validate: {},
      freezeTableName: false,
      id: 'INTEGER NOT NULL auto_increment PRIMARY KEY',
      title: 'VARCHAR(255) NOT NULL UNIQUE',
      text: 'TEXT',
```

```
        createdAt: 'DATETIME NOT NULL',
        updatedAt: 'DATETIME NOT NULL' },
    id: 14,
    title: 'A second object',
    text: 'second',
    createdAt: Sun, 08 Apr 2012 20:58:54 GMT,
    updatedAt: Sun, 08 Apr 2012 20:58:54 GMT,
    isNewRecord: false },...
```

Adding Several Objects Easily

Sequelize's asynchronous nature is definitely obvious from Example 10-8. Normally, the issue of nested callbacks won't be a problem because you won't be performing so many operations in a row—except if you're adding several new object instances. In that case, you can run into problems with the nested callbacks.

Luckily, Sequelize provides a simple way of chaining queries so that you can do something such as creating many new object instances and saving them all at once. The module provides a *chainer* helper where you can add `EventEmitter` tasks (such as a query), one after the other, and they won't be executed until you call `run`. Then the results of all operations are returned, either as a success or an error.

Example 11-9 demonstrates the chainer helper by adding three new object instances and then running a `findAll` on the database when the instances have been successfully saved.

Example 11-9. Using a chainer to simplify adding multiple object instances

```
var Sequelize = require('sequelize');

var sequelize = new Sequelize('databasenm',
            'username', 'password',
            { logging: false});

// define model
var Nodetest2 = sequelize.define('nodetest2',
  {id : {type: Sequelize.INTEGER, primaryKey: true},
   title : {type: Sequelize.STRING, allowNull: false, unique: true},
   text : Sequelize.TEXT,
   });

// sync
Nodetest2.sync().error(function(err) {
   console.log(err);
});
var chainer = new Sequelize.Utils.QueryChainer;
chainer.add(Nodetest2.create({title: 'A second object',text: 'second'}))
     .add(Nodetest2.create({title: 'A third object', text: 'third'}));

chainer.run()
     .error(function(errors) {
        console.log(errors);
     })
```

```
.success(function() {
    Nodetest2.findAll().success(function(tests) {
      console.log(tests);
    });
  });
```

This is much simpler, and much easier to read, too. Plus the approach makes it simpler to work with a user interface or an MVC application.

There is much more about Sequelize at the module's documentation website, including how to deal with associated objects (relations between tables).

Overcoming Issues Related to Going from Relational to ORM

When working with an ORM, you'll need to keep in mind that it makes certain assumptions about the data structure. One is that if the model object is named something like `Widget`, the database table is `widgets`. Another is an assumption that the table contains information about when a row is added or updated. However, many ORMs also know that both assumptions may not be met by an existing database system being converted from using a straight database binding to using an ORM.

One real issue with Sequelize is that it pluralizes the table names, no matter what you do. So if you define a model for the table, it wants to pluralize the model name for the table name. Even when you provide a table name, Sequelize wants to pluralize it. This isn't an issue when you don't have the database table, because a call to `sync` automatically creates the table. This *is* an issue if you're using an existing relational database—enough of an issue that I strongly recommend against using the module with anything other than a brand-new application.

CHAPTER 12

Graphics and HTML5 Video

Node provides numerous opportunities to work with several different graphics applications and libraries. Since it's a server technology, your applications can make use of any server-based graphics software, such as ImageMagick or GD. However, since it's also based on the same JavaScript engine that runs the Chrome browser, you can work with client-side graphics applications, such as Canvas and WebGL, too.

Node also has some support for serving up audio and video files via the new HTML5 media capabilities present in all modern browsers. Though we have limited capabilities with working directly with video and audio, we can serve files of both types, as we've seen in previous chapters. We can also make use of server-based technologies, such as FFmpeg.

No chapter on web graphics would be complete without mentioning PDFs at least once. Happily for those of us who make use of PDF documents in our websites, we have access to a very nice PDF generation Node module, as well as access to various helpful PDF tools and libraries installed on the server.

I'm not going to exhaustively cover every form of graphics or media implementation and management capability from Node. For one, I'm not familiar with all of them, and for another, some of the support is still very primitive, or the technologies can be extremely resource intensive. Instead, I'll focus on more stable technologies that make sense for a Node application: basic photo manipulation with ImageMagick, HTML5 video, working with and creating PDFs, and creating/streaming images created with Canvas.

Creating and Working with PDFs

Operating systems, versions of HTML, and development technologies may come and go, but one constant is the ubiquitous PDF. Regardless of the type of application or service you're creating, there's a good chance you'll need to provide PDF documents. And as Doctor Who would say, *PDFs are cool*.

You have a couple of options for working with PDFs from a Node application. One approach is to use a Node child process to access an operating system tool, such as the PDF Toolkit or wkhtmltopdf directly on Linux. Another approach is to use a module, such as the popular PDFKit. Or you can use always use both.

Accessing PDF Tools with Child Processes

Though there are few command-line tools to manipulate PDFs in the Windows world, there are several available for Linux and OS X. Fortunately, two I've worked with, PDF Toolkit and wkhtmltopdf, can be installed and accessed in all three environments.

Taking page snapshots with wkhtmltopdf

The wkhtmltopdf utility is a way of converting HTML into a PDF file using the WebKit rendering engine. It's a particularly handy way of taking a snapshot of a website, graphics and all. Some sites provide the ability to generate a PDF of content, but frequently do so by stripping out all the graphics. The wkhtmltopdf tool preserves the appearance of the page.

There are installation versions of this utility for OS X and Windows, and you can also download the source code for building in a Unix environment. If you're running the application on your server, you'll need to do some tweaks first, because of its X Windows dependency.

To work with wkhtmltopdf in my system (Ubuntu), I had to install supporting libraries:

```
apt-get install openssl build-essential xorg libssl-dev
```

Then I had to install a tool (xvfb) that allows wkhtmltopdf to run headless in a virtual X server (bypassing the X Windows dependency):

```
apt-get install xvfb
```

Next, I created a shell script, named *wkhtmltopdf.sh*, to wrap the wkhtmltopdf in xvfb. It contains one line:

```
xvfb-run -a -s "-screen 0 640x480x16" wkhtmltopdf $*
```

I then moved the shell script to */usr/bin*, and changed permissions with chmod a+x. Now I'm ready to access wkhtmltopdf from my Node applications.

The wkhtmltopdf tool supports a large number of options, but I'm going to demonstrate how to use the tool simply from a Node application. On the command line, the following takes a URL to a remote web page and then generates a PDF using all default settings (using the shell script version):

```
wkhtmltopdf.sh http://remoteweb.com/page1.html page1.pdf
```

To implement this in Node, we need to use a child process. For extensibility, the application should also take the name of the input URL, as well as the output file. The entire application is in Example 12-1.

Example 12-1. Simple Node application that wraps wkhtmltopdf

```
var    spawn = require('child_process').spawn;

// command line arguments
var url = process.argv[2];
var output = process.argv[3];

if (url && output) {
    var wkhtmltopdf = spawn('wkhtmltopdf.sh', [url, output]);

   wkhtmltopdf.stdout.setEncoding('utf8');
   wkhtmltopdf.stdout.on('data', function (data) {
       console.log(data);
   });

   wkhtmltopdf.stderr.on('data', function (data) {
       console.log('stderr: ' + data);
   });

   wkhtmltopdf.on('exit', function (code) {
       console.log('child process exited with code ' + code);
   });
} else {
   console.log('You need to provide a URL and output file name');
}
```

You typically wouldn't use wkhtmltopdf in a Node application by itself, but it can be a handy addition to any website or application that wants to provide a way to create a persistent PDF of a web page.

Accessing data about a PDF file with PDF Toolkit

PDF Toolkit, or pdftk, provides functionality to split apart (*burst*) a PDF document or merge several documents into one. It can also be used to fill a PDF form, apply a watermark, rotate a PDF document, apply or remove compression, or uncompress a PDF stream for editing. There are installers for both Mac and Windows, and simple-to-follow instructions for installing in most flavors of Unix.

PDF Toolkit can be accessed via Node child processes. As an example, the following code creates a child process that invokes PDF Toolkit's dump_data comment to discover information about a PDF, such as how many pages it contains:

```
    var    spawn = require('child_process').spawn;

    var pdftk = spawn('pdftk', [__dirname + '/pdfs/datasheet-node.pdf', 'dump_data']);


    pdftk.stdout.on('data', function (data) {

        // convert results to an object
        var array = data.toString().split('\n');
        var obj = {};
```

```
  array.forEach(function(line) {
    var tmp = line.split(':');
    obj[tmp[0]] = tmp[1];
  });

  // print out number of pages
  console.log(obj['NumberOfPages']);
});

pdftk.stderr.on('data', function (data) {
    console.log('stderr: ' + data);
});

pdftk.on('exit', function (code) {
    console.log('child process exited with code ' + code);
});
```

The PDF Toolkit data_dump returns results similar to the following:

```
stdout: InfoKey: Creator
InfoValue: PrintServer150&#0;
InfoKey: Title
InfoValue: &#0;
InfoKey: Producer
InfoValue: Corel PDF Engine Version 15.0.0.431
InfoKey: ModDate
InfoValue: D:20110914223152Z
InfoKey: CreationDate
InfoValue: D:20110914223152Z
PdfID0: 7fbe73224e44cb152328ed693290b51a
PdfID1: 7fbe73224e44cb152328ed693290b51a
NumberOfPages: 3
```

The format is easily converted into an object for simpler access of the individual properties.

PDF Toolkit is a reasonably responsive tool, but you'll want to use caution when holding up a web response waiting for it to finish. To demonstrate how to access PDF Toolkit from a Node web application, and how to deal with the expected lag time that working with a computationally expensive graphics application can cause, we'll build a simple PDF uploader.

Creating a PDF uploader and dealing with graphics lag time

PDF Toolkit's ability to burst a PDF or merge several PDFs into one is functionality that can be helpful at a website that allows users to upload and download PDF documents, and then provides individual access of each PDF page. Think of Google Docs, or a website such as Scribd, which allows PDF sharing.

The components to this type of application are:

* A form to select which PDF tool to upload
* A web service to receive the PDF document and then initiate the PDF processing

- A child process wrapper around PDF Toolkit to burst the PDF document into separate pages
- A response to the user providing links to the uploaded document and access to the individual pages

The component that bursts the PDF must first create a location for the pages and then determine what the pages will be named before it can perform the splitting action. This will require accessing the Node File System module to create the directory for the split files. Since larger files can take some time, rather than hold the web response waiting for PDF Toolkit to finish, the application sends an email to the user with URLs for the newly uploaded files. This requires the use of a module we've not used in previous chapters, Emailjs. This module provides basic email functionality.

You can install the Emailjs module via npm:

```
npm install emailjs
```

The form to upload the PDF is basic, needing little explanation. It uses a file input field in addition to a field for the person's name and email address, and sets the method to POST and the action to the web service. Since we're uploading a file, the enctype field must be set to multipart/form-data. The finished form page can be seen in Example 12-2.

Example 12-2. Form to upload a PDF file

```html
<!doctype html>
<html lang="en">
<head>
 <meta charset="utf-8" />
 <title>Upload PDF</title>
 <script>
   window.onload=function() {
      document.getElementById('upload').onsubmit=function() {
         document.getElementById('submit').disabled=true;
      };
   }
 </script>
</head>
<body>
<form id="upload" method="POST" action="http://localhost:8124"
enctype="multipart/form-data">
 <p><label for="username">User Name:</label>
   <input id="username" name="username" type="text" size="20" required /></p>
 <p><label for="email">Email:</label>
   <input id="email" name="email" type="text" size="20" required /></p>
 <p><label for="pdffile">PDF File:</label>
   <input type="file" name="pdffile" id="pdffile" required /></p>
 <p>
 <p>
 <input type="submit" name="submit" id="submit" value="Submit"/>
 </p>
```

```
    </form>
  </body>
```

We have a chance to brush up on our client-side JavaScript skills by disabling the submit button when the form is submitted. The form makes use of the HTML5 `required` attribute, which ensures that the proper data is provided.

The web service application that processes both the request for the form and the PDF upload uses the Connect middleware, this time without the Express framework.

In the service, the Connect static middleware is used to serve up static files, and the directory middleware is used to pretty-print a directory listing when a directory is accessed. The only other functionality that's needed is the process to parse out both the PDF file and the form data from the upload. The application uses the Connect `parse Body` method, which is capable of processing any type of posted data:

```
connect()
        .use(connect.bodyParser({uploadDir: __dirname + '/pdfs'}))
        .use(connect.static(__dirname + '/public'))
        .use(connect.directory(__dirname + '/public'))
        .listen(8124);
```

The data is then made available to a custom middleware named `upload`, which handles both the data and the PDF—invoking a custom module to process the PDF file. The `bodyParser` middleware makes the `username` and `email` available on the `request.body` object, and the uploaded file on the `request.files` object. If a file is uploaded, it's uploaded as an object named `pdffile` because that's the name of the file upload field. You'll need an additional test on the file `type` to ensure that the file uploaded is a PDF.

Example 12-3 has the complete code for the PDF service application.

Example 12-3. PDF upload web service application

```
var connect = require('connect');
var pdfprocess = require('./pdfprocess');

// if POST
// upload file, kick off PDF burst, respond with ack
function upload(req, res, next){
  if ('POST' != req.method) return next();

  res.setHeader('Content-Type', 'text/html');
  if (req.files.pdffile && req.files.pdffile.type === 'application/pdf') {
    res.write('<p>Thanks ' + req.body.username +
            ' for uploading ' + req.files.pdffile.name + '</p>');
    res.end("<p>You'll receive an email with file links when processed.</p>");

    // post upload processing
    pdfprocess.processFile(req.body.username, req.body.email,
                          req.files.pdffile.path, req.files.pdffile.name);
  } else {
    res.end('The file you uploaded was not a PDF');
  }
```

```
}
// in order
// static files
// POST - upload file
// otherwise, directory listing
connect()
        .use(connect.bodyParser({uploadDir: __dirname + '/pdfs'}))
        .use(connect.static(__dirname + '/public'))
        .use(upload)
        .use(connect.directory(__dirname + '/public'))
        .listen(8124);

console.log('Server started on port 8124');
```

The custom module *pdfprocess* is where the application performs the following steps to process the PDF file:

1. A directory is created for the user under the public *pdfs* subdirectory if none exists.
2. A timestamp value is used with the file to create a unique name for the current uploaded PDF.
3. The timestamp is used with the PDF filename to create a new subdirectory for the PDFs under the user's subdirectory.
4. The PDF is moved from the temporary upload directory to this new directory, and renamed the original PDF filename.
5. The PDF Toolkit burst operation is performed on this file, with all the individual PDFs placed in the *pdfs* directory.
6. An email is sent to the user providing a URL/link where he can access the new directory containing the original uploaded PDF and the individual PDF pages.

The filesystem functionality is provided by the Node File System module, the email functionality is handled by Emailjs, and the PDF Toolkit functionality is managed in a child process. There is no data returned from this child process, so the only events captured are child process **exit** and **error** events. Example 12-4 contains the code for this final piece of the application.

Example 12-4. Module to process PDF file and send user email with location of processed files

```
var fs = require('fs');
var spawn = require('child_process').spawn;
var emailjs = require('emailjs');

module.exports.processFile = function(username, email, path, filename) {

    // first, create user directory if doesn't exist
    fs.mkdir(__dirname + '/public/users/' + username, function(err) {

        // next create file directory if doesn't exist
        var dt = Date.now();

        // url for message later
```

```
    var url = 'http://examples.burningbird.net:8124/users/' +
            username + '/' + dt + filename;

// directory for file
var dir = __dirname + '/public/users/' + username + '/' +
        dt + filename;

fs.mkdir(dir, function(err) {
  if (err)
    return console.log(err);

  // now, rename file to new location
  var newfile = dir + '/' + filename;

  fs.rename(path, newfile, function(err) {
    if (err)
      return console.log(err);

    //burst pdf
    var pdftk = spawn('pdftk', [newfile, 'burst', 'output',
                    dir + '/page_%02d.pdf' ]);

    pdftk.on('exit', function (code) {
      console.log('child process ended with ' + code);
      if (code != 0)
        return;

      console.log('sending email');
      // send email

      var server = emailjs.server.connect({
          user : 'gmail.account.name',
          password : 'gmail.account.passwod',
          host : 'smtp.gmail.com',
          port : 587,
          tls : true
      });

      var headers = {
        text : 'You can find your split PDF at ' + url,
        from : 'youremail',
        to : email,
        subject: 'split pdf'
      };

      var message = emailjs.message.create(headers);

      message.attach({data:"<p>You can find your split PDF at " +
                    "<a href='" + url + "'>" + url + "</a></p>",
                    alternative: true});
```

```
        server.send(message, function(err, message) {
            console.log(err || message);
        });
        pdftk.kill();
    });

    pdftk.stderr.on('data', function (data) {
      console.log('stderr: ' + data);
    });

    });
   });
  });
};
```

The actual child process call to PDF Toolkit is in bold text in the code. The command-line syntax used is the following:

```
pdftk filename.pdf burst output /home/location/page_%02d.pdf
```

The filename is given first, then the operation, and then an output directive. The operation is, as mentioned earlier, the burst operation, which splits the PDF into separate pages. The `output` directive instructs PDF Toolkit to place the newly split PDF pages in a specific directory, and provides formatting for the page names—the first page would be *page_01.pdf*, the second *page_02.pdf*, and so on. I could have used Node's `process.chdir` to change the process to the directory, but it really wasn't necessary since I can make the PDF Toolkit operation place the files in a specified directory.

The email is sent using the Gmail SMTP server, which utilizes TLS (transport layer security), over port 587 and with a given Gmail username and password. You could, of course, use your own SMTP server. The message is sent both in plain text and with a given HTML-formatted attachment (for those folks who use an email reader capable of processing HTML).

The end result of the application is a link sent to the user that takes her to the directory where she'll find the uploaded PDF and the split pages. The Connect `directory` middleware ensures that the contents of the directory are attractively displayed. Figure 12-1 shows the results of uploading one very large PDF file on global warming.

With this approach—providing acknowledgment to the user in an email—the user doesn't have to wait around for (and the Node service isn't hung up waiting on) the PDF processing.

 Of course, the user still has to spend time uploading the PDF file—this application doesn't touch on the issues associated with large file uploads.

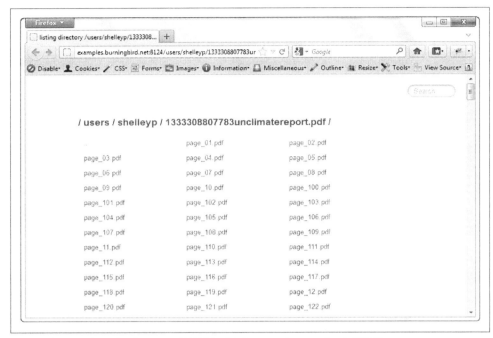

Figure 12-1. End result of running PDF Toolkit burst on large uploaded PDF

Creating PDFs with PDFKit

If using a child process and command-line tools isn't for you, or if you need to be able to create a PDF as well as manipulate existing PDFs, there are Node modules that provide PDF capability. Chief among them is PDFKit.

PDFKit is written in CoffeeScript, but you don't have to know CoffeeScript to use the module because the API is exposed to JavaScript. The module provides functionality to create a PDF document, add pages to it, incorporate text and graphics, and embed images. Future additions to the module should add other functionality, such as PDF outlines, gradients, tables, and other nice features.

Install PDFKit using npm like so:

```
npm install pdfkit
```

In your application, you start by creating a new PDF document:

```
var doc = new PDFDocument();
```

You can then add a font, a new web page, and graphics, all with the exposed API. The API methods can all be chained to simplify development.

To demonstrate how to use the module from JavaScript, I converted one of the CoffeeScript examples from the module developer into JavaScript. From the top, after the PDF document is created, a TrueType font is added to the document, the font size is set to 25 pixels, and text is drawn at *(x,y)* coordinates of 100, 100:

```
doc.font('fonts/GoodDog-webfont.ttf')
   .fontSize(25)
   .text('Some text with an embedded font!', 100, 100);
```

The application then adds a new PDF page, again changes the font size to 25 pixels, and draws new text at 100, 100:

```
doc.addPage()
   .fontSize(25)
   .text('Here is some vector graphics...', 100, 100);
```

The document coordinate system is saved, and the vector graphics functionality is used to draw a red triangle:

```
doc.save()
   .moveTo(100, 150)
   .lineTo(100, 250)
   .lineTo(200, 250)
   .fill("#FF3300");
```

The next section of code scales the coordinate system to 0.6, translates the origin, draws a path in the shape of a star, fills it with red, and then restores the document back to the original coordinate system and scale:

```
doc.scale(0.6)
   .translate(470, -380)
   .path('M 250,75 L 323,301 131,161 369,161 177,301 z')
   .fill('red', 'even-odd')
   .restore();
```

If you've worked with other vector graphics systems, such as Canvas, much of this should seem familiar. If you haven't, then you might want to check out the Canvas examples later in the book and then return to this example.

Another page is added, the fill color is changed to blue, and a link is added to the page. The document is then written out to a file named *output.pdf*:

```
doc.addPage()
   .fillColor("blue")
   .text('Here is a link!', 100, 100)
   .underline(100, 100, 160, 27, {color: "#0000FF"})
   .link(100, 100, 160, 27, 'http://google.com/');

doc.write('output.pdf');
```

It's tedious to create a PDF document manually. However, we can easily program the PDFKit API to take content from a data store and generate a PDF on the fly. We could also use PDFKit to generate a PDF document of web page content on demand, or to provide a persistent snapshot of data.

Be aware, though, that many of the module's methods are not asynchronous. You'll most likely be blocking as you're building the PDF, so plan accordingly.

Accessing ImageMagick from a Child Process

ImageMagick is a powerful command-line graphics tool available in the Mac, Windows, and Unix environments. It can be used to crop or resize an image, access image metadata, animate a sequence of images, and add any number of special effects. It's also very resource intensive, and depending on the size of the image and what you're doing with it, can take a noticeable amount of time.

There are ImageMagick Node modules. One of the first is imagemagick, which provides a wrapper for ImageMagick functionality. However, it hasn't been updated for some time. Another module is gm, which provides a set of predefined functions that work with ImageMagick in the background. You may find, though, that it's just as simple to work with ImageMagick directly. All you need to work with ImageMagick directly from a Node application is for ImageMagick to be installed, and a Node child process.

ImageMagick provides several different tools you can use to perform different functions:

animate
> Animates a sequence over an X server

compare
> Provides a mathematical and visual annotation of differences between an image and a reconstruction of the image after modification

composite
> Overlaps two images

conjure
> Executes scripts written in the Magick Scripting Language (MSL)

convert
> Converts an image using any number of possible conversions such as cropping, resizing, or adding an effect

display
> Displays an image on an X server

identify
> Describes the format and other characteristics of an image file or several image files

import
> Creates a screenshot of any visible window on an X server and saves to a file

mogrify
> Modifies an image in place (resizes, crops, dithers, etc.) and saves the effects in the existing image

---

```
montage
```
Creates a composite image from several

```
stream
```
Streams an image to storage, one pixel at a time

Several of the tools are related to an X server and make little sense from a Node application perspective. However, the `convert`, `mogrify`, `montage`, `identify`, and `stream` tools can have interesting uses in a Node application. In this section and the next, we'll focus on one: `convert`.

 Though we're focusing on `convert`, be aware that everything in this section also applies to `mogrify`, except that `mogrify` overwrites the original file.

The `convert` tool is the ImageMagick workhorse. With it, you can perform some pretty amazing transformations on an image and then save the results to a separate file. You can provide an adaptive blur, sharpen the image, annotate the image with text, position it on a backdrop, crop it, resize it, and even replace every pixel in the image with its color complement. There is little you can't do to an image with ImageMagick. Of course, not every operation is equal, especially if you're concerned about how long it will take. Some of the image conversions occur quickly, while others can take considerable time.

To demonstrate how to use `convert` from a Node application, the small, self-contained application in Example 12-5 specifies an image filename on the command line and scales that image so it fits into a space no more than 150 pixels wide. The image is also transformed into a PNG, regardless of its original type.

The command-line version of this process is:

```
convert photo.jpg -resize '150' photo.jpg.png
```

We'll need to capture four command arguments in the array for the child process: the original photo, the `-resize` flag, the value for the `-resize` flag, and the name of the new image.

Example 12-5. Node application to use a child process to scale an image with the ImageMagick convert tool

```
var spawn = require('child_process').spawn;

// get photo
var photo = process.argv[2];

// conversion array
var opts = [
photo,
'-resize',
```

```
'150',
photo + ".png"];

// convert
var im = spawn('convert', opts);

im.stderr.on('data', function (data) {
  console.log('stderr: ' + data);
});

im.on('exit', function (code) {
   if (code === 0)
      console.log('photo has been converted and is accessible at '
                      + photo + '.png');
});
```

The ImageMagick convert tool processes the image silently, so there is no child process data event to process. The only events we're interested in are the error and the exit, when the image processing is finished.

Where an application like ImageMagick can get tricky is when you're interested in doing a much more involved process. One of the more popular effects people have applied to images using ImageMagick is the *Polaroid effect*: rotating the image slightly around its center and adding a border and a shadow to make the image look like a Polaroid photo. The effect is now so popular that there's a predefined setting for it, but prior to this new setting, we had to use a command similar to the following (from the ImageMagick usage examples):

```
convert thumbnail.gif \
        -bordercolor white  -border 6 \
        -bordercolor grey60 -border 1 \
        -background  none    -rotate 6 \
        -background  black   \( +clone -shadow 60x4+4+4 \) +swap \
        -background  none    -flatten \
        polaroid.png
```

This is a lot of arguments, and the arguments are in a format you may not have seen previously. So how does this get converted into a child process arguments array?

Minutely.

What looks like a single argument on the command line (\(+clone -shadow 60x4+4+4 \)) is anything but to the Node child process. Example 12-6 is a variation of the conversion tool in Example 12-5, except now a Polaroid effect is being applied rather than the image being scaled. Pay particular attention to the line in bold text.

Example 12-6. Applying a Polaroid effect to a photo using ImageMagick from a Node application

```
var spawn = require('child_process').spawn;

// get photo
var photo = process.argv[2];
```

```
// conversion array
var opts = [
photo,
"-bordercolor", "snow",
"-border", "6",
"-background","grey60",
"-background", "none",
"-rotate", "6",
"-background", "black",
"(", "+clone", "-shadow", "60x4+4+4", ")",
"+swap",
"-background", "none",
"-flatten",
photo + ".png"];

var im = spawn('convert', opts);
```

The bolded code in the example demonstrates how what appears to be a single argument on the command line becomes five arguments to the child process. The end result of running the application is shown in Figure 12-2.

Figure 12-2. Result of running Node application to apply a Polaroid effect to a photo

It's unlikely that you'll use the Node application with an ImageMagick child process directly on the command line. After all, you can just run ImageMagick's tools directly. However, you can use the combined child process/ImageMagick tool to run several different conversions on a single image, or to provide services from a website (such as allowing a person to resize a photo to use as an avatar, or add annotations to uploaded images at a shared resource site).

The key to creating a web application that uses ImageMagick is the same as with the PDF demonstration applications from earlier in the chapter: if the process is going to be slow (especially with a larger number of concurrent users), you need to consider providing functionality that allows the individual to upload the image file and then provide a link to the finished project (either at a site, or via email) rather than block, waiting for everything to finish.

We can adapt the code in Example 12-3 and Example 12-4 to apply the Polaroid effect to any uploaded image. In particular, we can convert Example 12-3 into a module that can be applied for the same pattern of use: a file process that creates a new subdirectory for an uploaded file, runs a process, and deposits the resulting files in the same directory.

Properly Serving HTML5 Video with HTTP

In Chapter 6, we created a simple HTTP server that served static files and provided some basic directory and 404 handling. One of the web pages we tested with the server included an embedded HTML5 video. The web page also had a custom toolbar that allowed the user to click anywhere on a timeline to start the video at an intermediate position.

The HTML5 video application worked with the Connect module's static web server, but not the homemade web server. The reason is that the homemade web server didn't handle the concept of *HTTP ranges*. HTTP servers such as Apache and IIS have support for ranges, as does the Connect model; our static server did not.

In this section, we'll add support for ranges to the minimal web server we created back in Example 6-2.

 Support for ranges extends beyond serving HTML5 video. Ranges can also be used to download larger files.

Ranges are an HTTP header that provides a start and end position for loading a resource, such as a video file. Here are the steps we need to take to add support for HTTP ranges:

1. Signal willingness to accept range requests with response header `Accept-Ranges: bytes`.
2. Look for a range request in the request header.
3. If a range request is found, parse out the start and end values.

4. Validate that the start and end values are numbers, and that neither exceeds the length of the resource being accessed.

5. If no end value is provided, set it to the resource length; if no start value is provided, set it to zero (0).

6. Create a `Content-Range` response header consisting of start, end, and resource length values.

7. Create a `Content-Length` response header with a value calculated from subtracting the start value from the end value.

8. Change the status code from 200 to 206 (`Partial`).

9. Pass an object consisting of the start and end values to the `createReadStream` method.

When a web client accesses a resource from a web server, the web server can signal to the client that it supports ranges, and provide a range unit, with the following header:

```
Accept-Ranges: bytes
```

The first modification necessary for the minimal web server is to add the new header:

```
res.setHeader('Accept-Ranges','bytes');
```

The client will then send through range requests of the following format:

```
bytes=startnum-endnum
```

Where the *startnum*/*endnum* values are the starting and end numbers for the range. Several of these requests can be sent during playback. For example, the following are actual range requests sent from the web page with the HTML5 video after starting the video and then clicking around on the timeline during playback:

```
bytes=0-
bytes=7751445-53195861
bytes=18414853-53195861
bytes=15596601-18415615
bytes=29172188-53195861
bytes=39327650-53195861
bytes=4987620-7751679
bytes=17251881-18415615
bytes=17845749-18415615
bytes=24307069-29172735
bytes=33073712-39327743
bytes=52468462-53195861
bytes=35020844-39327743
bytes=42247622-52468735
```

The next addition to the minimal web server is to check to see if a range request has been sent, and if so, to parse out the start and end values. The code to check for a range request is:

```
if (req.headers.range) {...}
```

To parse the range start and end values, I created a function, processRange, that splits the string on the dash (-) and then extracts the numbers out of the two returned strings. The function also double-checks to ensure that a start value is provided and is a number, and isn't beyond the file length (returning a status code 416, Requested Range Not Satisfiable, if it is). It also checks to ensure that the end value is a number, and sets it to the video length if the value isn't provided. An object containing both start and end is returned by the function:

```
function processRange(res,ranges,len) {

  var start, end;

  // extract start and stop range
  var rangearray = ranges.split('-');

  start = parseInt(rangearray[0].substr(6));
  end = parseInt(rangearray[1]);

  if (isNaN(start)) start = 0;
  if (isNaN(end)) end = len -1;

  // start beyond end of file length
  if (start > len - 1) {
      res.setHeader('Content-Range', 'bytes */' + len);
      res.writeHead(416);
      res.end();
  }

  // end can't be beyond file length
  if (end > len - 1)
      end = len - 1;
  return {start:start, end:end};
}
```

The next component of the functionality is to prepare a Content-Range response header, providing the start and end values for the range, as well as the length of the resource, in the following format:

```
Content-Range bytes 44040192-44062881/44062882
```

The content length (Content-Length) response is also prepared, calculated as the end value minus the start value. In addition, the HTTP status code is set to 206, for Partial Content.

Last, the start and end values are also sent as an option to the createReadStream method call. This ensures that the stream is properly repositioned for streaming.

Example 12-7 pulls all of these pieces together into a modified minimal web server that can now serve HTML5 video (or other resource) ranges.

Example 12-7. The minimal web server, now with support for ranges

```
var http = require('http'),
    url = require('url'),
```

```
        fs   = require('fs'),
        mime = require('mime');

function processRange(res,ranges,len) {

  var start, end;

  // extract start and stop range
  var rangearray = ranges.split('-');

  start =  parseInt(rangearray[0].substr(6));
  end = parseInt(rangearray[1]);

  if (isNaN(start)) start = 0;
  if (isNaN(end)) end = len -1;

  // start beyond end of file length
  if (start > len - 1) {
      res.setHeader('Content-Range', 'bytes */' + len);
      res.writeHead(416);
      res.end();
  }

  // end can't be beyond file length
  if (end > len - 1)
     end = len - 1;

  return {start:start, end:end};
}
http.createServer(function (req, res) {

    pathname = __dirname + '/public' + req.url;

    fs.stat(pathname, function(err, stats) {
       if (err) {
         res.writeHead(404);
         res.write('Bad request 404\n');
         res.end();
       } else if (stats.isFile()) {

          var opt={};

          // assume no range
          res.statusCode = 200;

          var len = stats.size;

          // we have a Range request
          if (req.headers.range) {
             opt = processRange(res,req.headers.range,len);

             // adjust length
             len = opt.end - opt.start + 1;

             // change status code to partial
```

```
                res.statusCode = 206;

                // set header
                var ctstr = 'bytes ' + opt.start + '-' +
                            opt.end + '/' + stats.size;

                res.setHeader('Content-Range', ctstr);
            }

            console.log('len ' + len);
            res.setHeader('Content-Length', len);

            // content type
            var type = mime.lookup(pathname);
            res.setHeader('Content-Type', type);
            res.setHeader('Accept-Ranges','bytes');

            // create and pipe readable stream
            var file = fs.createReadStream(pathname,opt);
            file.on("open", function() {

                file.pipe(res);
            });
            file.on("error", function(err) {
              console.log(err);
            });

        } else {
          res.writeHead(403);
          res.write('Directory access is forbidden');
          res.end();
        }
    });
}).listen(8124);
console.log('Server running at 8124/');
```

Modifying the minimal web server demonstrates that HTTP and other network functionality isn't necessarily complicated—just tedious. The key is to break down each
task into separate tasks, and then add code to manage each subtask one at a time (testing
after each).

Now the web page (included in the examples) that allows the user to click around on
a timeline works correctly.

Creating and Streaming Canvas Content

The canvas element has become a favorite of game developers, graphic artists, and
statisticians because of the capability it provides for creating dynamic and interactive
graphics in client web pages. The canvas element is also supported in a Node environment via modules, such as the one covered in this section: node-canvas, or just plain

canvas (we'll use "node-canvas" here). The node-canvas module is based on Cairo, a cross-platform vector graphics library that's long been popular with developers.

To use node-canvas, install it via npm:

```
npm install canvas
```

All of the standard Canvas functionality you have in a client page is available via the node-canvas module. You create a Canvas object and then a context, do all your drawing in the context, and then either display the result or save the result in a file as a JPEG or PNG.

 Be aware that some of the functionality in Canvas, such as working with an image, requires a version of Cairo greater than 1.10.

There are also a couple of additional methods available on the server that you wouldn't have on the client. These allow us to stream a Canvas object to a file (either as a PNG or JPEG), persisting the results for later access (or serving in a web page). You can also convert the Canvas object to a data URI and include an img element in a generated HTML web page, or read an image from an external source (such as a file or a Redis database) and use it directly in the Canvas object.

Jumping right in to demonstrate how to use the node-canvas module, Example 12-8 creates a canvas drawing and then streams it to a PNG file for later access. The example uses a rotated graphic image from an example at the Mozilla Developer Network, and adds a border and shadow to it. Once finished, it's streamed to a PNG file for later access. Most of the functionality could be used in a client application as well as the Node application. The only real Node-specific component is persisting the graphic as a file in the end.

Example 12-8. Creating a graphic using node-canvas and persisting the result to a PNG file

```
var Canvas = require('canvas');
var fs = require('fs');

  // new canvas and context
  var canvas = new Canvas(350,350);
  var ctx = canvas.getContext('2d');

  // create filled rectangle with shadow
  // save context for later restore
  ctx.save();
  ctx.shadowOffsetX = 10;
  ctx.shadowOffsetY = 10;
  ctx.shadowBlur = 5;
  ctx.shadowColor='rgba(0,0,0,0.4)';

  ctx.fillStyle = '#fff';
  ctx.fillRect(30,30,300,300);
```

```
// done with shadow
ctx.restore();
ctx.strokeRect(30,30,300,300);

// MDN example: pretty graphic, inserted offset into
// previously created square
ctx.translate(125,125);
for (i=1;i<6;i++){
  ctx.save();
  ctx.fillStyle = 'rgb('+(51*i)+','+(255-51*i)+',255)';
  for (j=0;j<i*6;j++){
  ctx.rotate(Math.PI*2/(i*6));
  ctx.beginPath();
  ctx.arc(0,i*12.5,5,0,Math.PI*2,true);
  ctx.fill();
  }
  ctx.restore();
}
// stream to PNG file
var out = fs.createWriteStream(__dirname + '/shadow.png');
var stream = canvas.createPNGStream();

stream.on('data', function(chunk){
  out.write(chunk);
});

stream.on('end', function(){
  console.log('saved png');
});
```

Once you've run the Node application, access the *shadow.png* file from your favorite browser. Figure 12-3 shows the generated image.

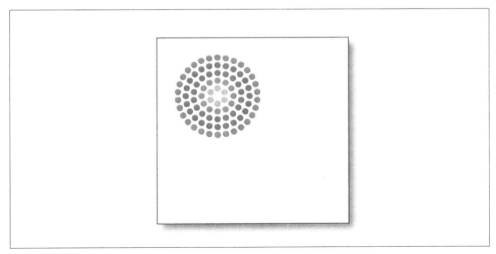

Figure 12-3. Image generated using node-canvas

You're not going to use the Canvas object in a Node application as you would a canvas element in a web page. One of the examples included with node-canvas is a dynamic clock that requires constant HTTP refreshes. If you want an active clock in the client, you should use the canvas element in the client.

Where canvas makes sense on the server is as a way of providing a graphical representation of a server activity, such as a database query, data in a Redis database, a logfile, or other data that originates on the server. By generating the graphic on the server, you not only can persist the graphic for multiple accesses, but you can also limit how much data flows to the client by being able to process a graphic on the server, rather than having to send the data to the client and then create the graphic.

Using canvas in a Node application also makes sense if you're generating game components that may need to adapt to user actions, particularly if the graphics need to be persisted for later access.

CHAPTER 13

WebSockets and Socket.IO

In this chapter, we're working in both the client and server environments, because both are necessary when it comes to WebSockets and Socket.IO.

WebSockets is a relatively new web technology that enables bidirectional, real-time communication directly from within a client to a server application, and back again. The communication occurs over TCP (Transmission Control Protocol), via sockets. The Socket.IO libraries provide the support necessary to implement this technology. Not only does Socket.IO provide a module to use in your Node application, but it also provides a client-side JavaScript library to enable the client end of the communication channel. For an added bonus, it also works as an Express middleware.

In this chapter I'll introduce WebSockets more fully by demonstrating how Socket.IO works, both in the client and in the server.

WebSockets

Before jumping into using Socket.IO, I want to provide a quick overview of WebSockets. To do that, I also need to explain *bidirectional full-duplex communication*.

The term *full duplex* describes any form of data transmission that allows communication in both directions. The term *bidirectional* means that both endpoints of a transmission can communicate, as opposed to *unidirectional* communication, when one end of a data transmission is a sender and all other endpoints are receivers. WebSockets provides the capability for a web client, such as a browser, to open up bidirectional full-duplex communication with a server application. And it does so without having to use HTTP, which adds unnecessary overhead to the communication process.

WebSockets is standardized as part of a specification called the WebSockets API at the World Wide Web Consortium (W3C). The technology has had a bumpy start, because no sooner had some browsers begun implementing WebSockets in 2009 than serious security concerns led those same browsers to either pull their implementation, or enable WebSockets only as an option.

The WebSockets protocol was revamped to address the security concerns, and Firefox, Chrome, and Internet Explorer support the new protocol. At this time, Safari and Opera support only the older versions of the technology, but you must enable WebSockets in the configuration settings. In addition, most mobile browers have only limited support, or support only the older WebSockets specification.

Socket.IO addresses the issue of uneven support for WebSockets by using several different mechanisms to enable the bidirectional communication. It attempts to use the following, in order:

- WebSockets
- Adobe Flash Socket
- Ajax long polling
- Ajax multipart streaming
- Forever iFrame for IE
- JSONP Polling

The key point to take away from this list is that Socket.IO supports bidirectional communication in most, if not all, browsers in use today—desktop and mobile.

 Though technically WebSockets isn't the mechanism used with all browsers in the applications in this chapter, I'll be using the name "WebSockets" to describe the communication technique. It's shorter than typing *bidirectional full-duplex communication*.

An Introduction to Socket.IO

Before we jump into code that implements the WebSockets application, you'll need to install Socket.IO on your server. Use npm to install the module and supporting Java-Script library:

```
npm install socket.io
```

A Socket.IO application requires two different components: a server and a client application. In the examples in this section, the server application is a Node application, and the client application is a JavaScript block in an HTML web page. Both are adaptions of example code provided at the Socket.IO website.

A Simple Communication Example

The client/server application demonstrated in this section sets up a communication between client and server, sending a text string back and forth that's published to the web page. The client always echoes the recent string to the server, which modifies the string and sends it back to the client.

The client application creates a new WebSockets connection, using the Socket.IO client-side library, and listens for any events labeled news. When an event is received, the application takes the text sent with the event and outputs it to the web page. It also echoes the text back to the server via an echo event. Example 13-1 shows the complete code for the client web page.

Example 13-1. Client HTML page in the Socket.IO application

```
<!doctype html>
<html lang="en">
<head>
  <meta charset="utf-8">
  <title>bi-directional communication</title>
  <script src="/socket.io/socket.io.js"></script>
  <script>
     var socket = io.connect('http://localhost:8124');
     socket.on('news', function (data) {
        var html = '<p>' + data.news + '</p>';
        document.getElementById("output").innerHTML=html;
        socket.emit('echo', { back: data.news });
    });
</script>
</head>
<body>
<div id="output"></div>
</body>
</html>
```

The server application uses HTTP to listen for incoming requests, and serves up only one file: the client HTML file. When a new socket connection is made, it emits a message to the client with the text of Counting... to an event labeled news.

When the server gets an echo event, it takes the text sent with the event and appends a counter value to it. The counter is maintained in the application and incremented every time the echo event is transmitted. When the counter gets to 50, the server no longer transmits the data back to the client. Example 13-2 contains all the code for the server application.

Example 13-2. Server application in the Socket.IO application

```
var app = require('http').createServer(handler)
  , io = require('socket.io').listen(app)
  , fs = require('fs')

var counter;

app.listen(8124);

function handler (req, res) {
  fs.readFile(__dirname + '/index.html',
  function (err, data) {
    if (err) {
      res.writeHead(500);
```

```
      return res.end('Error loading index.html');
    }
    counter = 1;
    res.writeHead(200);
    res.end(data);
  });
}
io.sockets.on('connection', function (socket) {
  socket.emit('news', { news: 'world' });
  socket.on('echo', function (data) {
    if (counter <= 50) {
      counter++;
      data.back+=counter;
      socket.emit('news', {news: data.back});
    }
  });
});
```

After the client application is loaded into the server, you can watch the counter update until it reaches the target end value. The web page doesn't have to be reloaded, and the user doesn't have to do anything special for the application to execute. The application exhibits the same behavior in all modern browsers, though the underlying technology that implements the effect differs by browser.

Both news and echo are custom events. The only socket events Socket.IO supports out of the box are connection, passed during the initial connection, and the following events on the server socket:

message
  Emitted whenever a message sent using socket.send is received

disconnect
  Emitted when either the client or server disconnects

And the following events on the client socket:

connect
  Emitted when the socket connection is made

connecting
  Emitted when the socket connection is being attempted

disconnect
  Emitted when the socket is disconnected

connect_failed
  Emitted when the connection fails

error
  Emitted when an error occurs

message
  Emitted when message sent with socket.send is received

`reconnect_failed`
  Emitted when Socket.IO fails to reestablish the connection if it is dropped

`reconnect`
  Emitted when a connection is reestablished after being dropped

`reconnecting`
  Emitted when attempting a reconnection after the connection is dropped

If you want WebSockets behavior, rather than use the `emit` method, you can use the `send` method and listen for the message. For instance, on the server, the application can use `send` to send the message to the client, and then listen for a response via the `message` event:

```
io.sockets.on('connection', function (socket) {
    socket.send("All the news that's fit to print");
    socket.on('message', function(msg) {
        console.log(msg);
    });
});
```

On the client, the application can also listen for the `message` event, and use `send` to communicate back:

```
socket.on('message', function (data) {
    var html = '<p>' + data + '</p>';
    document.getElementById("output").innerHTML=html;
    socket.send('OK, got the data');
});
```

This example uses `send` to manually acknowledge receipt of the message. If we want an automatic acknowledgment that the client received the event, we can pass a callback function in as the last parameter of the `emit` method:

```
io.sockets.on('connection', function (socket) {
    socket.emit('news', { news: "All the news that's fit to print" },
                    function(data) {
                        console.log(data);
                    });
});
```

In the client, we can then pass a message back using this callback function:

```
socket.on('news', function (data, fn) {
    var html = '<p>' + data.news + '</p>';
    document.getElementById("output").innerHTML=html;
    fn('Got it! Thanks!');
});
```

The socket passed as a parameter to the connection event handler is the unique connection between the server and the client, and persists as long as the connection persists. If the connection terminates, Socket.IO attempts to reconnect.

WebSockets in an Asynchronous World

The application works...to a point. Where it fails is in not taking into account Node's asynchronous nature. In the application, the counter used is one that's global to the application. If only one customer accesses the application at a time, it works fine. However, if two users access the application at the same time, you get odd results: one browser may end up with fewer numbers than the other, and neither is likely to get an expected result. Add in more concurrent users, and the results are worse.

What we need is a way of attaching data so it persists beyond events to the socket itself. Luckily, we have such a way—just by adding the data directly to the socket object that's created with each new connection. Example 13-3 is a modification of the code from Example 13-2, where the counter is now attached to the socket object directly, rather than floating about as a global variable. The changed code is bolded in the text.

Example 13-3. Modified server code incorporating the use of data persistence with the individual sockets

```
var app = require('http').createServer(handler)
  , io = require('socket.io').listen(app)
  , fs = require('fs')

app.listen(8124);

function handler (req, res) {
  fs.readFile(__dirname + '/index.html',
  function (err, data) {
    if (err) {
      res.writeHead(500);
      return res.end('Error loading index.html');
    }
    res.writeHead(200);
    res.end(data);
  });
}
io.sockets.on('connection', function (socket) {
  socket.counter = 1;
  socket.emit('news', { news: 'Counting...' });

  socket.on('echo', function (data) {
    if (socket.counter <= 50) {
      data.back+=socket.counter;
      socket.counter++;
      socket.emit('news', {news: data.back});
    }
  });
});
```

Now you can have several concurrent users, and they each get the exact same communication. The socket object exists until the socket connection is closed and can't be reestablished.

Each browser won't have *exactly* the same behavior. The counter could be faster or slower depending on the browser, because of the underlying mechanism used to manage the communication.

About That Client Code

For Socket.IO to work, the client side of the application must have access to the Socket.IO client-side JavaScript library. This library is included in the page with the following **script** element:

```
<script src="/socket.io/socket.io.js"></script>
```

You may be wondering if you have to specifically place this code in the top level of your web server—you don't.

In the server application, when the HTTP web server was created, it was passed to the Socket.IO's **listen** event:

```
var app = require('http').createServer(handler)
  , io = require('socket.io').listen(app)
```

What happens is that Socket.IO intercepts requests sent to the web server and listens for requests for:

```
/socket.io/socket.io.js
```

Socket.IO does a clever bit of behind-the-scenes finagling that determines what's returned in the response. If the client supports WebSockets, the JavaScript file returned is one that uses WebSockets to implement the client connection. If the client doesn't support WebSockets, but does support Forever iFrame (IE9), it returns that particular JavaScript client code, and so on.

 Don't modify the relative URL used for a Socket.IO application—your application won't work if you do.

Configuring Socket.IO

Socket.IO comes with several default settings that we usually won't need to change. In the examples in the preceding section, I didn't alter any of the default settings. If I wanted to, though, I could by using Socket.IO's **configure** method, which operates in a manner similar to what we've used with Express and Connect. You can even specify different configurations based on which environment the application is running.

Socket.IO contains a wiki page (at *https://github.com/learnboost/socket.io/wiki/*) that lists all of the options, and I don't want to repeat the rather extensive list here. Instead, I want to demonstrate a couple that you may want to consider modifying as you're learning to work with Socket.IO.

You can change the allowable transports by setting the `transports` option. By default, the allowable transports, in order of priority, are:

- `websocket`
- `htmlfile`
- `xhr-polling`
- `jsonp-polling`

Another transport option is Flash Socket, which is not enabled by default. If we add the following to Example 13-3, then when we access the application with Opera and IE, the application uses Flash Socket (rather than Ajax long polling and Forever iFrame, respectively):

```
io.configure('development', function() {
    io.set('transports', [
            'websocket',
            'flashsocket',
            'htmlfile',
            'xhr-polling',
            'jsonp-polling']);
});
```

You can also define different configurations for different environments, such as production and development:

```
io.configure('production', function() {
    io.set('transports', [
            'websocket',
            'jsonp-polling']);

});
io.configure('development', function() {
    io.set('transports', [
            'websocket',
            'flashsocket',
            'htmlfile',
            'xhr-polling',
            'jsonp-polling']);

});
```

Another option controls the amount of detail output to the logger (you'll notice the logger output as debug statements to the console on the server). If you want to turn off the logger output, you can set the `log level` option to 1:

```
io.configure('development', function() {
    io.set('log level', 1);
});
```

Some of the options—such as `store`, which determines where client data is persisted —have requirements other than just having an option in a configuration method call.

However, other than setting `log level` and `transports`, you should find the default settings sufficient as you're learning to work with Socket.IO.

Chat: The WebSockets "Hello, World"

Every technology has its own version of Hello, World—the first application people typically create when learning the technology—and the one for WebSockets and Socket.IO seems to be a chat client. The Socket.IO GitHub site provides a chat client (as well as an IRC, or Internet relay chat, client); searching on "Socket.IO and chat" lists several nice examples.

In this section, I'll demonstrate the code for a very simple chat client. It has no bells and whistles, and uses only Socket.IO (and no other library on the client or server), but it demonstrates how nicely Socket.IO facilitates an application that would be quite difficult to implement otherwise.

The application makes use of a couple of new methods to handle communication. In the earlier examples, the applications used either `send` or `emit` to send a communication between client and server. This type of communication is restricted to the socket, and is visible only to the user receiving the message, no matter how many other people are connected to the server.

To broadcast to every person connected to the server, you can use the `emit` method on the Socket.IO framework object:

```
io.sockets.emit();
```

Now anyone who has a socket connection to the server gets the message.

You can also broadcast a message to everyone but a specific individual by issuing a `broadcast.emit` on the socket of the person you don't want to see the message:

```
socket.broadcast.emit();
```

In the simple chat application, when a new client connects, the client application prompts for a name and then broadcasts to other connected clients that this person has now entered the chat room. The client application also provides a text field and button to send messages, and provides a place where new messages from all participants are printed. Example 13-4 shows the client application code.

Example 13-4. Client chat application

```
<!doctype html>
<html lang="en">
<head>
  <meta charset="utf-8">
  <title>bi-directional communication</title>
  <script src="/socket.io/socket.io.js"></script>
  <script>
    var socket = io.connect('http://localhost:8124');
    socket.on('connect', function() {
```

```
          socket.emit('addme', prompt('Who are you?'));
      });

      socket.on('chat',function(username, data) {
        var p = document.createElement('p');
        p.innerHTML = username + ':  ' + data;
        document.getElementById('output').appendChild(p);
      });
      window.addEventListener('load',function() {
          document.getElementById('sendtext').addEventListener('click',
              function() {
                  var text = document.getElementById('data').value;
                  socket.emit('sendchat', text);
              }, false);
      }, false);
</script>
</head>
<body>
<div id="output"></div>
<div id="send">
  <input type="text" id="data" size="100" /><br />
  <input type="button" id="sendtext" value="Send Text" />
</div>
</body>
</html>
```

Other than the addition of basic JavaScript functionality to capture the click event on the button, and the prompt to get the person's name, the functionality isn't much different than earlier examples.

In the server, the new person's username is attached as data to the socket. The server acknowledges the person directly, and then broadcasts the person's name to other chat room participants. When the server receives any new chat message, it attaches the username to the message so everyone can see who sent it. Finally, when a client disconnects from the chat room, another message is broadcast to all connected users indicating that the person is no longer participating. Example 13-5 has the complete code for the server application.

Example 13-5. Server chat application

```
var app = require('http').createServer(handler)
  , io = require('socket.io').listen(app)
  , fs = require('fs');

app.listen(8124);

function handler (req, res) {
  fs.readFile(__dirname + '/chat.html',
  function (err, data) {
    if (err) {
      res.writeHead(500);
      return res.end('Error loading chat.html');
    }
```

```
    res.writeHead(200);
    res.end(data);
  });
}

io.sockets.on('connection', function (socket) {

  socket.on('addme',function(username) {
    socket.username = username;
    socket.emit('chat', 'SERVER', 'You have connected');
    socket.broadcast.emit('chat', 'SERVER', username + ' is on deck');
  });

  socket.on('sendchat', function(data) {
    io.sockets.emit('chat', socket.username, data);
  });

  socket.on('disconnect', function() {
    io.sockets.emit('chat', 'SERVER', socket.username + ' has left the building');
  });

});
```

Figure 13-1 shows the results of the application when I tested it from four different browsers (Chrome, Firefox, Opera, and IE).

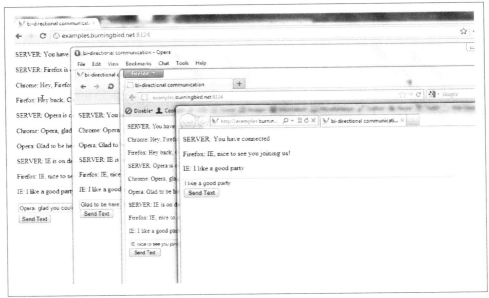

Figure 13-1. Trying out the chat application enabled by Socket.IO in several different browsers

An additional modification to the application might add a list of people currently connected so newcomers could see who is in the room when they enter. This could be a global array, since it, unlike the username, is accessible by all clients. I'll leave this last bit of code to you as an off-book exercise.

Using Socket.IO with Express

The examples up to this point used Node's HTTP as the web server. You can also easily incorporate Express into a Socket.IO application (or Socket.IO into an Express application). The key thing to remember is that Socket.IO must be able to listen for requests before they're processed by Express.

Example 13-6 converts the server component of the chat application from the last section into using Express to handle all web service requests. The line in the code that's essential to the integration of Socket.IO and Express is in bold. The actual communication components are not changed at all from the code in Example 13-5.

Example 13-6. Porting the chat server to Express

```
var express = require('express'),
    sio = require('socket.io'),
    http = require('http'),
    app = express();

var server = http.createServer(app);

app.configure(function () {
  app.use(express.static(__dirname + '/public'));
  app.use(app.router);
});

app.get('/', function (req, res) {
  res.send('hello');
});

var io = sio.listen(server);

server.listen(8124);

io.sockets.on('connection', function (socket) {

    socket.on('addme',function(username) {
        socket.username = username;
        socket.emit('chat', 'SERVER', 'You have connected');
        socket.broadcast.emit('chat', 'SERVER', username + ' is on deck');
    });

    socket.on('sendchat', function(data) {
        io.sockets.emit('chat', socket.username, data);
    });

    socket.on('disconnect', function() {
```

```
      io.sockets.emit('chat', 'SERVER', socket.username + ' has left the building');
   });

});
```

As the Express application is passed to the HTTP server, the HTTP server is in turn passed to Socket.IO. All three modules work together to ensure that all requests—whether web service or chat—are handled properly.

Though the chat client is a static page, it would be a simple matter to incorporate a template. The only issues are ensuring the integrity of the scripting block where the client application code resides, and remembering to include a link to the Socket.IO library.

CHAPTER 14

Testing and Debugging Node Applications

In previous chapters, the only debugging aid used in the examples was printing information to the console. For smaller and less complex applications that are still in development, this is sufficient. However, as your application grows and gets more complicated, you'll need to use other, more sophisticated tools for debugging.

You're also going to want to incorporate more formal testing, including the use of test-creation tools that can be used by others to test your module or application in their environments.

Debugging

Frankly, `console.log` will always remain my debugger of choice, but its usefulness does degrade as your application increases in size and complexity. Once you've moved beyond a simple application, you're going to want to consider using more sophisticated debugging tools. We'll go over some options in the sections that follow.

The Node.js Debugger

The V8 engine comes with a built-in debugger we can use with our Node applications, and Node provides a client that makes it simple to use. We start by adding debugger statements into our code anywhere we want a breakpoint:

```
// create the proxy that listens for all requests
httpProxy.createServer(function(req,res,proxy) {

    debugger;
    if (req.url.match(/^\/node\//)) 
       proxy.proxyRequest(req, res, {
          host: 'localhost',
          port: 8000
       });
```

```
    else
        proxy.proxyRequest(req,res, {
            host: 'localhost',
            port: 8124
        });
}).listen(9000);
```

We then run the application in debug mode:

```
node debug debugger.js
```

In debug mode, the application stops at the beginning of the file. To go to the first breakpoint, type **cont**, or its abbreviation, **c**. This causes the debugger to stop at the first breakpoint; the application then sits, waiting for input from the user (such as a web request):

```
< debugger listening on port 5858
connecting... ok
break in app2.js:1
  1 var connect = require('connect'),
  2     http = require('http'),
  3     fs = require('fs'),
debug> cont (--> note it is just waiting at this point for a web request)
break in app2.js:11
  9 httpProxy.createServer(function(req,res,proxy) {
 10
 11     debugger;
 12     if (req.url.match(/^\/node\//))
 13         proxy.proxyRequest(req, res, {
debug>
```

You have several options at this point. You can step through the code using the next (n) command, step into a function using step (s), or step out of a function using out (o). In the following code, the debugger stops at the breakpoint, and the next few lines are stepped over with next until line 13, which has a function call. I use step at this point to step into the function. I can then traverse the function code using next, and return to the application using out:

```
debug> cont
break in app2.js:11
  9 httpProxy.createServer(function(req,res,proxy) {
 10
 11     debugger;
 12     if (req.url.match(/^\/node\//))
 13         proxy.proxyRequest(req, res, {
debug> next
break in app2.js:12
 10
 11     debugger;
 12     if (req.url.match(/^\/node\//))
 13         proxy.proxyRequest(req, res, {
 14             host: 'localhost',
debug> next
break in app2.js:13
 11     debugger;
```

```
 12     if (req.url.match(/^\/node\//))
 13         proxy.proxyRequest(req, res, {
 14             host: 'localhost',
 15             port: 8000
debug> step
break in /home/examples/public_html/node/node_modules/http-proxy/lib/
node-http-proxy/routing-proxy.js:144
 142 //
 143 RoutingProxy.prototype.proxyRequest = function (req, res, options) {
 144   options = options || {};
 145
 146   //
debug> next
break in /home/examples/public_html/node/node_modules/http-proxy/lib/
node-http-proxy/routing-proxy.js:152
 150   // arguments are supplied to `proxyRequest`.
 151   //
 152   if (this.proxyTable && !options.host) {
 153     location = this.proxyTable.getProxyLocation(req);
 154
debug> out
break in app2.js:22
 20          port: 8124
 21       });
 22 }).listen(9000);
 23
 24 // add route for request for dynamic resource
```

You can also set a new breakpoint, either on the current line setBreakpoint (sb), or the first line in a named function or script file:

```
break in app2.js:22
 20          port: 8124
 21       });
 22 }).listen(9000);
 23
 24 // add route for request for dynamic resource
debug> sb()
 17     else
 18         proxy.proxyRequest(req,res, {
 19             host: 'localhost',
 20             port: 8124
 21       });
*22 }).listen(9000);
 23
 24 // add route for request for dynamic resource
 25 crossroads.addRoute('/node/{id}/', function(id) {
 26     debugger;
 27 });
```

Clear a breakpoint with clearBreakpoint (cb).

You can add an expression to a watch list and list out current watches, in addition to using REPL to examine variables:

```
break in app2.js:11
  9 httpProxy.createServer(function(req,res,proxy) {
 10
 11    debugger;
 12    if (req.url.match(/^\/node\//))
 13       proxy.proxyRequest(req, res, {
debug> repl
Press Ctrl + C to leave debug repl
> req.url
'/node/174'
debug>
```

The backtrace command is helpful for printing a *backtrace* (a list of currently active function calls) of the current execution frame:

```
debug> backtrace
#0 app2.js:22:1
#1 exports.createServer.handler node-http-proxy.js:174:39
```

Anytime you want to see which commands are available to you, type **help**:

```
debug> help
Commands: run (r), cont (c), next (n), step (s), out (o), backtrace (bt),
setBreakpoint (sb), clearBreakpoint (cb), watch, unwatch, watchers, repl, restart,
kill, list, scripts, breakpoints, version
```

The built-in debugger is very helpful, but sometimes you want a little bit more. You have other options, including accessing the V8 debugger directly by using the --debug command-line flag:

```
node --debug app.js
```

This starts up a TCP connection to the debugger, and you enter the V8 debug commands at the prompt. This is an interesting option, but does require a great deal of understanding of how the V8 debugger works (and what the commands are).

Another option is to use debugging via a WebKit browser—through an application such as Node Inspector, covered next.

Client-Side Debugging with Node Inspector

Node Inspector requires a little more setup to begin debugging, but the extra effort is worth it.

First, install Node Inspector globally using npm:

```
npm install -g node-inspector
```

To use the functionality, you'll first need to start the application using the V8 debugger flag:

```
node --debug app.js
```

Then you'll need to start the Node Inspector, in either the background or foreground:

```
node-inspector
```

When you start the application, you'll get the following message:

```
node-inspector
   info - socket.io started
visit http://0.0.0.0:8080/debug?port=5858 to start debugging
```

Using a WebKit-based browser (Safari or Chrome), access the debugging page. My example is running on my server, so I use the following URL:

http://examples.burningbird.net:8080/debug?port=5858

In the browser, the client-side debugger (part of the developer toolset) opens, and stops at the first breakpoint. Now you can use the tools you're probably already familiar with from your client-side JavaScript development efforts, such as stepping over a couple of lines of code and examining an object's properties, as shown in Figure 14-1.

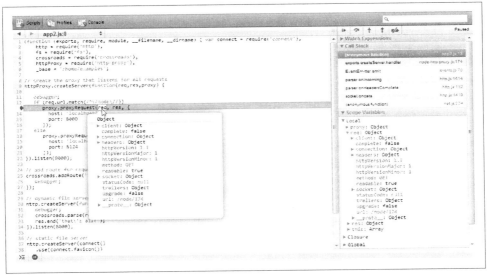

Figure 14-1. Running Node Inspector in Chrome on a Node application running on a remote server

Node Inspector is, by far, a superior approach to debugging the server application. Using the command line is OK, but being able to see all the code at once, and to use a toolset we're familiar with, more than compensates for the little extra effort necessary to enable the Node Inspector setup.

 If you eventually end up hosting your Node application in a cloud service, the service will usually provide its own form of development tools, including debuggers.

Unit Testing

Unit testing is a way of isolating specific components of an application for testing. Many of the tests that are provided in the *tests* subdirectory of Node modules are unit tests. The tests in the *test* subdirectory of the Node installation are *all* unit tests.

You can run a module's test scripts using npm. In the module subdirectory, type:

```
npm test
```

This command runs a module test script if one is provided. When I ran the test script in the subdirectory for node-redis (covered in Chapter 9), the resulting output displayed successful test results, such as the portion displayed here:

```
Connected to 127.0.0.1:6379, Redis server version 2.4.11

Using reply parser hiredis
- flushdb: 1 ms
- multi_1: 3 ms
- multi_2: 9 ms
- multi_3: 2 ms
- multi_4: 1 ms
- multi_5: 0 ms
- multi_6: 7 ms
- eval_1:Skipping EVAL_1 because server version isn't new enough.
 0 ms
- watch_multi: 0 ms
```

Many of these unit tests are built using the Assert module, which we'll go over next.

Unit Testing with Assert

Assertion tests evaluate expressions, the end result of which is a value of either true or false. If you're testing the return from a function call, you might first test that the return is an array (first assertion). If the array contents should be a certain length, you perform a conditional test on the length (second assertion), and so on. There's one Node built-in module that facilitates this form of assertion testing: Assert.

You include the Assert module in an application with the following:

```
var assert = require('assert');
```

To see how to use Assert, let's look at how existing modules use it. The following test is in the *test.js* script found with the node-redis installation:

```
var name = "FLUSHDB";
client.select(test_db_num, require_string("OK", name));
```

The test uses a function, require_string, which returns a function that uses the Assert module methods assert.equal and assert.stringEqual:

```
function require_string(str, label) {
    return function (err, results) {
        assert.strictEqual(null, err, "result sent back unexpected error: " + err);
```

```
        assert.equal(str, results, label + " " + str + " does not match " + results);
        return true;
    };
}
```

The first test, `assert.stringEqual`, fails if the `err` object returned in the Redis test isn't `null`. The second test using `assert.equal` fails if results are not equal to the expected string. Only if both tests are successful (i.e., neither test fails) does the code fall through to the `return true` statement.

What is actually tested is whether the Redis `select` command succeeds. If an error occurs, the error is output. If the result of the selection isn't what's expected (a return value of `OK`), a message is output to that effect, including the test label where the test failed.

The Node application also makes use of the Assert module in its module unit tests. For instance, there's a test application called *test-util.js* that tests the Utilities module. The following code is the section that tests the `isArray` method:

```
// isArray
assert.equal(true, util.isArray([]));
assert.equal(true, util.isArray(Array()));
assert.equal(true, util.isArray(new Array()));
assert.equal(true, util.isArray(new Array(5)));
assert.equal(true, util.isArray(new Array('with', 'some', 'entries')));
assert.equal(true, util.isArray(context('Array')()));
assert.equal(false, util.isArray({}));
assert.equal(false, util.isArray({ push: function() {} }));
assert.equal(false, util.isArray(/regexp/));
assert.equal(false, util.isArray(new Error));
assert.equal(false, util.isArray(Object.create(Array.prototype)));
```

Both the `assert.equal` and the `assert.strictEqual` methods have two mandatory parameters: an expected response and an expression that evaluates to a response. In the earlier Redis test, the `assert.strictEqual` test expects a result of `null` for the `err` argument. If this expectation fails, the test fails. In the `assert.equal isArray` test in the Node source, if the expression evaluates to `true`, and the expected response is `true`, the `assert.equal` method succeeds and produces no output—the result is *silent*.

If, however, the expression evaluates to a response other than what's expected, the `assert.equal` method responds with an exception. If I take the first statement in the `isArray` test in the Node source and modify it to:

```
assert.equal(false, util.isArray([]));
```

then the result is:

```
node.js:201
        throw e; // process.nextTick error, or 'error' event on first tick
        ^
AssertionError: false == true
    at Object.<anonymous> (/home/examples/public_html/node/chap14/testassert.js:5:8)
    at Module._compile (module.js:441:26)
    at Object..js (module.js:459:10)
```

```
at Module.load (module.js:348:31)
at Function._load (module.js:308:12)
at Array.0 (module.js:479:10)
at EventEmitter._tickCallback (node.js:192:40)
```

The `assert.equal` and `assert.strictEqual` methods also have a third optional parameter, a message that's displayed rather than the default in case of a failure:

```
assert.equal(false, util.isArray([]), 'Test 1Ab failed');
```

This can be a useful way of identifying exactly which test failed if you're running several in a test script. You can see the use of a message (a label) in the node-redis test code:

```
assert.equal(str, results, label + " " + str + " does not match " + results);
```

The message is what's displayed when you catch the exception and print out the message.

The following Assert module methods all take the same three parameters, though how the test value and expression relate to each other varies, as the name of the test implies:

`assert.equal`
    Fails if the expression results and given value are not equal

`assert.strictEqual`
    Fails if the expression results and given value are not strictly equal

`assert.notEqual`
    Fails if the expression results and given value are equal

`assert.notStrictEqual`
    Fails if the expression results and given value are strictly equal

`assert.deepEqual`
    Fails if the expression results and given value are not equal

`assert.notDeepEqual`
    Fails if the expression results and given value are equal

The latter two methods, `assert.deepEqual` and `assert.notDeepEqual`, work with complex objects, such as arrays or objects. The following succeeds with `assert.deepEqual`:

```
assert.deepEqual([1,2,3],[1,2,3]);
```

but would not succeed with `assert.equal`.

The remaining `assert` methods take differing parameters. Calling `assert` as a method, passing in a value and a message, is equivalent to calling `assert.isEqual`, passing in `true` as the first parameter, an expression, and a message. The following:

```
var val = 3;
assert(val == 3, 'Equal');
```

is equivalent to:

```
assert.equal(true, val == 3, 'Equal');
```

Another variation of the exact same method is `assert.ok`:

```
assert.ok(val == 3, 'Equal');
```

The `assert.fail` method throws an exception. It takes four parameters: a value, an expression, a message, and an operator, which is used to separate the value and expression in the message when an exception is thrown. In the following code snippet:

```
try {
  var val = 3;
  assert.fail(3, 4, 'Fails Not Equal', '==');
} catch(e) {
  console.log(e);
}
```

the console message is:

```
{ name: 'AssertionError',
  message: 'Fails Not Equal',
  actual: 3,
  expected: 4,
  operator: '==' }
```

The `assert.ifError` function takes a value and throws an exception only if the value resolves to anything but `false`. As the Node documentation states, it's a good test for the error object as the first argument in a callback function:

```
assert.ifError(err); //throws only if true value
```

The last `assert` methods are `assert.throws` and `assert.doesNotThrow`. The first expects an exception to get thrown; the second doesn't. Both methods take a code block as the first required parameter, and an optional error and message as the second and third parameters. The error object can be a constructor, regular expression, or validation function. In the following code snippet, the error message is printed out because the error regular expression as the second parameter doesn't match the error message:

```
assert.throws(
  function() {
    throw new Error("Wrong value");
  },
  /something/
  )
} catch(e) {
  console.log(e.message);
}
```

You can create sophisticated tests using the Assert module. The one major limitation with the module, though, is the fact that you have to do a lot of wrapping of the tests so that the entire testing script doesn't fail if one test fails. That's where using a higher-level unit testing framework, such as Nodeunit (discussed next), comes in handy.

Unit Testing with Nodeunit

Nodeunit provides a way to script several tests. Once scripted, each test is run serially, and the results are reported in a coordinated fashion. To use Nodeunit, you're going to want to install it globally with npm:

```
npm install nodeunit -g
```

Nodeunit provides a way to easily run a series of tests without having to wrap everything in try/catch blocks. It supports all of the Assert module tests, and provides a couple of methods of its own in order to control the tests. Tests are organized as test cases, each of which is exported as an object method in the test script. Each test case gets a control object, typically named **test**. The first method call in the test case is to the **test** element's **expect** method, to tell Nodeunit how many tests to expect in the test case. The last method call in the test case is to the **test** element's **done** method, to tell Nodeunit the test case is finished. Everything in between composes the actual test unit:

```
module.exports = {
   'Test 1' : function(test) {
     test.expect(3); // three tests
     ... // the tests
     test.done();
   },
   'Test 2' : function (test) {
     test.expect(1); // only one test
     ... // the test
     test.done();
   }
};
```

To run the tests, type **nodeunit**, followed by the name of the test script:

```
nodeunit thetest.js
```

Example 14-1 has a small but complete testing script with six assertions (tests). It consists of two test units, labeled Test 1 and Test 2. The first test unit runs four separate tests, while the second test unit runs two. The **expect** method call reflects the number of tests being run in the unit.

Example 14-1. Nodeunit test script, with two test units, running a total of six tests

```
var util = require('util');

module.exports = {
    'Test 1' : function(test) {
        test.expect(4);
        test.equal(true, util.isArray([]));
        test.equal(true, util.isArray(new Array(3)));
        test.equal(true, util.isArray([1,2,3]));
        test.notEqual(true, (1 > 2));
        test.done();
    },
    'Test 2' : function(test) {
        test.expect(2);
```

```
            test.deepEqual([1,2,3], [1,2,3]);
            test.ok('str' === 'str', 'equal');
            test.done();
        }
};
```

The result of running the Example 14-1 test script with Nodeunit is:

```
example1.js
✓ Test 1
✓ Test 2

OK: 6 assertions (3ms)
```

Symbols in front of the tests indicate success or failure: a check for success, and an *x* for failure. None of the tests in this script fails, so there's no error script or stack trace output.

 For CoffeeScript fans, the newest version of Nodeunit supports Coffee-Script applications.

Other Testing Frameworks

In addition to Nodeunit, covered in the preceding section, there are several other testing frameworks available for Node developers. Some of the tools are simpler to use than others, and each has its own advantages and disadvantages. Next, I'll briefly cover three frameworks: Mocha, Jasmine, and Vows.

Mocha

Install Mocha with npm:

```
npm install mocha -g
```

Mocha is considered the successor to another popular testing framework, Espresso.

Mocha works in both browsers and Node applications. It allows for asynchronous testing via the done function, though the function can be omitted for synchronous testing. Mocha can be used with any assertion library.

The following is an example of a Mocha test, which makes use of the should.js assertion library:

```
should = require('should')
describe('MyTest', function() {
  describe('First', function() {
    it('sample test', function() {
      "Hello".should.equal("Hello");
    });
```

```
    });
  });
```

You need to install the should.js library before running the test:

```
npm install should
```

Then run the test with the following command line:

```
mocha testcase.js
```

The test should succeed:

```
✓ 1 test complete (2ms)
```

Jasmine

Jasmine is a behavior-driven development (BDD) framework that can be used with many different technologies, including Node with the node-jasmine module. The node-jasmine module can be installed with npm:

```
npm install jasmine-node -g
```

 Note the module name: jasmine-node, rather than the format of node-*modulename* (or the shortened form, *modulename*) that you've seen so far in the book.

The jasmine-node GitHub repository includes examples in the *specs* subdirectory. As with most other testing frameworks, the Jasmine Node module also accepts a done function as a callback in order to allow asynchronous testing.

There are some environmental requirements to using jasmine-node. First, the tests must be in a *specs* subdirectory. The jasmine-node module is a command-line application, and you'll be able to specify the root directory, but it does expect the tests to be in *specs*.

Next, the tests must be named in a specific format. If the test is written in JavaScript, the test filename must end in *.spec.js*. If the test is written in CoffeeScript, the name of the file must end in *.spec.coffee*. You can use subdirectories in the *specs* directory. When you run jasmine-node, it runs all tests in all directories.

To demonstrate, I created a simple test script that uses Zombie (discussed later) to make a request against a web server and access the page contents. I named the file *tst.spec.js* and placed it in the *specs* directory in my development environment:

```
var zombie = require('zombie');

describe('jasmine-node', function(){

    it("should respond with Hello, World!", function(done) {
      zombie.visit("http://examples.burningbird.net:8124",
                                        function(error, browser, status){
        expect(browser.text()).toEqual("Hello, World!\n");
```

```
            done();
        });
    });
});
```

The web server is from Chapter 1, and all it does is return the "Hello, World!" message. Note the use of the newline character—the test will fail if you don't include it.

I ran the test with the following command line:

```
jasmine-node --test-dir /home/examples/public_html/node
```

The result was the following output:

```
Finished in 0.133 seconds
1 test, 1 assertion, 0 failures
```

A successful test.

 Jasmine uses `path.existsSync`, which is deprecated in favor of `js.exist sSync` in Node 0.8. Again, hopefully a fix will be in soon.

If the script had been in CoffeeScript, I would have added the `--coffee` parameter:

```
jasmine-node --test-dir /home/examples/public_html/node --coffee
```

Vows

Vows is another BDD testing framework, and has one advantage over others: more comprehensive documentation. Testing is composed of testing suites, themselves made up of batches of sequentially executed tests. A batch consists of one or more contexts, executed in parallel, and each consisting of a topic, which is when we finally get to the executable code. The test within the code is known as a *vow*. Where Vows prides itself on being different from the other testing frameworks is by providing a clear separation between that which is being tested (topic) and the test (vow).

I know those are some strange uses of familiar words, so let's look at a simple example to get a better idea of how a Vows test works. First, though, we have to install Vows:

```
npm install vows
```

To try out Vows, I'm using the simple circle module I created earlier in the book, now edited to set precision:

```
var PI = Math.PI;

exports.area = function (r) {
  return (PI * r * r).toFixed(4);
};

exports.circumference = function (r) {
  return (2 * PI * r).toFixed(4);
};
```

I needed to change the precision on the result because I'm going to be doing an equality assertion test on the results in the Vows application.

In the Vows test application, the circle object is the topic, and the area and circumference methods are the vows. Both are encapsulated as a Vows context. The suite is the overall test application, and the batch is the test instance (circle and two methods). Example 14-2 shows the entire test.

Example 14-2. Vows test application with one batch, one context, one topic, and two vows

```
var vows = require('vows'),
    assert = require('assert');

var circle = require('./circle');

var suite = vows.describe('Test Circle');

suite.addBatch({
    'An instance of Circle': {
        topic: circle,
        'should be able to calculate circumference': function (topic) {
            assert.equal (topic.circumference(3.0), 18.8496);
        },
        'should be able to calculate area': function(topic) {
            assert.equal (topic.area(3.0), 28.2743);
        }
    }
}).run();
```

Running the application with Node runs the test because of the addition of the `run` method at the end of the `addBatch` method:

```
node example2.js
```

The results should be two successful tests:

```
·· ✓ OK » 2 honored (0.003s)
```

The topic is always an asynchronous function or a value. Instead of using `circle` as the topic, I could have directly referenced the object methods as topics—with a little help from function closures:

```
var vows = require('vows'),
    assert = require('assert');

var circle = require('./circle');

var suite = vows.describe('Test Circle');

suite.addBatch({
    'Testing Circle Circumference': {
        topic: function() { return circle.circumference;},
        'should be able to calculate circumference': function (topic) {
            assert.equal (topic(3.0), 18.8496);
        },
```

```
        },
        'Testing Circle Area': {
            topic: function() { return circle.area;},
            'should be able to calculate area': function(topic) {
                assert.equal (topic(3.0), 28.2743);
            }
        }
    }).run();
```

In this version of the example, each context is the object given a title: Testing Circle Circumference and Testing Circle Area. Within each context, there's one topic and one vow.

You can incorporate multiple batches, each with multiple contexts, which can in turn have multiple topics and multiple vows.

Acceptance Testing

Acceptance testing differs from unit testing in that the former's primary purpose is to determine if the application meets user requirements. Unit tests ensure that the application is *robust*, while acceptance tests ensure that the application is *useful*.

Acceptance testing can be accomplished through the use of predefined scripts that users actually design and implement in a coordinated setting. Acceptance testing can also be automated—again through the use of scripts, but scripts that are implemented by tools rather than people. These tools don't completely satisfy all aspects of acceptance testing because they can't measure subjective perspectives ("This web page form is awkward to use"), nor can they pinpoint those difficult-to-find bugs that users always seem to drive out, but they can make sure program requirements are met.

Selenium Testing with Soda

If you want a higher level of sophistication in your testing, using actual browsers rather than emulators, and you're willing to pay for a subscription to a testing service, then you might want to check out Selenium, Sauce Labs, and the Node module Soda.

Selenium emerged out of a desire to automate testing tools. It consists of a core library, a Selenium remote control (RC), and a Selenium integrated development environment (IDE). The Selenium IDE is a Firefox plug-in, while the RC is a Java *.jar* file. The first version of Selenium (Selenium 1) is based in JavaScript, which was also one of the problems with the tool suite: whatever limitations JavaScript had, Selenium shared. Another effort to provide an automated test suite is WebDriver, a project that came about because of an interest in working around Selenium's limitations. Work is currently under way for Selenium 2 (Selenium WebDriver), which is a merge of Selenium 1 and WebDriver.

Sauce Labs provides a host for Selenium 1 testing. It offers a way of testing your application with various web browsers in various environments, such as Opera on Linux, or IE9 on Windows 7. It does have two major limitations: no Mac OS X support, and no mobile test environment. However, it is a way of testing an application with multiple versions of browsers, such as IE, which is difficult (if not impossible) if you have only one machine.

Sauce Labs provides various subscription plans, including a basic, free subscription plan for trying out the service. The basic plan allows for two concurrent users, and provides 200 OnDemand minutes a month and 45 Scout minutes a month—more than sufficient for a developer trying things out. The site is geared toward Ruby developers, but there is a Node module, Soda, that you can use.

Soda provides a Node wrapper for Selenium testing. An example of using Soda, included in the module documentation, is the following:

```
var soda = require('soda');

var browser = soda.createClient({
    host: 'localhost'
  , port: 4444
  , url: 'http://www.google.com'
  , browser: 'firefox'
});

browser.on('command', function(cmd, args){
  console.log(' \x1b[33m%s\x1b[0m: %s', cmd, args.join(', '));
});

browser
  .chain
  .session()
  .open('/')
  .type('q', 'Hello World')
  .end(function(err){
    browser.testComplete(function() {
      console.log('done');
      if(err) throw err;
    });
  });
```

The code is actually quite intuitive. First, you create a browser object, specifying which browser to open, the name of the host and port, and what website is being accessed. Start a new browser session, load a web page ('/'), and type a phrase into an input field with a given identifier of q. When finished, print done to the console.log, and throw any error that occurs.

To run a Soda application, you'll need to ensure that Java is installed. Then, copy the Selenium RC Java .jar file to your system and run it:

```
java -jar selenium.jar
```

The application expects Firefox to be installed, since this is the browser specified in the application. While I didn't have it on my Linux box, I did on my Windows laptop and was able to easily get the application running. It's rather fascinating but a little disconcerting to see windows pop up and suddenly disappear as the Selenium RC does its thing.

Another approach is to use Sauce Labs as a remote testing environment, specifying which browser to use for a given test. You'll need to create an account first, and then find your account username and application programming interface (API) key. The username is displayed in the top toolbar, and you can find the API key under the Account tab, after clicking the "View my API Key" link. This is also where you can track your remaining OnDemand and Scout minutes (the testing applications we're creating use OnDemand minutes).

To try the remote testing out, I created a simple test for a login form that we'll build in Chapter 15. The login form has two text fields and two buttons. The text field values are username and password, and one of the buttons has a value of Submit. The test script is testing failure, not success, so the testing script (scenario) would be:

1. Access web application (*http://examples.burningbird.net:3000*).
2. Open login (*/login*).
3. Type **Sally** into the username field.
4. Type **badpassword** into the password field.
5. The page should display "Invalid Password."

These are the steps encoded into Example 14-3.

Example 14-3. Test case for the login form with bad password

```
var soda = require('soda');

var browser = soda.createSauceClient({
    'url': 'http://examples.burningbird.net:3000/'
  , 'username': 'your username'
  , 'access-key': 'your access key'
  , 'os': 'Linux'
  , 'browser': 'firefox'
  , 'browser-version': '3.'
  , 'max-duration': 300 // 5 minutes
});

// Log commands as they are fired
browser.on('command', function(cmd, args){
  console.log(' \x1b[33m%s\x1b[0m: %s', cmd, args.join(', '));
});

browser
  .chain
  .session()
  .setTimeout(8000)
  .open('/login')
  .waitForPageToLoad(5000)
  .type('username', 'Sally')
  .type('password', 'badpassword')
```

```
.clickAndWait('//input[@value="Submit"]')
.assertTextPresent('Invalid password')
.end(function(err){
  browser.setContext('sauce:job-info={"passed": ' + (err === null) + '}', function(){
    browser.testComplete(function(){
      console.log(browser.jobUrl);
      console.log(browser.videoUrl);
      console.log(browser.logUrl);
      if (err) throw err;
    });
  });
});
```

In the test application, a browser object is created with a given browser, browser version, and operating system—in this case, Firefox 3.x on Linux. Note also the different browser client: soda.createSauceClient, not soda.createClient. In the browser object, I'm restricting testing time to no more than five minutes; the site accessed is *http://examples.burningbird.net:3000*; and we've just covered where to get the username and API key.

As each command is issued, it's logged. We want to have a log so we can check responses and look for failures and abnormalities:

```
// Log commands as they are fired
browser.on('command', function(cmd, args){
  console.log(' \x1b[33m%s\x1b[0m: %s', cmd, args.join(', '));
});
```

Last is the actual test. Typically, the tests would have to be nested callbacks (since this is an asynchronous environment), but Soda provides a chain *getter* that greatly simplifies adding tasks. The very first task is to start a new session, and then each separate item in the testing script is encoded. In the end, the application prints out the URLs for the job, log, and video of the test.

The output from running the application is:

```
setTimeout: 8000
open: /login
waitForPageToLoad: 5000
type: username, Sally
type: password, badpassword
clickAndWait: //input[@value="Submit"]
assertTextPresent: Invalid password
setContext: sauce:job-info={"passed": true}
testComplete:
https://saucelabs.com/jobs/d709199180674dc68ec6338f8b86f5d6
https://saucelabs.com/rest/shelleyjust/jobs/d709199180674dc68ec6338f8b86f5d6/
results/video.flv
https://saucelabs.com/rest/shelleyjust/jobs/d709199180674dc68ec6338f8b86f5d6/
results/selenium-server.log
```

You can access the results directly, or you can log into Sauce Labs and see the results of all your tests, as shown in Figure 14-2.

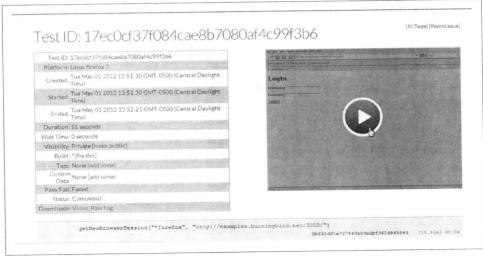

Figure 14-2. *Results of running Soda test against Sauce Labs Selenium core*

As mentioned earlier, Soda is a Selenium wrapper, so there's little documentation of the Selenium commands in the module. You'll need to find these at the Selenium website and extrapolate how they'd work with Soda.

 Access the Selenium website at *http://seleniumhq.org/*.

Emulating a Browser with Tobi and Zombie

Rather than using any specific browser, you can do acceptance testing with Node modules that emulate a browser. Both Tobi and Zombie provide this capability. The primary advantage to these modules is that you can run the applications in an environment that doesn't have a browser installed. In this section, I'll briefly demonstrate how you can use Zombie for acceptance testing.

First, install Zombie using npm:

```
npm install zombie
```

Zombie resembles Soda in that you create a browser and then run tests that emulate the actions of a user at a browser. It even supports chained methods to circumvent the issues with nested callbacks.

I converted the test case against the login form in Example 14-3 to Zombie, except this time the test uses the proper password and tests for success rather than failure (the user is redirected to the */admin* page). Example 14-4 has the code for this acceptance test.

Example 14-4. Testing the login form with Zombie

```
var Browser = require('zombie');
var assert = require('assert');

var browser = new Browser();

browser.visit('http://examples.burningbird.net:3000/login', function() {
   browser.
   fill('username', 'Sally').
   fill('password', 'apple').
   pressButton('Submit', function() {
      assert.equal(browser.location.pathname, '/admin');
   });
});
```

The test is silent, since the `assert` at the end is successful—the browser location is */admin*, which is the page that should open if the login works, signaling a successful test.

 Several of the examples are dependent on the popular Node module jsdom. Again, this module had some problems with the 0.7.10 unstable Node build, but should, hopefully, be quickly compatible with Node 0.8.x.

Performance Testing: Benchmarks and Load Tests

A robust application that meets all the user's needs is going to have a short life if its performance is atrocious. We need the ability to *performance test* our Node applications, especially when we make tweaks as part of the process to improve performance. We can't just tweak the application, put it out for production use, and let our users drive out performance issues.

Performance testing consists of benchmark testing and load testing. *Benchmark testing*, also known as *comparison testing*, is running multiple versions or variations of an application and then determining which is better. It's an effective tool to use when you're tweaking an application to improve its efficiency and scalability. You create a standardized test, run it against the variations, and then analyze the results.

Load testing, on the other hand, is basically stress testing your application. You're trying to see at what point your application begins to fail or bog down because of too many demands on resources, or too many concurrent users. You basically want to drive the application until it fails. Failure is a success with load testing.

There are existing tools that handle both kinds of performance testing, and a popular one is ApacheBench. It's popular because it's available by default on any server where Apache is installed—and few servers don't have Apache installed. It's also an easy-to-use, powerful little testing tool. When I was trying to determine whether it's better to create a static database connection for reuse or to create a connection and discard it with each use, I used ApacheBench to run tests.

ApacheBench works against web applications, which means you provide a URL rather than an application name. If we prefer a Node solution, or an application that can run applications (not just query websites), there's another combination command-line tool/module: Nodeload. Nodeload can interact with a stats module, output graphics of results, and provide real-time monitoring. It also supports distributed load testing.

 In the next couple of sections, the test applications are working with Redis, so if you haven't read Chapter 9, you may want to do that now.

Benchmark Testing with ApacheBench

ApacheBench is commonly called ab, and I'll use that name from this point forward. ab is a command-line tool that allows us to specify the number of times an application is run, and by how many concurrent users. If we want to emulate 20 concurrent users accessing a web application a total of 100 times, we'd use a command like the following:

```
ab -n 100 -c 20 http://somewebsite.com/
```

It's important to provide the final slash, as ab expects a full URL, including path.

ab provides a rather rich output of information. An example is the following output (excluding the tool identification) from one test:

```
Concurrency Level:      10
Time taken for tests:   20.769 seconds
Complete requests:      15000
Failed requests:        0
Write errors:           0
Total transferred:      915000 bytes
HTML transferred:       345000 bytes
Requests per second:    722.22 [#/sec] (mean)
Time per request:       13.846 [ms] (mean)
Time per request:       1.385 [ms] (mean, across all concurrent requests)
Transfer rate:          43.02 [Kbytes/sec] received

Connection Times (ms)
              min  mean[+/-sd] median   max
Connect:        0    0   0.1      0       4
Processing:     1   14  15.7     12     283
Waiting:        1   14  15.7     12     283
Total:          1   14  15.7     12     283

Percentage of the requests served within a certain time (ms)
  50%     12
  66%     14
  75%     15
  80%     16
```

```
90%    18
95%    20
98%    24
99%    40
100%   283 (longest request)
```

The test ran 15,000 times, with 10 concurrent users.

The lines we're most interested in (in bold text) are those having to do with how long each test took, and the cumulative distribution at the end of the test (based on percentages). According to this output, the average time per request (the first value with this label) is 13.846 milliseconds. This is how long the average user could expect to wait for a response. The second line has to do with throughput, and is probably not as useful as the first.

The cumulative distribution provides a good look into the percentage of requests handled within a certain time frame. Again, this indicates what we can expect for an average user: response times between 12 and 283 milliseconds, with the vast majority of responses handled in 20 milliseconds or less.

The last value we're looking at is the requests per second—in this case, 722.22. This value can somewhat predict how well the application will scale, because it gives us an idea of the maximum requests per second—that is, the upper boundaries of application access. However, you'll need to run the test at different times, and under different ancillary loads, especially if you're running the test on a system that serves other uses.

The application tested consists of a web server listening for requests. Each request triggers a query to a Redis data store. The application creates a persistent connection to the Redis data store that it maintains throughout the lifetime of the Node application. The test application is shown in Example 14-5.

Example 14-5. Simple Redis access application used to test persistent Redis connection

```
var redis = require("redis"),
    http = require('http');

// create Redis client
var client = redis.createClient();

client.on('error', function (err) {
    console.log('Error ' + err);
});

// set database to 1
client.select(1);

var scoreServer = http.createServer();

// listen for incoming request
scoreServer.on('request', function (req, res) {

  console.time('test');
```

```
req.addListener("end", function() {

    var obj = {
            member : 2366,
            game : 'debiggame',
            first_name : 'Sally',
            last_name : 'Smith',
            email : 'sally@smith.com',
            score : 50000 };

    // add or overwrite score
    client.hset(obj.member, "game", obj.game, redis.print);
    client.hset(obj.member, "first_name", obj.first_name, redis.print);
    client.hset(obj.member, "last_name", obj.last_name, redis.print);
    client.hset(obj.member, "email", obj.email, redis.print);
    client.hset(obj.member, "score", obj.score, redis.print);

    client.hvals(obj.member, function (err, replies) {
        if (err) {
            return console.error("error response - " + err);
        }

        console.log(replies.length + " replies:");
        replies.forEach(function (reply, i) {
          console.log("    " + i + ": " + reply);
        });
    });

    res.end(obj.member + ' set score of ' + obj.score);
    console.timeEnd('test');
  });
});

scoreServer.listen(8124);

// HTTP server closes, close client connection
scoreServer.on('close', function() {
   client.quit();
});

console.log('listening on 8124');
```

I was curious about performance if I changed one parameter in the application: from maintaining a persistent connection to Redis to grabbing a connection when the web service was accessed, and releasing it as soon as the request was finished. That led to the second version of the application, shown in Example 14-6. The changes from the first are in bold text.

Example 14-6. Modified application with nonpersistent Redis connections

```
var redis = require("redis"),
    http = require('http');
```

```
var scoreServer = http.createServer();

// listen for incoming request
scoreServer.on('request', function (req, res) {

  console.time('test');

  // create Redis client
  var client = redis.createClient();

  client.on('error', function (err) {
    console.log('Error ' + err);
  });

  // set database to 1
  client.select(1);

  req.addListener("end", function() {

      var obj = {
          member : 2366,
          game : 'debiggame',
          first_name : 'Sally',
          last_name : 'Smith',
          email : 'sally@smith.com',
          score : 50000 };

      // add or overwrite score
      client.hset(obj.member, "game", obj.game, redis.print);
      client.hset(obj.member, "first_name", obj.first_name, redis.print);
      client.hset(obj.member, "last_name", obj.last_name, redis.print);
      client.hset(obj.member, "email", obj.email, redis.print);
      client.hset(obj.member, "score", obj.score, redis.print);

      client.hvals(obj.member, function (err, replies) {
         if (err) {
            return console.error("error response - " + err);
         }

         console.log(replies.length + " replies:");
         replies.forEach(function (reply, i) {
           console.log("    " + i + ": " + reply);
         });
      });

      res.end(obj.member + ' set score of ' + obj.score);
      client.quit();
      console.timeEnd('test');
   });
});

scoreServer.listen(8124);

console.log('listening on 8124');
```

I ran the ab test against this second application, and the relevant test results are as follows:

```
Requests per second:    515.40 [#/sec] (mean)
Time per request:       19.402 [ms] (mean)
...
Percentage of the requests served within a certain time (ms)
   50%    18
   66%    20
   75%    21
   80%    22
   90%    24
   95%    27
   98%    33
   99%    40
  100%   341 (longest request)
```

The tests give us a fairly good indication that maintaining a persistent connection enhances performance. This is further borne out, in rather dramatic fashion, with a second test.

When I ran the test 100,000 times, with 1,000 concurrent users, the Node application that maintained a persistent connection to Redis finished the test, while the other option actually failed; too many concurrent users backed up at Redis, and it started rejecting connections. Exactly 67,985 tests completed before the application went toes up.

Load Testing with Nodeload

Nodeload provides a command-line tool that performs the same type of testing as ab, but with the addition of some nice graphics of the results. It also provides a module you can use to develop your own performance testing applications.

 Another application also goes by the name Nodeload, and is responsible for building and delivering Git repositories as *.zip* files. To ensure that you're accessing the correct Nodeload, install it with the following:

```
npm install nodeload -g
```

When Nodeload is installed globally, you can access the command-line version (*nl.js*) of the module application anywhere. The command-line arguments it takes are similar to what we've used with ab:

```
nl.js -c 10 -n 10000 -i 2 http://examples.burningbird.net:8124
```

The application accesses the website 10,000 times, emulating 10 concurrent users. The -i flag alters how frequently the statistics are reported (every 2 seconds rather than the default 10 seconds). Here is the complete set of flags:

-n --number
    Number of requests to make

-c --concurrency
    Number of concurrent users

-t --time-limit
    Time limit for the test

-m --method
    HTTP method to use

-d --data
    Data to send with PUT or POST request

-r --request-generator
    Path to module for getRequest function (if a custom one is provided)

-q --quiet
    Suppress display of progress

-h --help
    Help

What's fun about Nodeload is the live graphics that are displayed while the test is running. If you access port 8000 of the test server (*http://localhost:8000* or via domain), you can see a graphic display of the results as they are happening. Figure 14-3 shows a snapshot of the display during one test.

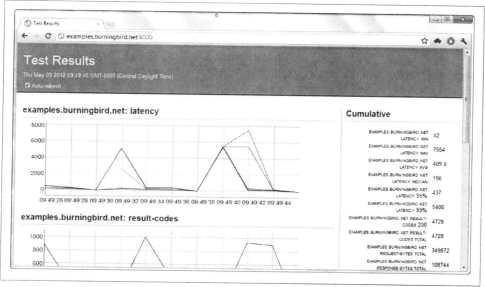

Figure 14-3. Live graphics of ongoing Nodeload test

The graphics file is also persisted for later access, as is a logfile of the test results. At the end of the test, summary results are given that are very close to ab in nature. An example of one output is the following:

```
Server:                               examples.burningbird.net:8124
HTTP Method:                          GET
Document Path:                        /
Concurrency Level:                    100
Number of requests:                   10000
Body bytes transferred:              969977
Elapsed time (s):                     19.59
Requests per second:                  510.41
Mean time per request (ms):           192.74
Time per request standard deviation:  47.75

Percentages of requests served within a certain time (ms)
   Min: 23
   Avg: 192.7
   50%: 191
   95%: 261
   99%: 372
   Max: 452
```

If you want to provide your own custom test, you can use the Nodeload module to develop a testing application. The module provides live monitoring, graphics capability, statistics, as well as distributed testing capability.

 Nodeload currently uses `http.createClient`, which is deprecated in favor of `http.request` in Node 0.8.x. Although it still seemed to work, it should be upgraded shortly.

Refreshing Code with Nodemon

Before leaving this chapter, I want to introduce one more module: Nodemon. Though not technically related to either testing or debugging, it is a handy development tool.

First, install it with npm:

```
npm install nodemon
```

Nodemon wraps your application. Instead of using Node to start the application, use Nodemon:

```
nodemon app.js
```

Nodemon sits quietly monitoring the directory (and any contained directories) where you ran the application, checking for file changes. If it finds a change, it restarts the application so that it picks up the recent changes.

You can pass parameters to the application:

```
nodemon app.js param1 param2
```

You can also use the module with CoffeeScript:

```
nodemon someapp.coffee
```

If you want Nodemon to monitor some directory other than the current one, use the
--watch flag:

```
nodemon --watch dir1 --watch libs app.js
```

There are other flags, documented with the module. The module can be found at *https:*
//github.com/remy/nodemon/.

 Chapter 16 demonstrates how to use Nodemon with Forever, which
restarts your application if it shuts down for some reason.

CHAPTER 15

Guards at the Gate

Security in web applications goes beyond ensuring that people don't have access to the application server. Security can be complex, and even a little intimidating. Luckily, when it comes to Node applications, most of the components we need for security have already been created. We just need to plug them in, in the right place and at the right time.

In this chapter, I break down security into four major components: encryption, authentication and authorization, attack prevention, and sandboxing:

Encryption
Ensures that data transmitted over the Internet is safe, even if it is intercepted midroute. The only receiver that can actually decrypt the data is the system that has the proper credentials (typically a key). Encryption is also used for data that must be stored confidentially.

Authentication and authorization
Consist of the logins we get whenever we need to access protected areas of an application. Not only do these logins ensure that a person has access to a section of an application (authorization), they also ensure the person is who she says she is (authentication).

Attack prevention
Ensures that someone who is submitting data via a form isn't trying to tack on text that can attack the server or the database you're using.

Sandboxing
Barricades script so it doesn't have access to the system resources—it operates only within a limited context.

Encrypting Data

We send a lot of data over the Internet. Most of it isn't anything essential: Twitter updates, web page history, comments on a blog post. Much of the data, though, is private, including credit card data, confidential email messages, or login information to our servers. The only way to ensure that these types of data transmissions are kept private, and aren't hacked in any way during transit, is to use encryption with the communication.

Setting Up TSL/SSL

Secure, tamper-resistant communication between a client and a server occurs over SSL (Secure Sockets Layer), and its upgrade, TLS (Transport Layer Security). TSL/SSL provides the underlying encryption for HTTPS, which I cover in the next section. However, before we can develop for HTTPS, we have to do some environment setup.

A TSL/SSL connection requires a *handshake* between client and server. During the handshake, the client (typically a browser) lets the server know what kind of security functions it supports. The server picks a function and then sends through an *SSL certificate*, which includes a public key. The client confirms the certificate and generates a random number using the server's key, sending it back to the server. The server then uses its private key to decrypt the number, which in turn is used to enable the secure communication.

For all this to work, you'll need to generate both the public and private key, as well as the certificate. For a production system, the certificate would be signed by a *trusted authority*, such as our domain registrars, but for development purposes you can make use of a *self-signed certificate*. Doing so generates a rather significant warning in the browser, but since the development site isn't being accessed by users, there won't be an issue.

The tool used to generate the necessary files is OpenSSL. If you're using Linux, it should already be installed. There's a binary installation for Windows, and Apple is pursuing its own Crypto library. In this section, I'm just covering setting up a Linux environment.

To start, type the following at the command line:

```
openssl genrsa -des3 -out site.key 1024
```

The command generates the private key, encrypted with Triple-DES and stored in PEM (privacy-enhanced mail) format, making it ASCII readable.

You'll be prompted for a password, and you'll need it for the next task, creating a certificate-signing request (CSR).

When generating the CSR, you'll be prompted for the password you just created. You'll also be asked a lot of questions, including the country designation (such as US for United States), your state or province, city name, company name and organization, and email address. The question of most importance is the one asking for the Common Name. This is asking for the hostname of the site—for example, *burningbird.net* or *yourcompany.com*. Provide the hostname where the application is being served. In my example code, I created a certificate for examples.burningbird.net.

```
openssl req -new -key site.key -out site.csr
```

The private key wants a *passphrase*. The problem is, every time you start up the server, you'll have to provide this passphrase, which is an issue in a production system. In the next step, you'll remove the passphrase from the key. First, rename the key:

```
mv site.key site.key.org
```

Then type:

```
openssl rsa -in site.key.org -out site.key
```

If you do remove the passphrase, make sure your server is secure by ensuring that the file is readable only by root.

The next task is to generate the self-signed certificate. The following command creates one that's good only for 365 days:

```
openssl x509 -req -days 365 -in site.csr -signkey site.key -out final.crt
```

Now you have all the components you need in order to use TLS/SSL and HTTPS.

Working with HTTPS

Web pages that ask for user login or credit card information had better be served as HTTPS, or we should give the site a pass. HTTPS is a variation of the HTTP protocol, except that it's also combined with SSL to ensure that the website is who and what we think it is, that the data is encrypted during transit, and the data arrives intact and without any tampering.

Adding support for HTTPS is similar to adding support for HTTP, with the addition of an options object that provides the public encryption key, and the signed certificate. The default port for an HTTPS server differs, too: HTTP is served via port 80 by default, while HTTPS is served via port 443.

Example 15-1 demonstrates a very basic HTTPS server. It does little beyond sending a variation of our traditional Hello, World message to the browser.

Example 15-1. Creating a very simple HTTPS server

```
var   fs = require("fs"),
      https = require("https");

var privateKey = fs.readFileSync('site.key').toString();
var certificate = fs.readFileSync('final.crt').toString();
```

```
var options = {
    key: privateKey,
    cert: certificate
};

https.createServer(options, function(req,res) {
    res.writeHead(200);
    res.end("Hello Secure World\n");
}).listen(443);
```

The public key and certificate are opened, and their contents are read synchronously. The data is attached to the `options` object, passed as the first parameter in the `https.createServer` method. The callback function for the same method is the one we're used to, with the server request and response object passed as parameters.

Accessing the page demonstrates what happens when we use a self-signed certificate, as shown in Figure 15-1. It's easy to see why a self-signed certificate should be used only during testing.

Figure 15-1. What happens when you use Chrome to access a website using HTTPS with a self-signed certificate

The browser address bar demonstrates another way that the browser signals that the site's certificate can't be trusted, as shown in Figure 15-2. Rather than displaying a lock indicating that the site is being accessed via HTTPS, it displays a lock with a red x showing that the certificate can't be trusted. Clicking the icon opens an information window with more details about the certificate.

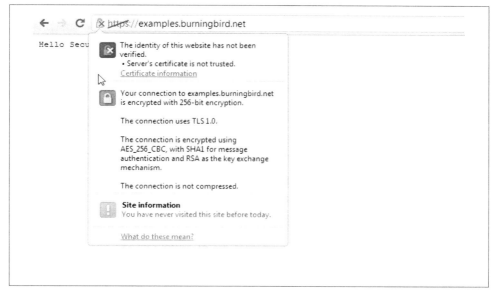

Figure 15-2. More information about the certificate is displayed when the lock icon is clicked

Encrypting communication isn't the only time we use encryption in a web application. We also use it to store user passwords and other sensitive data.

Safely Storing Passwords

Node provides a module used for encryption: Crypto. According to the module's documentation:

> The crypto module requires OpenSSL to be available on the underlying platform. It offers a way of encapsulating secure credentials to be used as part of a secure HTTPS net or http connection.

> It also offers a set of wrappers for OpenSSL's `hash`, `hmac`, `cipher`, `decipher`, `sign`, and `verify` methods.

The functionality we're interested in is the module's OpenSSL hash support.

One of the most common tasks a web application has to support is also one of the most vulnerable: storing a user's login information, including password. It probably only took five minutes after the first username and password were stored in plain text in a web application database before someone came along, cracked the site, got the login information, and had his merry way with it.

You do not store passwords in plain text. Luckily, you don't need to store passwords in plain text with Node's Crypto module.

You can use the Crypto module's `createHash` method to encrypt the password. An example is the following, which creates the hash using the sha1 algorithm, uses the hash to encode a password, and then extracts the digest of the encrypted data to store in the database:

```
var hashpassword = crypto.createHash('sha1')
                         .update(password)
                         .digest('hex');
```

The digest encoding is set to hexadecimal. By default, encoding is binary, and base64 can also be used.

Many applications use a hash for this purpose. However, there's a problem with storing plain hashed passwords in a database, a problem that goes by the innocuous name of *rainbow table*.

Put simply, a rainbow table is basically a table of precomputed hash values for every possible combination of characters. So, even if you have a password that you're sure can't be cracked—and let's be honest, most of us rarely do—chances are, the sequence of characters has a place somewhere in a rainbow table, which makes it much simpler to determine what your password is.

The way around the rainbow table is with *salt* (no, not the crystalline variety), a unique generated value that is concatenated to the password before encryption. It can be a single value that is used with all the passwords and stored securely on the server. A better option, though, is to generate a unique salt for each user password, and then store it with the password. True, the salt can also be stolen at the same time as the password, but it would still require the person attempting to crack the password to generate a rainbow table specifically for the one and only password—adding immensely to the complexity of cracking any individual password.

Example 15-2 is a simple application that takes a username and a password passed as command-line arguments, encrypts the password, and then stores both as a new user in a MySQL database table. The table is created with the following SQL:

```
CREATE TABLE user (userid INT NOT NULL AUTO_INCREMENT, PRIMARY KEY(userid),
username VARCHAR(400) NOT NULL, password VARCHAR(400) NOT NULL);
```

The salt consists of a date value multiplied by a random number and rounded. It's concatenated to the password before the resulting string is encrypted. All the user data is then inserted into the MySQL user table.

Example 15-2. Using Crypto's createHash method and a salt to encrypt a password

```
var mysql = require('mysql'),
    crypto = require('crypto');

var client = mysql.createClient({
  user: 'username',
  password: 'password'
});
```

```
client.query('USE databasenm');

var username = process.argv[2];
var password = process.argv[3];

var salt = Math.round((new Date().valueOf() * Math.random())) + '';

var hashpassword = crypto.createHash('sha512')
                      .update(salt + password)
                      .digest('hex');
// create user record
client.query('INSERT INTO user ' +
    'SET username = ?, password = ?, salt = ?',
    [username, hashpassword, salt], function(err, result) {
        if (err) console.log(err);
        client.end();
});
```

The application to test a username and password, shown in Example 15-3, queries the database for the password and salt based on the username. It uses the salt to, again, encrypt the password. Once the password has been encrypted, it's compared to the password stored in the database. If the two don't match, the user isn't validated. If they match, then the user's in.

Example 15-3. Checking a username and a password that has been encrypted

```
var mysql = require('mysql'),
    crypto = require('crypto');

var client = mysql.createClient({
   user: 'username',
   password: 'password'
  });

client.query('USE databasenm');

var username = process.argv[2];
var password = process.argv[3];

client.query('SELECT password, salt FROM user WHERE username = ?',
    [username], function(err, result, fields) {
    if (err) return console.log(err);

    var newhash = crypto.createHash('sha512')
                    .update(result[0].salt + password)
                    .digest('hex');


    if (result[0].password === newhash) {
      console.log("OK, you're cool");
    } else {
      console.log("Your password is wrong. Try again.");
    }
```

```
    client.end();
});
```

Trying out the applications, we first pass in a username of `Michael`, with a password of `applef*rk13*`:

```
node password.js Michael apple*frk13*
```

We then check the same username and password:

```
node check.js Michael apple*frk13*
```

and get back the expected result:

```
OK, you're cool
```

Trying it again, but with a different password:

```
node check.js Michael badstuff
```

we get back the expected result again:

```
Your password is wrong. Try again
```

Of course, we don't expect our users to log in via the command line. Neither do we always use a local password system to authenticate people. We'll go over the authentication process next.

Authentication/Authorization with Passport

Are you the person you say you are? Do you have the authority to do this action? Can this action cause harm? Answering these questions is the work of two different technical components: authentication and authorization.

Authentication is concerned with ensuring that you are who you say you are. When Twitter attaches a verification flag to an account, it's signaling that the person flagged is the genuine article. *Authorization*, on the other hand, is related to ensuring that you have access only to what you need to access. Of a dozen users at a Drupal site, half may have only the ability to post comments, five others can post articles and comments, but only one has control over everything. The site may not care who user Big Daddy is, only that he can post comments but not delete posts.

It's not unusual for both authorization and authentication to be combined into the same function. Typically, when attempting to do some action, you're challenged to provide some means of authenticating who you are. You're probably going to be asked to provide a username and a password. Then, once you've proved who you are, your actions are further limited by the application: the person identified by your username can access only certain pages or perform only certain operations.

Sometimes the authentication is done through a third party. An example of third-party authentication is the use of OpenID. Rather than have your users create a username and password at your site, you authenticate them with OpenID and then give them application access.

Other times, both authentication and authorization occur at a third-party site. For instance, if an application wants to access a Twitter or Facebook account, either to post messages or to get information, the users have to authenticate with these sites, and then your application has to be authorized for the access. This authorization occurs via another strategy, OAuth.

The functionality for all of these scenarios can be met with the Passport module and one or more Passport strategies.

 Passport isn't the only module that provides authentication and authorization, but I found it to be the easiest to use.

Authorization/Authentication Strategies: OAuth, OpenID, Username/ Password Verification

Let's take a closer look at our three different types of authorization/authentication strategies.

When you're accessing the administrative section of a content management system (CMS) such as Drupal or an online site such as Amazon, you're using basic credential verification. You're supplying a username and a password, both of which are verified by the site before you're given access. This is still the most widely implemented authorization/authentication strategy. And for the most part, it's an effective one.

Earlier in the chapter, I demonstrated how user passwords can be protected in the database. Even if the user system is compromised, the data thieves won't have access to your password in plain text. Of course, they could crack your password, but if you used a combination of letters, symbols, and numbers in a relatively meaningless way, it would take a lot of time and CPU power to crack the password.

OAuth is a way of accessing data, such as a person's Twitter account data, without the person having to give direct access to the account password. It's a way of authorizing data access without the person's credentials having to be stored in various locations— which increases the likelihood of the person's credentials eventually being compromised. It also gives the user greater control, because she can usually rescind the authorization from her primary account at any time.

OAuth is involved almost exclusively with authorization—of data access. OpenID is different in that its primary focus is on authentication, though authorization does come along for the ride.

OpenID is not as widely used as OAuth, and is used primarily in comment systems and in user registration at various media sites. One of the problems with comment systems is that individuals may say they're a person, but there's no way to verify they are who they say they are. With OpenID, a person can sign into a comment system or register as a user, and the OpenID system ensures that the person authenticates, at least within the OpenID system.

OpenID is also a way of registering at different locations without having to create a different username and password with each. You just provide your OpenID, it's verified, the information the system needs is pulled from the OpenID provider, and you're done.

None of these three strategies precludes the use of the other two. Many applications incorporate support for all three: local credential verification for administrative tasks, OAuth to share data or post to sites such as Facebook and Twitter, and OpenID to allow user registration and comments.

There are several modules that can provide all forms of authentication and authorization, but I'm going to focus on one: Passport. Passport is middleware that works with both Connect and Express to provide both authentication and authorization. You can install it with npm:

```
npm install passport
```

Passport utilizes strategies that are installed independently from the framework. All Passport strategies have the same basic requirements:

- The strategy must be installed.
- The strategy must be configured in the application.
- As part of the configuration, the strategy incorporates a callback function, used to verify the user's credentials.
- All strategies require additional work depending on the authority vetting the credentials: Facebook and Twitter require an account and account key, while the local strategy requires a database with usernames and passwords.
- All strategies require a local data store that maps the authority's username with an application username.
- Passport-provided functionality is used to persist the user login session.

In this chapter, we're looking at two Passport strategies: local authentication/authorization, and authentication through Twitter using OAuth.

The Local Passport Strategy

We can install the local Passport strategy module (passport-local) with npm:

```
npm install passport-local
```

Passport is middleware, and must be instantiated like middleware within the Express application. After including both the passport and passport-local modules, like so:

```
var express = require('express');
var passport = require('passport');
var localStrategy = require('passport-local').Strategy;
```

initiate the Passport middleware as follows:

```
var app = express();

app.configure(function(){
    ...
    app.use(passport.initialize());
    app.use(passport.session());
    ...
});
```

Then configure the local strategy. The format for configuring the local strategy is the same as that for configuring all other strategies: a new instance of the strategy is passed to Passport via the use method, similar to the approach utilized by Express:

```
passport.use(new localStrategy( function (user, password, done) { ... }
```

The passport-local module expects that the username and password are passed to the web application via a posted form, and that the values are contained in fields named username and password. If you want to use two other field names, pass them as an option when creating the new strategy instance:

```
var options =
 { usernameField : 'appuser',
    passwordField : 'userpass'
  };
passport.use(new localStrategy(options, function(user, password, done) { ... }
```

The callback function passed to the strategy construction is called after the username and password have been extracted from the request body. The function performs the actual authentication, returning:

- An error, if an error occurs
- A message that the user doesn't authenticate if he fails authentication
- The user object, if the user does authenticate

Whenever a user tries to access a protected site, Passport is queried to see if he is authorized. In the following code, when the user tries to access the restricted admin page, a function named ensureAuthenticated is called to determine whether he is authorized:

```
app.get('/admin', ensureAuthenticated, function(req, res){
    res.render('admin', { title: 'authenticate', user: req.user });
});
```

The ensureAuthenticated function checks the result of the req.isAuthenticated method that Passport has added as an extension to the request object. If the response is false, the user is redirected to the login page:

```
function ensureAuthenticated(req, res, next) {
  if (req.isAuthenticated()) { return next(); }
  res.redirect('/login')
}
```

To persist the login for the session, Passport provides two methods, `serializeUser` and `deserializeUser`. We have to provide the functionality in the callback function that is passed to these two methods. Basically, `passport.serializeUser` serializes the user's identifier, while `passport.deserializeUser` uses this identifier to find the user in whatever data store we're using, and return an object with all the user information:

```
passport.serializeUser(function(user, done) {
  done(null, user.id);
});

passport.deserializeUser(function(id, done) {
  ...
});
```

Serialization to the session isn't a requirement for Passport. If you don't want to serialize the user, don't include the `passport.session` middleware:

```
app.use(passport.session());
```

If you do decide to serialize the user to the session (and you should; otherwise, you'll have a very annoyed user, as he'll keep getting login requests), you must ensure that the Passport middleware is included after the Express session middleware:

```
app.use(express.cookieParser('keyboard cat'));
app.use(express.session());
app.use(passport.initialize());
app.use(passport.session());
```

If you don't maintain the proper order, the user never authenticates.

The last chunk of functionality is handling what happens when the person doesn't validate. During the authentication, if a user's username isn't found in the data store, an error message is generated. If the username is found, but the password doesn't match what's stored, an error is generated. We need to communicate these error messages back to the user.

Passport uses the Express 2.x `req.flash` method to queue error messages for display back to the user. I didn't cover `req.flash` in earlier chapters because the functionality was deprecated in Express 3.x. However, to ensure that Passport works with Express 2.x and 3.x, the Passport developer created a new module, connect-flash, that adds this functionality back in.

The connect-flash module can be installed with npm:

```
npm install connect-flash
```

used in the application:

```
var flash = require('connect-flash');
```

and then integrated as middleware with Express:

```
app.use(flash());
```

Now, in the POST login route, if the user doesn't authenticate, he's redirected to the login form and given a notification that an error occurred:

```
app.post('/login',
    passport.authenticate('local', { failureRedirect: '/login', failureFlash: true }),
    function(req, res) {
        res.redirect('/admin');
});
```

The error message(s) generated via the authentication process can be passed on to the views engine via `req.flash` when the login form is rendered:

```
app.get('/login', function(req, res){
    var username = req.user ? req.user.username : '';
    res.render('login', { title: 'authenticate', username: username,
                message: req.flash('error') });
});
```

The views engine can then display the error message in addition to the login form elements, as this Jade template demonstrates:

```
extends layout

block content
  h1 Login
  if message
    p= message
  form(method="POST"
      action="/login"
      enctype="application/x-www-form-urlencoded")
    p Username:
        input(type="text"
            name="username"
            id="username"
            size="25"
            value="#{username}"
            required)
    p Password:
        input(type="password"
            name="password"
            id="password"
            size="25"
            required)
        input(type="submit"
            name="submit"
            id="submit"
            value="Submit")
        input(type="reset"
            name="reset"
            id="reset"
            value="reset")
```

To demonstrate all of these pieces, I incorporated the command-line authentication application from Example 15-3 into an Express application, shown in Example 15-4, with authentication provided by Passport. The only routes the application supports are the login route for the login form display and authentication, and access to a restricted admin page and the top-level index page.

The MySQL code from Example 15-3 is incorporated directly into the authentication routine (though normally this would be split out in a more formal application). Additional MySQL access code is used to find the user information given an identifier, when the user is deserialized.

Example 15-4. Combining password hash, MySQL user table, and Passport authentication into one Express application

```
// modules
var express = require('express')
  , flash = require('connect-flash')
  , passport = require('passport')
  , LocalStrategy = require('passport-local').Strategy
  , http = require('http');

var mysql = require('mysql')
  , crypto = require('crypto');

// check user authentication

function ensureAuthenticated(req, res, next) {
  if (req.isAuthenticated()) { return next(); }
  res.redirect('/login')
}

// serialize user to session
passport.serializeUser(function(user, done) {
  done(null, user.id);
});

// find user in MySQL database
passport.deserializeUser(function(id, done) {

  var client = mysql.createClient({
    user : 'username',
    password: 'password'
  });

  client.query('USE databasenm');

  client.query('SELECT username, password FROM user WHERE userid = ?',
        [id], function(err, result, fields) {
    var user = {
        id : id,
        username : result[0].username,
        password : result[0].password};
    done(err, user);
    client.end();
```

```
    });
});

// configure local strategy
// authenticate user against MySQL user entry
passport.use(new LocalStrategy(
  function(username, password, done) {

    var client = mysql.createClient({
      user : 'username',
      password: 'password'
    });

    client.query('USE nodetest2');

    client.query('SELECT userid, password, salt FROM user WHERE username = ?',
          [username], function(err, result, fields) {

      // database error
      if (err) {
        return done(err);

      // username not found
      } else if (result.length == 0) {
        return done(null, false, {message: 'Unknown user ' + username});

      // check password
      } else {
        var newhash = crypto.createHash('sha512')
                      .update(result[0].salt + password)
                      .digest('hex');

        // if passwords match
        if (result[0].password === newhash) {
          var user = {id : result[0].userid,
                      username : username,
                      password : newhash };
          return done(null, user);

        // else if passwords don't match
        } else {
          return done(null, false, {message: 'Invalid password'});
        }
      }
      client.end();
    });
}));

var app = express();

app.configure(function(){
  app.set('views', __dirname + '/views');
  app.set('view engine', 'jade');
  app.use(express.favicon());
  app.use(express.logger('dev'));
```

```
  app.use(express.bodyParser());
  app.use(express.methodOverride());
  app.use(express.cookieParser('keyboard cat'));
  app.use(express.session());
  app.use(passport.initialize());
  app.use(passport.session());
  app.use(flash());
  app.use(app.router);
  app.use(express.static(__dirname + '/public'));
});

app.get('/', function(req, res){
  res.render('index', { title: 'authenticate', user: req.user });
});

app.get('/admin', ensureAuthenticated, function(req, res){
  res.render('admin', { title: 'authenticate', user: req.user });
});

app.get('/login', function(req, res){
  var username = req.user ? req.user.username : '';
  res.render('login', { title: 'authenticate', username: username,
              message: req.flash('error') });
});

app.post('/login',
  passport.authenticate('local', { failureRedirect: '/login', failureFlash: true }),
  function(req, res) {
    res.redirect('/admin');
});

http.createServer(app).listen(3000);

console.log("Express server listening on port 3000");
```

Example 15-4 is a longer example than I normally like to include in a book, but stubbing in the data source portions of the example wouldn't give you a real feel for how the Passport component works with the password hashing component, discussed earlier.

Let's take a closer look at the authentication method. Once the application has queried for the user record given the username, it invokes the callback function with the database error, if an error occurs. If an error does not occur, but the username isn't found, the application invokes the callback function with the username set to false to signal that the username wasn't found, and provides an appropriate message. If the user is found, but the passwords don't match, the same thing happens: a value of false is returned for the user and a message is generated.

Only when no database error occurred, the user exists in the user table, and the passwords match is a user object created and returned via the callback function:

```
// database error
if (err) {
  return done(err);
```

```
    // username not found
    } else if (result.length == 0) {
        return done(null, false, {message: 'Unknown user ' + username});

    // check password
    } else {
        var newhash = crypto.createHash('sha512')
                    .update(result[0].salt + password)
                    .digest('hex');

        // if passwords match
        if (result[0].password === newhash) {
            var user = {id : result[0].userid,
                        username : username,
                        password : newhash };
            return done(null, user);

        // else if passwords don't match
        } else {
            return done(null, false, {message: 'Invalid password'});
        }
    }
}
```

This user object is then serialized to the session, and the user is given access to the admin page. He'll continue to have access without challenge to the admin page as long as the session is alive.

The Twitter Passport Strategy (OAuth)

Rather than store usernames and passwords locally and perform our own authentication, we can use another service, such as Twitter. This is also a way to integrate a site more closely with Twitter (or Facebook, Google+, or another third-party site).

Passport authentication using Twitter is supported through the passport-twitter module. It can be installed with npm:

```
npm install passport-twitter
```

To use OAuth to authenticate a user through Twitter, you need to set up a developer's account at Twitter, and get a consumer key and a consumer secret. These are used in the application to form part of the OAuth request.

Once you have your consumer key and secret, use these, in addition to the callback URL, to create the Twitter strategy:

```
passport.use(new TwitterStrategy(
    { consumerKey: TWITTER_CONSUMER_KEY,
      consumerSecret: TWITTER_CONSUMER_SECRET,
      callbackURL: "http://examples.burningbird.net:3000/auth/twitter/callback"},
    function(token, tokenSecret,profile,done) {
        findUser(profile.id, function(err,user) {
            console.log(user);
            if (err) return done(err);
            if (user) return done(null, user);
```

```
            createUser(profile, token, tokenSecret, function(err, user) {
              return done(err,user);
            });
          })
        })
    );
```

Though Twitter provides authentication, you're still most likely going to need a way to store information about the user. In the Twitter strategy code block, notice that the callback function passed lists several parameters: token, tokenSecret, profile, and then the last callback function. Twitter provides the token and tokenSecret parameters when it responds to the request for authentication. The token and tokenSecret values can then be used to interact with the individual's Twitter account—for example, to republish recent tweets, tweet to her account, or discover information about her lists and followers. The Twitter API exposes all the information the user herself sees when she interacts with Twitter directly.

The profile object, though, is the object we're interested in here. It contains a wealth of information about the person: her Twitter screen name, full name, description, location, avatar image, number of followers, number of people followed, number of tweets, and so on. It's this data that we're going to mine in order to store some relevant information about the user in our local database. We're not storing a password; OAuth doesn't expose the individual's authentication information. Rather, we're just storing information we may want to use in our web applications to personalize the individual's experience at our sites.

When the person first authenticates, the application does a lookup on her Twitter identifier in the local database. If the identifier is found, an object is returned with the information stored about the person locally. If it's not found, a new database record is created for the person. Two functions are created for this process: findUser and crea teUser. The findUser function is also used when Passport deserializes the user from the session:

```
passport.deserializeUser(function(id, done) {
    findUser(id, function(err, user) {
        done(err,user);
    });
});
```

There is no longer a login page, because Twitter provides the login form. In the application, the only login provided is a link to authenticate via Twitter:

```
extends layout

block content
    h1= title
    p
        a(href='/auth/twitter') Login with Twitter
```

If the person isn't logged into Twitter, she's presented a login page like the one shown in Figure 15-3.

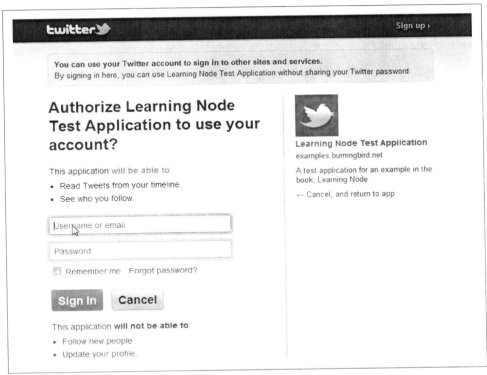

Figure 15-3. Twitter login and authorization page for the Node application

Once the user is logged in, the web page is then redirected to the application, which then displays the administrative page for the user. Now, however, the page is personalized with data drawn directly from Twitter, including the person's display name and avatar:

```
extends layout

block content
  h1 #{title} Administration
  p Welcome to #{user.name}
  p
    img(src='#{user.img}',alt='avatar')
```

This data is some of what's stored when the person first authenticates. If you look into your Twitter account settings page and then click through to the Apps, you'll see the application among those listed, as shown in Figure 15-4.

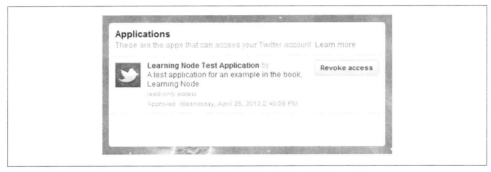

Figure 15-4. Twitter Apps Settings displaying the entry for our Node application

Example 15-5 has the complete application code for authenticating the user via Twitter and storing her data in a MySQL database. You can, of course, also store the data in MongoDB, or even Redis, if you persist your Redis data. The Crypto module is no longer needed, because we're no longer storing passwords—a distinct advantage to authenticating via a third-party service.

Example 15-5. Complete application authenticating a user via Twitter

```
var express = require('express')
  , flash = require('connect-flash')
  , passport = require('passport')
  , TwitterStrategy = require('passport-twitter').Strategy
  , http = require('http');

var mysql = require('mysql');

var TWITTER_CONSUMER_KEY = "yourkey";
var TWITTER_CONSUMER_SECRET = "yoursecret";

var client = mysql.createClient({
   user : 'username',
   password : 'password'
});

client.query('USE nodetest2');

function findUser(id, callback) {
   var user;

   client.query('SELECT * FROM twitteruser WHERE id = ?',
            [id], function(err, result, fields) {
      if (err) return callback(err);
      user = result[0];
      console.log(user);
      return callback(null,user);
   });
};
```

```
function createUser(profile, token, tokenSecret, callback) {

    var qryString = 'INSERT INTO twitteruser ' +
                    '(id, name, screenname, location, description,' +
                    'url, img, token, tokensecret)' +
                    ' values (?,?,?,?,?,?,?,?,?)';
    client.query(qryString, [
            profile.id,
            profile.displayName,
            profile.username,
            profile._json.location,
            profile._json.description,
            profile._json.url,
            profile._json.profile_image_url,
            token,
            tokenSecret], function(err, result) {
                if (err) return callback(err);
                var user = {
                  id : profile.id,
                  name : profile.displayName,
                  screenname : profile.screen_name,
                  location : profile._json.location,
                  description: profile._json.description,
                  url : profile._json.url,
                  img : profile._json.profile_image_url,
                  token : token,
                  tokensecret : tokenSecret};
                  console.log(user);
                  return callback(null,user);
            });
};

function ensureAuthenticated(req, res, next) {
  if (req.isAuthenticated()) { return next(); }
  res.redirect('/auth/twitter')
}

passport.serializeUser(function(user, done) {
  done(null, user.id);
});

passport.deserializeUser(function(id, done) {
    findUser(id, function(err, user) {
        done(err,user);
    });
});

passport.use(new TwitterStrategy(
        { consumerKey: TWITTER_CONSUMER_KEY,
          consumerSecret: TWITTER_CONSUMER_SECRET,
          callbackURL: "http://examples.burningbird.net:3000/auth/twitter/callback"},
        function(token, tokenSecret,profile,done) {
            findUser(profile.id, function(err,user) {
                console.log(user);
                if (err) return done(err);
```

```
              if (user) return done(null, user);
              createUser(profile, token, tokenSecret, function(err, user) {
                return done(err,user);
              });
          })
      })
);

var app = express();


app.configure(function(){
  app.set('views', __dirname + '/views');
  app.set('view engine', 'jade');
  app.use(express.favicon());
  app.use(express.logger('dev'));
  app.use(express.bodyParser());
  app.use(express.methodOverride());
  app.use(express.cookieParser('keyboard cat'));
  app.use(express.session());
  app.use(passport.initialize());
  app.use(passport.session());
  app.use(flash());
  app.use(app.router);
  app.use(express.static(__dirname + '/public'));
});

app.get('/', function(req, res){
  res.render('index', { title: 'authenticate', user: req.user });
});

app.get('/admin', ensureAuthenticated, function(req, res){
  res.render('admin', { title: 'authenticate', user: req.user });
});

app.get('/auth', function(req,res) {
  res.render('auth', { title: 'authenticate' });
});

app.get('/auth/twitter',
  passport.authenticate('twitter'),
  function(req, res){
  });

app.get('/auth/twitter/callback',
  passport.authenticate('twitter', { failureRedirect: '/login' }),
  function(req, res) {
    res.redirect('/admin');
  });

http.createServer(app).listen(3000);

console.log("Express server listening on port 3000");
```

You can use the same steps you took with the Twitter Passport strategy with other OAuth services. As an example, you can use the exact same code to authenticate the user with Facebook that you used with the Twitter application. The only difference is that you have to supply a Facebook key and secret, rather than the one Twitter provides. Because of the similarity in code and processing, many applications today let you authenticate with a variety of OAuth services.

Passport does its best to reformat the data returned by the different services so that the functionality to process the profile has to change very little. However, you'll need to investigate the profile returned by each service in order to determine what's consistently provided before deciding what you do, and don't, want to store.

Then there's the issue of the user revoking application access in the service. Of course, the only time this impacts the web application is if the person decides to authenticate with the same application using another service—in which case, her new information is stored, and the application continues on its merry way. The only negative consequence is a now-defunct database record containing the previous authentication information for the person, and it wouldn't be that much extra work to modify the application to generate an application-specific identifier for her, and update the record if she changes authentication servers. I'll leave this for an off-book exercise. Now it's time to look at another aspect of application security: cleaning form data.

Protecting Applications and Preventing Attacks

As a JavaScript developer, you quickly learned about the hazards of accepting input from the user and passing it directly to an eval statement call. As a web developer, you also learned about the hazards of taking text from users and appending it directly as a where clause in a SQL statement.

Node applications have all the vulnerability of client-side JavaScript applications, as well as the additional vulnerabilities associated with server-side applications that use database systems, especially relational database systems.

To ensure that your applications are safe, you need to provide good authorization and authentication systems, as described in the last section. But you also need to protect your application against injection attacks and other attempts to use openings in your system to gain access to your important, and confidential, data.

Earlier, the login form accepted text directly from the user and pasted it into a SQL query. This isn't the wisest thing to do, because the person could attach text that can cause harm in a SQL database. For instance, if the text is forming the data in a WHERE clause, and is appended directly to a WHERE clause string:

```
var whereString = "WHERE name = " + name;
```

and the name string contains the following:

```
'johnsmith; drop table users'
```

You could have a problem.

The same occurs when processing text or JSON from the user or source in a JavaScript eval statement—the incoming string could be more harmful than helpful.

Both types of vulnerabilities demand that we scrub input before using it in circumstances that can cause harm. Both also require that we make use of tools and techniques to ensure the safest possible applications.

Don't Use eval

One simple rule can make a difference in your JavaScript applications, regardless of whether they're Node or not: don't use eval. The eval function is the least restrictive, most permissive component of JavaScript, and we should view its use with fear and trepidation.

In most cases, we don't need to use eval. The one instance where we might be tempted to use it is when we're converting a JSON string into an object. However, a simple approach to protect against a JavaScript injection attack when converting a string into an object is to use JSON.parse, rather than eval, to process incoming JSON. An eval statement isn't discriminatory about what's included in the text, while JSON.parse validates that the JSON is *only* JSON:

```
var someObj = JSON.parse(jsonString);
```

Since Node is using the V8 engine, we know that we have access to the JSON object, so we don't have to worry about cross-browser workarounds.

Do Use Checkboxes, Radio Buttons, and Drop-Down Selections

A second simple rule for developing web applications is to minimize the opportunities for writing free text in a web form. Provide drop-down selections and checkboxes or radio buttons rather than open text fields. You'll not only ensure safer data, but you'll most likely ensure more consistent and reliable data, too.

Years ago, I was cleaning up a database table where all the data came from a form that the client (aeronautical engineers) used. All the inputs in the form were open text. One field required part identifiers, if this data was applicable. The "if applicable" part was the application's downfall.

The engineers decided to use the field for "notes and whatever," because the form didn't have such a field designated. I ended up finding data ranging from part identifiers to a reminder from one engineer about a lunch reservation with a vendor. It was entertaining reading, but not particularly helpful to the company. And it was extremely difficult to clean, because part numbers from different vendors weren't similar enough that we could use regular expressions to clean up the data.

This is an example of *unintentional* harm. An example of *intentional* harm was described in the last section, where a SQL statement to drop a database table was attached to the user's login name.

If you must require free text from a user for fields, such as his username when he's logging into a system, then you're going to want to scrub the data before using it in a data update or query.

Scrub Your Data and Sanitize It with node-validator

If you must support text input fields, scrub the data before you use it. The node-mysql module provides a method, `client.escape`, that escapes the incoming text and protects against potential SQL injection attacks. You can also disable potentially destructive functionality. In Chapter 10's discussion on MongoDB, I mentioned how you can flag that a JavaScript function should be serialized when stored.

You can also use a validation tool that not only ensures that incoming data is safe, but also that it's consistent. One such validation tool that stands out is node-validator.

Install node-validator using npm:

```
npm install node-validator
```

The module exports two objects, `check` and `sanitize`:

```
var check = require('validator').check,
    sanitize = require('validator').sanitize;
```

You can check that the incoming data is of a format consistent with its use, such as checking to ensure that incoming text is an email:

```
try {
    check(email).isEmail();
} catch (err) {
    console.log(err.message); // Invalid email
}
```

The node-validator application throws an error whenever the data doesn't check out. If you want a better error message, you can provide it as an optional second parameter in the check method:

```
try {
    check(email, "Please enter a proper email").isEmail();
} catch (err) {
    console.log(err.message); // Please enter a proper email
}
```

The `sanitize` filter ensures that the string is sanitized according to whatever method you use:

```
var newstr = sanitize(str).xss(); // prevent XSS attack
```

Example 15-6 uses both objects to check and sanitize three different strings.

Example 15-6. Checking out node-validator's methods

```
var check = require('validator').check,
    sanitize = require('validator').sanitize;

var email = 'shelleyp@burningbird.net';
var email2 = 'this is a test';

var str = '<SCRIPT SRC=http://ha.ckers.org/xss.js></SCRIPT>';
try {
   check(email).isEmail();
   check(email2).isEmail();
} catch (err) {
   console.log(err.message);
}

var newstr = sanitize(str).xss();
console.log(newstr);
```

The result of running this application is:

```
Invalid email
[removed][removed]
```

There's also Express middleware support for node-validator: express-validator. When you include this in your Express application:

```
var expressValidator = require('express-validator');
...
app.use(expressValidator);
```

You can access the check, sanitize, and other provided methods directly on the request object:

```
app.get('/somepage', function (req, rest) {
   ...
   req.check('zip', 'Please enter zip code').isInt(6);
   req.sanitize('newdata').xss();
   ...
});
```

Sandboxed Code

The vm Node module provides a way to safely sandbox JavaScript. It provides access to a new V8 virtual machine in which you can run JavaScript passed as a parameter.

 Sandboxing typically means isolating code from anything it can use to do harm.

There are a couple of approaches to using vm. The first is using `vm.createScript` with the script passed as a parameter to the method. The vm module compiles it and returns a script object representing the script:

```
var vm = require('vm');
var script_obj = vm.createScript(js_text);
```

You can then run the script in a separate context, passing in any data it might need as an optional object:

```
script_obj.runInNewContext(sandbox);
```

Example 15-7 has a small but complete example of using vm to compile a JavaScript statement, utilizing two sandbox object properties, and creating a third.

Example 15-7. Simple example of using Node's vm module to sandbox a script

```
var vm = require('vm');
var util = require('util');

var obj = { name: 'Shelley', domain: 'burningbird.net'};

// compile script
var script_obj = vm.createScript("var str = 'My name is ' + name + ' at ' + domain",
                                 'test.vm');

// run in new context
script_obj.runInNewContext(obj);

// inspect sandbox object
console.log(util.inspect(obj));
```

Running the application returns the following output:

```
{ name: 'Shelley',
  domain: 'burningbird.net',
  str: 'My name is Shelley at burningbird.net' }
```

The object passed to the new context is the point of connection between the calling application and the sandboxed script. The script has no other access to the parent context. If you tried to use a global object, such as `console`, in your sandboxed Java-Script, you'd get an error.

To demonstrate, Example 15-8 modifies the Example 15-7 to load a script in from a file and run it. The script being loaded is nothing but a slight variation of what we had in the preceding example, with the addition of a `console.log` request:

```
var str = 'My name is ' + name + ' from ' + domain;
console.log(str):
```

The `vm.createScript` can't read in the file directly. The second (optional) parameter isn't an actual file, but a name used as a label in a stack trace—it's for debugging purposes only. We'll need to use the filesystem's `readFile` to read in the script file contents.

Example 15-8. Modification of code to use vm to sandbox script read in from a file

```
var vm = require('vm');
var util = require('util');
var fs = require('fs');

fs.readFile('suspicious.js', 'utf8', function(err, data) {
  if (err) return console.log(err);

  try {

    console.log(data);
    var obj = { name: 'Shelley', domain: 'burningbird.net'};

    // compile script
    var script_obj = vm.createScript(data, 'test.vm');

    // run in new context
    script_obj.runInNewContext(obj);

    // inspect sandbox object
    console.log(util.inspect(obj));
  } catch(e) {
    console.log(e);
  }
});
```

Running the application returns the following:

```
[SyntaxError: Unexpected token :]
```

The error occurs—and rightly so—because there is no console object within the virtual machine; it's a V8 virtual machine, not a Node virtual machine. We've seen how we can implement any process with child processes in a Node application. We certainly don't want to expose that kind of power to sandboxed code.

We can run the script within a V8 context, which means it has access to the global object. Example 15-9 re-creates the application from Example 15-8, except this time the runInContext method is used, with a context object passed to the method. The context object is seeded with the object that has the parameters the script is expecting. Printing out the inspection results on the object after the script execution, though, shows that the newly defined property, str, is no longer present. We need to inspect the context to see the object as it exists both in the current context and the sandbox context.

Example 15-9. Running the code in context, with context object passed to vm

```
var vm = require('vm');
var util = require('util');
var fs = require('fs');

fs.readFile('suspicious.js', 'utf8', function(err, data) {
  if (err) return console.log(err);
```

```
try {

    var obj = { name: 'Shelley', domain: 'burningbird.net' };

    // compile script
    var script_obj = vm.createScript(data, 'test.vm');

    // create context
    var ctx = vm.createContext(obj);

    // run in new context
    script_obj.runInContext(ctx);

    // inspect object
    console.log(util.inspect(obj));


    // inspect context
    console.log(util.inspect(ctx));

  } catch(e) {
      console.log(e);
  }
});
```

The examples used a precompiled script block, which is handy if you're going to run the script multiple times. If you want to run it just once, though, you can access both the runInContext and runInThisContext methods directly off the virtual machine. The difference is that you have to pass in the script as the first parameter:

```
var obj = { name: 'Shelley', domain: 'burningbird.net' };

// create context
var ctx = vm.createContext(obj);

// run in new context
vm.runInContext(data,ctx,'test.vm');

// inspect context
console.log(util.inspect(ctx));
```

Again, within a supplied context, the sandbox script does have access to a global object defined via createContext, seeded with any data the sandboxed code needs. And any resulting data can be pulled from this context after the script is run.

CHAPTER 16

Scaling and Deploying Node Applications

At some point in time, you're going to want to take your Node application from development and testing to production. Depending on what your application does and what services it provides (or needs), the process can be simple, or it can be very complex.

I'm going to briefly touch on the possible combinations and issues related to production deployment of a Node application. Some require only minimal effort on your part, such as installing Forever to ensure that your Node application runs, well, forever. Others, though, such as deploying your application to a cloud server, can take considerable time and advance planning.

Deploying Your Node Application to Your Server

Taking your application from development to production isn't overly complicated, but you do need to prepare for the move, and make sure that your application is staged in such a way as to maximize its performance and minimize any potential downtimes.

Deploying a Node application has several prerequisites:

- Your application must be well tested by users as well as developers.
- You need to be able to deploy your application safely, and ensure well-coordinated changes and fixes.
- Your application must be secure.
- You need to ensure that your application restarts if some event causes a failure.
- You may need to integrate your Node applications with other servers, such as Apache.
- You must monitor your application's performance, and be ready to adjust application parameters if the performance begins to degrade.
- You need to take the fullest advantage of your server's resources.

Chapter 14 covered unit, acceptance, and performance testing, and Chapter 15 covered security. Here, we'll look at implementing the other necessary components of deploying a Node application to production on your own server.

Writing That package.json File

Each Node module has a *package.json* file that contains information about the module, as well as code dependencies the module might have. I briefly touched on the *package.json* file with the discussion of modules in Chapter 4. Now I want to take a closer look at this file, especially as you can use it to deploy your application.

As its name implies, *package.json* must be proper JSON. You can jump-start the *package.json* process by running `npm init` and answering the questions. When I ran `npm init` in Chapter 4, I didn't provide any dependencies, but most Node applications will have them.

As a case in point, the widget application we built over several chapters in the book is an example of an application, albeit a small one, that we might consider deploying. What would its *package.json* look like?

 I'm not covering all the possible data values in *package.json*, only those meaningful for a Node application.

To start, we need to provide the application's basic information, including its name, version, and primary author:

```
{
    "name": "WidgetFactory",
    "preferGlobal": "false",
    "version": "1.0.0",
    "author": "Shelley Powers <shelley.just@gmail.com> (http://burningbird.net)",
    "description": "World's best Widget Factory",
```

Note that the `name` property value cannot have any whitespace.

The author values could also be split out, as follows:

```
    "author": { "name": "Shelley Powers",
                "email": "shelley.just@gmail.com",
                "url": "http://burningbird.net"},
```

though it is simpler to use the single value format.

If there are other contributors to the application, you can list them out in an array with the `contributors` keyword, with each person identified in the same manner as the author.

If the Widget Factory had a binary application, you could list it with the `bin` property. An example of the use of `bin` is in the Nodeload (covered in Chapter 14) *package.json*:

```
"bin": {
      "nodeload.js": "./nodeload.js",
      "nl.js": "./nl.js"
              },
```

What this setting tells me is that when the module is installed globally, I can run the Nodeload application just by typing `nl.js`.

The widget application doesn't have a command-line tool. It also doesn't have any scripts. The `scripts` keyword identifies any scripts that are run during the package life cycle. There are several events that can happen during the life cycle, including `prein stall`, `install`, `publish`, `start`, `test`, `update`, and so on, and scripts can be run with each.

If you issue the following npm command in a Node application or module directory:

```
npm test
```

the script *test.js* is run:

```
"scripts": {
   "test": "node ./test.js"
},
```

You should include any unit test script for the widget application in `scripts`, in addition to any other script necessary for installation (such as scripts to set up the environment for the application). Though the Widget Factory doesn't have a start script yet, your application should, especially if it is going to be hosted in a cloud service (discussed later in the chapter).

If you don't provide a script for some values, npm provides defaults. For the start script, the default is to run the application with Node:

```
node server.js
```

if the application has a *server.js* file in the root of the package.

The `repository` property provides information about the tool used to manage the source code control for the application, and the `url` property provides the location of the source, if it is published online:

```
"repository": {
   "type": "git",
   "url": "https://github.com/yourname/yourapp.git"
},
```

The `repository` property isn't essential unless you're publishing your application source (though you can restrict source access to a specific group of people). One of the advantages of providing this information is that users can access your documentation with `npm docs`:

```
npm docs packagename
```

On my Ubuntu system, I first set the browser configuration option to Lynx:

```
npm config set browser lynx
```

Then I opened the docs for Passport, the authentication module covered in Chapter 15:

```
npm docs passport
```

The `repository` setting helps npm find the documentation.

One of the more important designations in the *package.json* file is what version of Node your application can run in. You specify this with the `engine` property. In the case of the Widget Factory, it's been tested in stable release 0.6.x and 0.8.2, which means it should work with future versions of 0.8, too. Being ever hopeful, I set the engine option to:

```
"engines": {
  "node": ">= 0.6.0 < 0.9.0"
},
```

The widget application has several different dependencies, for both production and development environments. These are listed individually—the former in `devDependencies`, the latter in `dependencies`. Each module dependency is listed as the property, and the version needed as the value:

```
"dependencies": {
  "express": "3.0",
  "jade": "*",
  "stylus": "*",
  "redis": "*",
  "mongoose": "*"
},
"devDependencies": {
  "nodeunit": "*"
}
```

If there are any operating system or CPU dependencies, we can also list these:

```
"cpu" : ["x64", "ia32"],
"os": ["darwin","linux"]
```

There are some publishing values, including `private`, to ensure that the application isn't accidentally published:

```
"private": true,
```

And `publishConfig` is used for setting npm configuration values.

By the time we're done, the Widget Factory *package.json* file looks like Example 16-1.

Example 16-1. The package.json file for the Widget Factory application

```
{
  "name": "WidgetFactory",
  "version": "1.0.0",
  "author": "Shelley Powers <shelley.just@gmail.com> (http://burningbird.net)",
  "description": "World's best Widget Factory",
```

```
  "engines": {
    "node": ">= 0.6.0"
  },
  "dependencies": {
    "express": "3.0",
    "jade": "*",
    "stylus": "*",
    "redis": "*",
    "mongoose": "*"
  },
  "devDependencies": {
    "nodeunit": "*"
  },
  "private": true
}
```

We can test the *package.json* file by copying the Widget Factory's code to a new location and then typing **npm install -d** to see if all the dependencies are installed and the application runs.

Keeping Your Application Alive with Forever

You do the best you can with your application. You test it thoroughly, and you add error handling so that errors are managed gracefully. Still, there can be gotchas that come along—things you didn't plan for that can take your application down. If this happens, you need to have a way to ensure that your application can start again, even if you're not around to restart it.

Forever is just such a tool—it ensures that your application restarts if it crashes. It's also a way of starting your application as a daemon that persists beyond the current terminal session. Forever can be used from the command line or incorporated as part of the application. If you use it from the command line, you'll want to install it globally:

```
npm install forever -g
```

Rather than start an application with Node directly, start it with Forever:

```
forever start -a -l forever.log -o out.log -e err.log httpserver.js
```

The preceding command starts a script, *httpserver.js*, and specifies the names for the Forever log, the output log, and the error log. It also instructs the application to append the log entries if the logfiles already exist.

If something happens to the script to cause it to crash, Forever restarts it. Forever also ensures that a Node application continues running, even if you terminate the terminal window used to start the application.

Forever has both options and actions. The **start** value in the command line just shown is an example of an action. All available actions are:

```
start
```
> Starts a script

```
stop
```
> Stops a script

```
stopall
```
> Stops all scripts

```
restart
```
> Restarts the script

```
restartall
```
> Restarts all running Forever scripts

```
cleanlogs
```
> Deletes all log entries

```
logs
```
> Lists all logfiles for all Forever processes

```
list
```
> Lists all running scripts

```
config
```
> Lists user configurations

```
set <key> <val>
```
> Sets configuration key value

```
clear <key>
```
> Clears configuration key value

```
logs <script|index>
```
> Tails the logs for <script|index>

```
columns add <col>
```
> Adds a column to the Forever list output

```
columns rm <col>
```
> Removes a column from the Forever list output

```
columns set <cols>
```
> Sets all columns for the Forever list output

An example of the list output is the following, after *httpserver.js* is started as a Forever daemon:

```
info:    Forever processes running
data:        uid  command script        forever pid  logfile                        uptime
data:    [0] ZRYB node     httpserver.js 2854    2855 /home/examples/.forever/forever.log
         0:0:9:38.72
```

There are also a significant number of options, including the logfile settings just demonstrated, as well as running the script (-s or --silent), turning on Forever's verbosity (-v or --verbose), setting the script's source directory (--sourceDir), and others, all of which you can find just by typing:

```
forever --help
```

You can incorporate the use of Forever directly in your code, as demonstrated in the documentation for the application:

```
var forever = require('forever');

var child = new (forever.Monitor)('your-filename.js', {
  max: 3,
  silent: true,
  options: []
});

child.on('exit', this.callback);
child.start();
```

Additionally, you can use Forever with Nodemon (introduced in Chapter 14), not only to restart the application if it unexpectedly fails, but also to ensure that the application is refreshed if the source is updated. You simply wrap Nodemon within Forever and specify the --exitcrash option to ensure that if the application crashes, Nodemon exits cleanly, passing control to Forever:

```
forever nodemon --exitcrash httpserver.js
```

If the application does crash, Forever starts Nodemon, which in turn starts the Node script, ensuring that not only is the running script refreshed if the source is changed, but also that an unexpected failure doesn't take your application permanently offline.

If you want your application to start when your system is rebooted, you need to set it up as a daemon. Among the examples provided for Forever is one labeled initd-example. This example is the basis of a script that starts your application with Forever when the system is rebooted. You'll need to modify the script to suit your environment and also move it to /etc/init.d, but once you've done so, even if the system is restarted, your application restarts without your intervention.

Using Node and Apache Together

All the examples in this book start as a port other than 80, the default web service port. Some start at port 3000, others at port 8124. In my system, I have to use another port because Apache processes web requests on port 80. People are not going to want to have to specify a port, though, when they access a website. What we need is a way for Node applications to coexist with another web service, be it Apache, Nginx, or another web server.

If the system is running Apache, and you aren't able to change the Apache port, you can use an .htaccess file to rewrite the web requests for Node, redirecting the applications to the proper port without the user being aware of the redirection:

```
<IfModule mod_rewrite.c>

    RewriteEngine on

    # Redirect a whole subdirectory:
    RewriteRule ^node/(.+) http://examples.burningbird.net:8124/$1 [P]

</IfModule>
```

If you have the proper permissions, you can also create a subdomain specifically for your Node application and have Apache proxy all requests to the Node application. This is an approach used in other environments of this type, such as running Apache and Tomcat together:

```
<VirtualHost someipaddress:80>
    ServerAdmin admin@server.com
    ServerName examples.burningbird.net
    ServerAlias www.examples.burningbird.net

    ProxyRequests off

    <Proxy *>
        Order deny,allow
        Allow from all
    </Proxy>

    <Location />
        ProxyPass http://localhost:8124/
        ProxyPassReverse http://localhost:8124/
    </Location>
</VirtualHost>
```

These will work, and the performance should be more than acceptable if you don't expect your Node application to be accessed frequently. The problem with both approaches, though, is that all requests are channeled through Apache, which spins off a process to handle each. The whole point of Node is to avoid this costly overhead. If you expect your Node application to get heavy use, another approach—but one that's dependent on your having root control of your system—is to modify the Apache *ports.conf* file and change which port Apache listens to, from:

```
Listen 80
```

to whatever your preferred port is, such as 78:

```
Listen 78
```

Then use a Node proxy, like http-proxy, to listen for and proxy requests to the appropriate port. As an example, if Apache is to handle all requests to subdirectory *public*, and Node handles all requests to *node*, you could create a standalone proxy server that takes incoming requests and routes them accordingly:

```
var httpProxy = require('http-proxy');

var options = {
```

```
    router: {
        'burningbird.net/public_html' : '127.0.0.1:78',
        'burningbird.net/node' : '127.0.0.1:3000'
    }
};

var proxyServer = httpProxy.createServer(options);
proxyServer.listen(80);
```

The user never sees any of the port magic that is happening behind the scenes. The http-proxy module also works with WebSocket requests, as well as HTTPS.

Why continue to use Apache? Because applications such as Drupal and others use *.htaccess* files to control access to their contents. In addition, several subdomains at my site use *.htpasswd* to password-protect the contents. These are all examples of Apache constructs that have no equivalence in Node server applications.

We have a long-established history with Apache. Tossing it aside in favor of Node applications is more complicated than just creating a static server using Express.

Improving Performance

There are additional steps you can take to boost the performance of your Node application, depending on your system's resources. Most are not trivial, and all are beyond the scope of this book.

If your system is multicore, and you're willing to use experimental technology, you can use Node clustering. The Node.js documentation contains an example of clustering, whereby each process is spawned on a different CPU, though all are listening for incoming requests on the same port.

In some future version of Node, we'll be able to automatically take advantage of a multicore environment just by passing a parameter of --balance when starting the application.

You can also take advantage of a distributed computing architecture, utilizing a module such as hook.io.

There are tricks and techniques to improve your Node application's performance. Most will take a considerable amount of work. Instead, you can host your application on a cloud service and take advantage of whatever performance improvements the host provides. We'll go over that option next.

Deployment to a Cloud Service

An increasingly popular choice for running an application is deploying the application to a cloud service rather than hosting it on your own servers. The reasons for doing so are many and include:

- Enhanced security (it's like having your own personal security team)
- 24-hour monitoring (so you can go to bed)
- Immediate scalability (if your application suddenly peaks in popularity, your server doesn't crash)
- Cost (it frequently can be cheaper to host in a cloud service rather than your own server)
- Deployment tools (clouds provide tools that can simplify Node app deployment)
- Being cool (the only reason on this list *not* to deploy your Node application to a cloud service)

Of course, there are disadvantages, too. One is the necessary limitations on what you can do with your application. For instance, if your application wants to use a tool like ImageMagick, most clouds won't have this installed or allow you to install it. In addition, if your application is based in Node 6.x (or 8.x, or whatever), the cloud service may only be set up for another version (such as 4.x).

It can also be cumbersome to set up your application on a cloud. Some cloud services provide tools so that deployment basically consists of typing in a location and pushing a button. Others, though, can require a great deal of preparation—preparation, I should add, that may or may not be well documented.

In this last section, I'm going to briefly introduce some of the more commonly used cloud services that provide hosting for Node applications, and touch on any aspect that makes one unique from the others.

Deploying to Windows Azure via Cloud9 IDE

If your environment is Windows-based, and you've used Windows functionality previously (such as developing applications with .NET), then you're definitely going to want to explore hosting a Node application in Windows Azure. To make it simpler to post Node applications to Azure, you can use the Cloud9 IDE (integrated development environment) in order to post a project.

Cloud9 is a web-based IDE that can, among other things, interface with your GitHub account. When you open the application, you're presented with the project management interface, as shown in Figure 16-1.

From the project management page, clicking on a project opens it into a separate page, where you can select any of the project files for editing, as shown in Figure 16-2. You can clone an existing project in GitHub directly from the IDE.

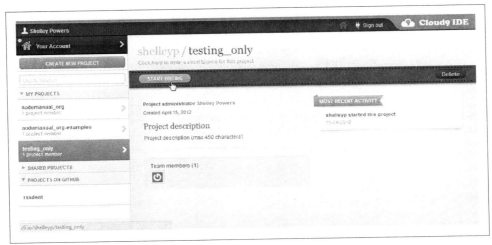

Figure 16-1. Cloud9 IDE project management page

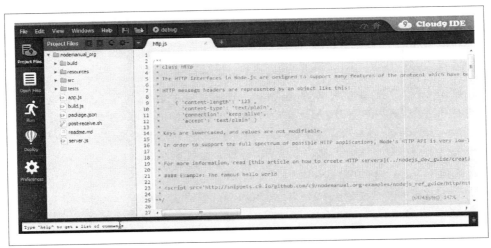

Figure 16-2. Cloud9 IDE project editing page

You can add and edit files, and then run the application directly in the IDE. Cloud9 also supports debugging.

The Cloud9 IDE is free to start working with an application, but you'll need to sign up for premium service if you want to deploy. It supports a variety of languages, though it's primarily focused on HTML and Node applications. It also supports multiple repositories, including GitHub, Bitbucket, Mercurial repositories, Git repositories, and FTP servers.

The Cloud9 IDE interface simplifies moving an application to Azure (and other services—more on this a little later). If you have an Azure account, moving a Node application to Azure is as simple as clicking the Deploy button and providing information in the dialogs that open. Be forewarned: you should be familiar with Azure first. There is a 90-day free trial to try out the service before committing.

How much Azure costs is dependent on the number of compute instances, the size of the SQL Server database instance, the blob storage amount, and bandwidth. The service also provides a decent set of documents to get you started, including a nice tutorial on creating an Express application on Azure.

I mentioned a few paragraphs back that Cloud9 IDE can deploy to multiple clouds. It supports three at this time:

- Windows Azure
- Heroku
- Joyent

I'll introduce you to the Joyent Development SmartMachine and Heroku next.

Joyent Development SmartMachines

Joyent SmartMachines are virtual machines, running either Linux or Windows, that come prebuilt and optimized for running a Node application. The folks at Joyent also provide a Node.js Development SmartMachine that lets Node developers host an application in a cloud service without any charge. If you're ready to go to production, then you can upgrade to the production environment.

Joyent provides a detailed how-to on getting started with a Node.js Development SmartMachine. It includes the following steps:

1. Create a Joyent cloud account.
2. Create an SSH (secure shell) key if you don't already have one.
3. Update the *~/.ssh/config* file to reflect the unique port number for your machine.
4. Deploy the application to the SmartMachine with Git.
5. Ensure that the application has a *package.json* file, and identify a start script.

Again, the Node.js Development SmartMachine is for development purposes only.

So, what does the Joyent Development SmartMachine provide? Well, for a start, no upfront cost. This is actually a smart move—it gives developers a chance to try cloud hosting without significant cost.

Joyent also provides for simplified Git deployment to multiple machines at the same time, as well as npm support to manage application dependencies.

Heroku

I like cloud services where you don't have to pay anything in order to try them out, and a Heroku account is both free and instant. If you decide to use the service for your production system, it's configurable, just like Azure. The cloud server also has very good documentation, and tools you can install in your development environment to simplify deploying the application to Heroku (if you're not using Cloud9 IDE).

The cloud service comes with prepackaged add-ons you can add to your account, including support for one of my favorite data stores, Redis. The concept of the add-on in Heroku is very well managed, and many of the add-ons are also free while you're trying them out.

The Heroku documentation, as mentioned, is some of the best among the cloud servers, and the development tools really simplify deployment. You create the application, write the *package.json* file listing out dependencies, declare a process type via a simple Procfile (which usually has something like `web: node app.js`), and then start the application with one of the tools supplied as part of the Heroku toolkit.

To deploy, commit the application to Git, and then deploy the application using Git. Simple.

Amazon EC2

Amazon Elastic Compute Cloud, or EC2, has some history behind it now, which makes it an attractive option. It also doesn't impose a lot of requirements on the Node developer looking to host an application in this cloud service.

Setting up on Amazon EC2 is little different than setting up on a more traditional VPN (virtual private network). You specify your preferred operating system, update it with the necessary software to run Node, deploy the application using Git, and then use a tool like Forever to ensure that the application persists.

The Amazon EC2 service has a website that can make it simple to set up the instance. It doesn't provide a free service like Joyent does, but the charges are reasonable—about 0.02 an hour while you're trying out the service.

If your application is using MongoDB, the MongoDB website provides very detailed Amazon EC2 setup instructions.

Nodejitsu

Nodejitsu is currently in beta, and is offering beta accounts. Like many of the other excellent cloud services, it lets you try out the service for free.

Like Heroku, Nodejitsu provides a tool, jitsu, to simplify the deployment process. You install it using npm. Log into Nodejitsu with jitsu, and deploy simply by typing:

```
jitsu deploy
```

The tool gets what it needs from the *package.json* file and asks a couple of minor questions, and then you're good to go.

Nodejitsu also provides its own web-based IDE, though I haven't had a chance to try it out. It does seem to be much simpler than Cloud9 IDE.

Node, Git, and GitHub

Git is a version control system, similar to CVS (Concurrent Versioning System) or Subversion. Where Git differs from the other, more conventional version control systems is how it maintains the source as you make modifications. A version control system like CVS stores version changes as differences from a base file. Git, on the other hand, stores snapshots of the code at a specific point in time. If a file isn't changed, Git just links to the previous snapshot.

To begin using Git, you first need to install it on your system. There are binaries for Windows and Mac OS X, as well as source code for various flavors of Unix. Installing it on my Linux (Ubuntu 10.04) server required only one command:

```
sudo apt-get install git
```

All dependencies are automatically downloaded and installed.

 The commands from this point on assume you're using a Unix-based terminal to enter them. There is a graphical interface for Git on Windows. You'll need to follow the documentation that comes with the interface to set up your system, but the general procedures are the same in all environments.

Once Git is installed, it needs to be configured. You'll need to provide a Git username (typically, your first and last name) and an email address. These form the two components of the *commit author*, used to mark your edits:

```
git config --global user.name "your name"
git config --global user.email "your email"
```

Since you're going to be working with GitHub, the hosting service that houses most (if not all) Node modules, you're also going to need to set up a GitHub account. You can use whatever GitHub username you want—it doesn't have to match the username you just specified. You'll also need to generate an SSH (secure shell) key to provide GitHub, following the documentation outlined in the GitHub help documentation.

Most Git tutorials start you out by creating a simple *repository* (or *repo* to use common terminology) of your own work. Since we're interested mainly in Git with Node, we'll start out by cloning an existing repository rather than creating our own. Before you can clone the source, though, you must first *fork* (obtain a working snapshot) the repository at the GitHub website by clicking the Fork button located on the upper-right side of the repository's main GitHub web page, as shown in Figure A-1.

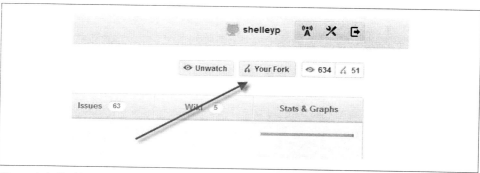

Figure A-1. Forking an existing Node module in GitHub

Then you can access the forked repository in your profile. You'll also access the Git URL in the newly forked repository web page. For instance, when I forked the node-canvas module (covered in Chapter 12), the URL was *git@github.com:shelleyp/node-canvas.git*. The command to clone the forked repository is `git clone URL`:

```
git clone git@github.com:shelleyp/node-canvas.git
```

You can also clone over HTTP, though the GitHub folks don't recommend it. However, it is a good approach to use if you want a read-only copy of the repository source because you want examples and other material that may not be included when you install the module with npm (or if you want to access a copy of the module in work that hasn't yet been pushed out to npm).

Access the HTTP read-only URL from each repository's web page, such as the following for node-canvas:

```
git clone https://github.com/username/node-whatever.git
```

 You can also install a module by specifying a Git URL:

```
npm install git://github.com/username/node-whatever.git
```

Now you have a copy of the node-canvas repository (or whatever repository you want to access). You can make changes in any of the source files if you wish. You add new or changed files by issuing the command `git add`, and then commit those changes by issuing `git commit` (using the -m flag to provide a brief comment about the change made):

```
git add somefile.js
git commit -m 'note about what this change is'
```

If you want to see if the file is staged and ready to commit, you can type the `git status` command:

```
git status
```

If you want to submit the changes to be included back as part of the original repository, you'll issue a *pull request*. To do so, open the forked repository on which you want to issue the request in your browser, and look for the button labeled Pull Request, as shown in Figure A-2.

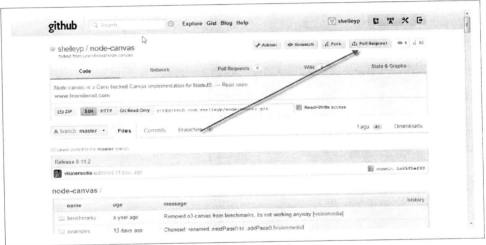

Figure A-2. Click the Pull Request button at GitHub to initiate a pull request

Clicking the Pull Request link opens up a Pull Request preview pane, where you can enter your name and a description of the change, as well as preview exactly what's going to be committed. You can change the commit range and destination repository at this time.

Once satisfied, send the request. This puts the item in the Pull Request queue for the repository owner to merge. The repository owner can review the change; have a discussion about the change; and, if he decides to merge the request, do a fetch and merge of the change, a patch and apply, or an automerge.

> GitHub has documentation on how to merge in changes, as well as other aspects of using Git with the hosting site.

If you create your own Node module and want to share it with others, you'll want to create a repository. You can do this through GitHub, too, by clicking the New Repository button from your main GitHub web page and providing information about the module, including whether it is private or public.

Initialize an empty repository using the `git init` command:

```
mkdir ~/mybeautiful-module
cd ~/mybeautiful-module
git init
```

Provide a README for the repository, using your favorite text editor. This is the file that is displayed when a user clicks Read More in a module page at GitHub. Once the file is created, add it and commit it:

```
git add README
git commit -m 'readme commit'
```

To connect your repository to GitHub, you'll need to establish a remote repository for the module and push the commits to it:

```
git remote add origin git@github.com:username/MyBeautiful-Module.git
git push -u origin master
```

Once you've pushed your new module to GitHub, you can begin the fun of promoting it by ensuring that it gets listed in the Node module listings as well as the npm registry.

This is a quick run-through of the documentation that you can find at the GitHub website, under the Help link.

Index

Symbols

" (double quotes), 100
$set modifier, 217, 218
& (ampersand), 11
' (single quotes), 100
* (asterisk), 137
--balance parameter, 353
--debug flag, 290
--exitcrash option, 351
--global option, 66
-d flag, 68, 112
-g option, 66
-m flag, 360
-s option, 350
-v option, 351
/c flag, 54
/K flag, 54
=== (strict equality operator), 100
> prompt, 29
\n, 48
_ (underscore), 22, 73
__dirname variable, 104, 110
{} (curly braces), 24, 101

A

A record, 54
acceptance testing, 301–306
    with Soda module, 301–305
    with Tobi module, 305–306
    with Zombie module, 305–306
addCallback method, 82
addErrback method, 82
addListener method, 62
Advanced Packaging Tool (APT), 2

allowHalfOpen parameter, 42
Amazon EC2 (Elastic Compute Cloud), 357
Apache web server, 1
ApacheBench module, 307–311
app.js file, 8, 129–132
Apricot tool, 69
APT (Advanced Packaging Tool), 2
arrow keys in REPL, 26
Assert module, 292–295
Async module, 70, 95–99
asynchronous functionality, 13–19
    and MongoDB, 220–221
    and program flow, 16–19
    and WebSockets, 278–279
    asynchronous I/O, ix
    benefits of, 19
    defined, 13
    patterns for, 91–99
    reading files, 14–16
attacks, 337–340
    avoiding eval function, 338
    avoiding open text fields, 338–339
    sanitizing data, 339–340
audience for this book, x
authentication
    defined, 322
    with Passport module, 322–337
        locally stored, 324–331
        using OAuth, 323–324, 331–337
        using OpenID, 323–324
authorization
    defined, 322
    with Passport module, 322–337
        locally stored, 324–331
        using OAuth, 323–324, 331–337

ImageMagick, 260–264
img element, 106, 269
immediate flag, 114
include directive, 175, 192
incr method, 201
indenting code, 100
index function, 134, 135
index.js file, 159
inherits method, 56–58, 60, 61, 77
injection attacks, 337–338
insert method, 211, 235, 236, 240
inspect method, 56
install event, 347
installing
    development environment
        on Linux (Ubuntu), 2–4
        on Mac, 1
        on Windows 7, 4–9
    Express framework, 128
    libraries, 2
    Redis module, 188–190
integrated development environment (IDE),
    354
IPC (interprocess communication), 44
isAuthenticated method, 325
isEqual method, 294

J

Jade file, 192
Jade module, 70
Jade template system, 172–180
    modularizing views in, 174–180
    syntax for, 172–174
Janczuk, Tomasz, 5
Jasmine framework, 298–299
JavaScript as basis for Node, ix, 1
JavaScript Gateway Interface (JSGI), 111
journaling option, 214
Joyent SmartMachines, 356
.js files for modules, 64
JSDOM module, 71
JSGI (JavaScript Gateway Interface), 111
.json files for modules, 64

K

keepGoing option, 213
keyboard shortcuts in REPL, 27

L

la option, 67
last argument callbacks, 83
.leave command, 48
length parameter, 40
length property, 166, 177
libraries
    defined, 127
    installing, 2
    requirements, 2
libssl-dev, 2
limit option, and findOne method, 216
Linux
    installing development environment on, 2–
    4
    making REPL executable, 32
list option, 67
listen method, 11–13, 15
listening event, 13, 15
ll option, 67
load
    balancing using reverse proxy, 124
    testing with Nodeload module, 311–313
loading modules, 63–65
local installation of modules, 66
log method, 25, 31, 37, 47, 88
log, changing colors in, 71
logger middleware module, 114–115, 116, 119,
    131
lookup method, 54
ls option, 67

M

-m flag, 360
Mac, installing on, 1
main property, 75
map function, 95
maxLength option, 133
maxObjects option, 133
maxSockets property, 45
McMahon, Caolan, 95
Memcached key/value store, 187
memoization, 95
memoryUsage method, 39
Mercurial repositories, 330
message event, 47
message queue
    defined, 196

load testing with, 311–313
Nodemon module, 313–314
Nodeunit module, 296–297
NODE_ENV variable, 130
node_modules folder, 64
normalize method, 162
NoSQL databases, 187, 207
npm (Node Package Manager), xi, 65
.npmignore list, 79
NS record, 54
Nvm (Node Version Manager), 9

O

OAuth, 323–324, 331–337
object-relational mapping (ORM), 229
ODM (object-document mapping), 221
offset parameter, 40
on method, 42, 59, 61, 62
onclick event handler, 81
open event, 105
open method, 154
open text fields, avoiding, 338–339
OpenFeint, 190
OpenID, 323–324
OpenSSL, 316
Optimist module, 70, 72–73
ORM (object-relational mapping), 229
os module, 32
out command, 288
output stream, 112
overhead of single thread process, 19

P

package.json files
    deploying to servers, 346–349
    for custom modules, 75–78
    generating, 76
    required fields in, 75
packaging directory, 75
parallel method, 95, 98, 193
parse method, 55, 338
parseBody method, 254
parseCookie middleware module, 115–118
passphrase, 317
Passport module, 322–337
    storing locally with, 324–331
    using OAuth with, 323–324, 331–337
    using OpenID with, 323–324

passwords, encrypting, 319–322
PATH environment variable, 3
path routing in Express framework, 136–138
pattern attribute, 140
PDF files, 249–260
    using PDF Toolkit
        accessing data about file with, 251–252
        creating files with, 258–260
        creating page to upload files, 252–257
        wkhtmltopdf utility, 250–251
PEM (privacy-enhanced mail) format, 316
performance
    benchmark testing with ApacheBench
        module, 307–311
    improving, 353
    load testing with Nodeload module, 311–313
picklist
    defined, 165
    generating, 165–166
pipe
    defined, 48
    method, 105
placeholders, 233
platform method, 38
Polaroid effect, 262
poolSize option, 208
port parameter, 188
post method, 134, 140
POST verb, 134, 139
prefix configuration option, 3
prefork MPM (prefork multiprocessing model), 13
preinstall event, 347
print method, 189, 190
privacy-enhanced mail (PEM) format, 316
private keys, 316
process method, 39
process object, 38–39
Procfile, 337
profile parameter, 332
program flow and asynchronous functionality, 16–19
promises vs. callback functions, 81–84
proxies, 123–126, 123
public keys, 316
publish event, 347
pull request, 361
put method, 146

setBreakpoint command, 289
setEncoding method, 39, 40, 43, 48, 51
setInterval function, 41
setMaxListeners method, 62
setTimeout function, 17, 39, 40, 41
sha1 algorithm, 320
shared hosting, 4
showStack flag, 132
sign method, 319
SimpleDB, 207
single quotes, 100
single thread
    for Node, ix
    overhead of, 19
Socket.IO module, 70
    and WebSockets, 274–279
    configuring, 279–281
    using with Express, 284–285
sockets, 41
Soda module, 301–305
sorted set, 190
spawn method, 50–52, 50
SSH (secure shell), 356, 359
SSL (Secure Sockets Layer), 316–317
stack property, 87
Standard IO (STDIO), 36
start event, 347
start method, 29
startnum/endnum values, 265
stat command, 89
static files
    routing to, 161–162
    server for, 103–110
static middleware module, 113–114, 131
static middleware option, 113, 114
staticCache middleware module, 133
stats method, 89, 98
stats middleware module, 201–205
stderr stream, 38, 50, 51, 132
stdin stream, 38, 46, 48, 51, 61
STDIO (Standard IO), 36
stdout stream, 38, 48, 50, 51, 114
step command, 288
Step module, 92–95
Strata framework, 151
stream interface, 48–50
stream option, 30
strict equality operator, 100
strictEqual method, 293, 294

stringEqual method, 293
strings, encodings for, 40
.styl files, 182
style tag, 192
Stylus
    in template systems, 180–184
    no dynamic CSS views in, 181
Subversion, 359–362
success event, 232, 233
sudo command, 4
superConstructor argument, 56
superuser privileges, 4
syntax for EJS template system, 154–155

T

tail command, 197
TCP (Transmission Control Protocol), 40, 273
template systems
    EJS (embedded JavaScript) template system,
        153–172
        filters for, 157–158
        for Node, 155–156
        syntax for, 154–155
        using with Express, 158–172
    Jade template system, 172–180
        modularizing views in, 174–180
        syntax for, 172–174
    Stylus in, 180–184
test event, 347
testing
    acceptance testing, 301–306
        with Soda module, 301–305
        with Tobi module, 305–306
        with Zombie module, 305–306
    in all browsers, 107
    performance testing, 306–313
        benchmark testing with ApacheBench
            module, 307–311
        load testing with Nodeload module,
            311–313
    unit testing, 292–301
        with Assert module, 292–295
        with Jasmine framework, 298–299
        with Mocha framework, 297–298
        with Nodeunit module, 296–297
        with Vows framework, 299–301
text/html content type, 107
third-party authentication/authorization, 322
this context keyword, 58, 93

time-consuming operations, 15
timer functions, 40–41
TLS (Transport Layer Security), 41, 257, 316–317
Tobi module, 305–306
token parameter, 332
tokenSecret parameter, 332
toString method, 47
Tower.js framework, 151
transactions support, 239–242
Transmission Control Protocol (TCP) (see TCP (Transmission Control Protocol))
Transport Layer Security (TLS) (see TLS (Transport Layer Security))
transports option, 280
Triple-DES encryption, 316
trusted authorities, 316
try blocks, 85
Twitter, 331
type parameter, 122

U

Ubuntu, 2–4
UDP (User Datagram Protocol), 41, 46–47
Uglify-js module, 70
Underscore module, 70, 73–74
unidirectional, 273
unit testing, 292–301
    with Assert module, 292–295
    with Jasmine framework, 298–299
    with Mocha framework, 297–298
    with Nodeunit module, 296–297
    with Vows framework, 299–301
update event, 347
update method, 217–221, 235, 236, 240
update modifiers for MongoDB, 218–219
upload files page, 252–257
uppercase, use of, 100
upserts
    defined, 217
    parameter, 219
URL module, 55
url property, 104
use method, 112
useGlobal flag, 37
User Datagram Protocol (UDP) (see UDP (User Datagram Protocol))
Utilities module, 32, 56–59

V

-v option, 351
var keyword, 19, 20, 22, 24, 100
verify method, 319
version method, 38
video element, 106, 264–268
virtual private network (VPN), 357
VOIP (Voice over Internet Protocol), 46
Vows framework, 299–301
VPN (virtual private network), 357

W

W3C (World Wide Web Consortium), 273
waterfall method, 92, 95, 96, 193
WebDriver, 301
WebGL, 249
WebSockets protocol, 273–274
    and Socket.IO, 274–279
    browser support for, 274
    client side requirements, 279
    Hello, World example, 281–284
    in asynchronous application, 278–279
    simple example using, 274–277
where method, 236
Widget Factory, 337
Windows 7
    child processes in, 53–54
    installing development environment on, 4–9
Windows Azure, 354–356
wkhtmltopdf utility, 250–251
worker MPM (prefork multiprocessing model), 13
World Wide Web Consortium (W3C), 273
write method, 40, 43, 136, 137
writeFile method, 94, 96, 98
writeHead method, 12

Z

zero-sized chunk, 44
Zombie module, 305–306
zrange method, 192

About the Author

Shelley Powers has been working with, and writing about, web technologies—from the first release of JavaScript to the latest graphics and design tools—for more than 12 years. Her recent O'Reilly books have covered the semantic web, Ajax, JavaScript, and web graphics. She's an avid amateur photographer and web development aficionado, who enjoys applying her latest experiments on her many websites.

Colophon

The animal on the cover of *Learning Node* is a hamster rat (*Beamys*). There are two species of hamster rats: the greater hamster rat (*Beamys major*) and the lesser hamster rat (*Beamys hindei*).

The hamster rat inhabits the African forests from Kenya to Tanzania. This large rodent prefers to make its home in moist environments: along riverbanks and in thickly-forested areas. It thrives in coastal or mountainous regions, although deforestation threatens its natural habitat. Hamster rats live in multichambered burrows and are excellent climbers.

This rodent has a very distinct appearance: it can be 7 to 12 inches long and weigh up to a third of a pound. It has a short head and gray fur overall, with a white belly and a mottled black and white tail. The hamster rat, like other rodents, has a variable diet; it possesses cheek pouches for food storage.

The cover image is from *Shaw's Zoology*. The cover font is Adobe ITC Garamond. The text font is Linotype Birka; the heading font is Adobe Myriad Condensed; and the code font is LucasFont's TheSansMonoCondensed.

Have it your way.

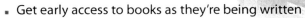

Get even more for your money.

Join the O'Reilly Community, and register the O'Reilly books you own. It's free, and you'll get:

- $4.99 ebook upgrade offer
- 40% upgrade offer on O'Reilly print books
- Membership discounts on books and events
- Free lifetime updates to ebooks and videos
- Multiple ebook formats, DRM FREE
- Participation in the O'Reilly community
- Newsletters
- Account management
- 100% Satisfaction Guarantee

Signing up is easy:

1. **Go to: oreilly.com/go/register**
2. **Create an O'Reilly login.**
3. **Provide your address.**
4. **Register your books.**

Note: English-language books only

To order books online:

oreilly.com/store

For questions about products or an order:

orders@oreilly.com

To sign up to get topic-specific email announcements and/or news about upcoming books, conferences, special offers, and new technologies:

elists@oreilly.com

For technical questions about book content:

booktech@oreilly.com

To submit new book proposals to our editors:

proposals@oreilly.com

O'Reilly books are available in multiple DRM-free ebook formats. For more information:

oreilly.com/ebooks

O'REILLY®

Spreading the knowledge of innovators   oreilly.com

CPSIA information can be obtained at www.ICGtesting.com
Printed in the USA
BVOW062358260912

301315BV00001B/11/P